KINGDOM
LIVING

With Gratitude

I WANT TO SAY a word of thanks to my friends and editors, Philip Rawley and Heather Hair, for their excellent help in the preparation of this original manuscript two decades ago and then the most recent update, as well as to Greg Thornton, Cheryl Molin, Kevin Mungons, and the rest of the team at Moody Publishers for their encouragement and quality work on this project.

Introduction

ONE DAY I WAS WALKING through my yard with a workman who was going to cut down and remove some dead trees. I showed him one tree that I wanted him to cut down because it appeared dead to me.

"Oh, sir," he said quickly. "You don't need to cut this tree down. It's still alive." Then he proceeded to show me some small green buds on the tree that I had not noticed. What looked like death to me was really stunted growth. Because this tree had not been properly nurtured and developed, it appeared to have no life at all.

Countless Christians today are like that underdeveloped tree on my property. At first glance they may appear to have no spiritual life at all, but upon closer observation their problem is seen to be severely inhibited development. Too many Christians are not experiencing the abundant life Jesus promised because of their lack of spiritual growth.

This book is about kingdom living. If you have truly trusted the Lord Jesus Christ to be your Sin-bearer, and you are looking to Him alone for forgiveness and the gift of eternal life, then you have life abiding in you. What is needed now is more growth, not more life.

The problem, however, is that many Christians either don't know how spiritual growth occurs, or they refuse to allow it to occur. My goal in this book is to motivate and educate you in the essential elements of kingdom living, so you can grow into a mature spiritual adult, one who consistently aligns his or her life under God and His kingdom agenda.

You will see the word *grace* appear throughout this book. This is because your spiritual development is directly tied to your understanding of and response to God's grace. The grace that saved you is the grace that will transform you as you grow.

Spiritual growth is guaranteed to every true believer. No child of God has to remain stagnant and spiritually underdeveloped. In the pages to follow, you will discover how to cooperate with God's grace in order to experience maximum spiritual growth.

It is my hope that this book will incite and excite you to pursue the full experience of your new life in Christ and discover the joy of being transformed into the image of God's Son. Then you will know the blessed experience of Christ being formed in you (Gal. 4:19). As a result, you will impact the world around you for the glory of God and the good of others as you serve as a testimony of what it means to model kingdom living to everyone around you.

1

The Importance of Kingdom Living

AS DIFFICULT AS IT MAY BE to write this opening paragraph, it is equally as full of joy. I only say it is difficult because it reveals how long I've been on earth, over seven decades now! But it is equally as joyful because, as the Bible says, "Behold, children are a gift of the LORD, the fruit of the womb is a reward" (Ps. 127:3). That being said, my late wife Lois and I can count ourselves as highly rewarded. With four kids, we have also been blessed with thirteen grandkids and now four great-grandkids!

Each birth brings with it new hope and new expectations. What will this child grow up to live out? How will the Lord bless and use this new baby for His glory? Thoughts run through our minds as we cradle each new life. I'm sure you've experienced the same or similar feelings and thoughts.

Families look ahead with excitement to a new child's future because inherent in every birth is the hope and expectation that this baby is going to grow and develop. Once a child has been conceived and born, growth is anticipated, because that's the way God designed the human body to work. No parents I know are content simply to say, "Well, we conceived a child, and that's all that matters," or "We have a healthy baby, so it doesn't matter if there is no growth." Parents who are excited about the conception and birth of their child are also excited about seeing that child grow.

One reason that parents can tolerate the 1:00 a.m. feedings is that they know this phase of childhood won't last forever. The same can be said for each stage of a child's growth—and aren't we all glad that the teenage years with their ups and downs and major crises every week don't last forever? We grew past all those stages, and so will our children, because growth is the normal and expected outcome of a new birth. In fact, if a child doesn't grow, we want to know why. That child is taken to the doctor for tests to be run to try to identify the cause of the lack of development, whether it is physical, emotional, or mental.

Now if human parents are concerned about the growth of their children, then we ought not be surprised that God, our Father, is concerned about the growth of His children as well. It is God's desire that we all grow in maturity to the point where kingdom living is a natural way of life. If the Holy Spirit, using the Word of God, brought about conviction in your heart and you put your faith in Jesus Christ alone for your salvation, then God is your Father by virtue of your new birth. He wants to make sure that you are growing in spiritual maturity.

We're going to begin our study of kingdom living by talking about the nature and importance of spiritual growth. But before we can begin to build a solid biblical understanding of spiritual growth, we need to clear away the rubble that can come from confused thinking. There is an enormous amount of confusion on this matter of how Christians grow spiritually. We need to address some of these issues, because if we don't get our thinking right, we can actually stifle instead of enhance our own spiritual growth, as well as that of others.

For example, some people view spiritual growth as primarily a matter of learning the correct biblical information. This group believes that if you attend enough Christian seminars, read enough books, belong to enough small groups, and study the Bible enough, then growth in Christ will follow automatically.

I can identify with this group as a person who spent years studying the Bible in college and seminary. But any seminary student can tell you that studying the Bible and accumulating knowledge can actually lead to spiritual dryness and stymie growth if and when that "head knowledge" is not accompanied by inner spiritual transformation in response to God's truth. I found that to be true in my case. After nearly a decade of formal study day in and day out, even going so far as learning the original languages of Scripture, I felt more distant from God than when I had begun. Spiritual maturity is not contingent on book knowledge. It's entirely contingent on your connection with the King.

Jesus said to the people of His day, "You search the Scriptures because you think that in them you have eternal life; it is these that testify about Me; and you are unwilling to come to Me so that you may have life" (John 5:39–40). These individuals studied Scripture. They were the theological scholars of their time. Regardless, they didn't know Jesus. Their study, even of the Bible's accurate data, did not lead them to the One who is the source of truth and life.

Other people believe that spiritual growth is the result of following a certain well-defined process. They want to know the ten steps to spiritual growth, or the eight surefire keys to achieving maturity in Christ. Lists like these often contain good ideas, but when you have a lot of steps to climb, you get weary after a while. And if you miss a step, you get tripped up and everything gets out of sync.

I'm not saying there aren't some clearly defined stages or steps in our spiritual growth. The problem comes when we try to reduce a living process to a mechanical list of steps that everybody has to follow. People simply don't grow at the same rate, so a "one size fits all" approach to spiritual growth won't fit everyone.

One other misconception about the nature of spiritual growth is important to mention, because it has such a long history in the church. Most people in modern Western culture are inclined toward action and want to know what they can do to achieve a desired result. But another group of people is convinced that spirituality is achieved by what you avoid rather than what you do. These are people who work hard to give up certain things, deny themselves certain pleasures, and abstain from certain activities.

This approach to spiritual growth is known as asceticism, and it's almost as old as Christianity itself. Some ascetics live in cloistered monasteries to escape the world and its temptations. They may also systematically deny food to their bodies and anything else that could be considered a worldly pleasure. They avoided them because they didn't want to defile their souls.

During certain periods of church history, ascetics did spectacular and even bizarre things to try to conquer their sinful flesh and get closer to God. Some whipped themselves to punish their flesh, while history tells us of one man who went so far as to sit on a high pole for years to free himself from the evil world.

But asceticism by itself fails to produce lasting spiritual growth because our problem is that the sinful desires and impulses that mess us up come from within, from our hearts, rather than just from the outside. There's nothing wrong with avoiding sinful activities and worldly lusts that inflame wrong desires. But even monks are prone to discover that we still have to wrestle with sin even if we are sitting in a bare cell in a monastery.

If you have ever tried to grow spiritually using any or all of these methods, believing that they will do the job, then you have probably experienced some degree of frustration in your desire to grow in Christ. There is some truth in all of the methods we have mentioned, but the Bible's teaching on spiritual growth is bigger and more exciting than a list of dos and don'ts. My goal is to approach the subject in a way that is both biblically sound and applicable to your life.

THE NECESSITY OF SPIRITUAL GROWTH

Getting a handle on spiritual growth is crucial for at least two reasons. First, it is God's command and, therefore, His will for us. And second, the alternative to growth is stagnation and eventual deformity. There's a good reason you won't find a hymn called "Backwards Christian Soldiers" being sung in any churches. Failing to grow is not an option for believers—at least not if we want to please God.

It may help to begin with a definition of spiritual growth that will serve as the basis for this book. Spiritual growth can be defined as *that transformational process by which we allow the indwelling Christ to increasingly express Himself in and through us, resulting in a greater capacity on our part to bring God greater glory, be a blessing to others, and advance His kingdom on earth.*

Spiritual growth involves more of Christ being expressed in your life and less of you. John the Baptist said it best. As Jesus' ministry and popularity grew and John began to step into the background, John's disciples came to him and said, "Do you realize what's going on here?" (John 3:22–26). John responded, "He [Jesus] must increase, but I must decrease" (v. 30). We are growing spiritually when more of Jesus is being expressed through us than us ourselves.

Spiritual Growth Demands Nourishment

It often helps to follow a definition with an illustration of what we're talking about. One obvious way to illustrate spiritual growth is by looking at its physical counterpart. Going back to our topic of newborn babies, I'm sure you know that every infant not only wants but also often demands food. Everything within that child cries out, "Give me something to eat. I've got some growing to do!"

If you have ever heard a newborn baby cry out of hunger, you can appreciate the apostle Peter's words of admonition to Christians:

"Like newborn babies, long for the pure milk of the word, so that by it you may grow in respect to salvation" (1 Peter 2:2). This is one of the best one-sentence descriptions of spiritual growth you'll find in the Bible. We may not know exactly how spiritual growth works, but this verse helps us because it compares spiritual growth to physical growth.

The issue for a newborn baby is the development of the life he or she has been given. Now that may seem so simple and obvious that you wonder why I even mention it. But it has been my experience as a pastor that this key principle of spiritual growth is often overlooked for exactly that reason. Spiritual growth is not first and foremost a program or a curriculum, as I said above, but the nourishment and development of a life.

Now I can hear someone saying, "Well, a baby may not be following a program, but her mom certainly is." That's true. There is a well-established, proven program of nourishment that any mom needs to follow if she wants her baby to experience healthy growth. That's why I said there is nothing wrong with various programs or steps *as long as they are facilitating the growth of spiritual life.* The goal of spiritual growth is to feed the life you were given by the Holy Spirit at the moment of your conversion, or new birth, so that you may, as Peter wrote, "grow in respect to salvation" (1 Peter 2:2). Paul put it this way: "We are to grow up in all aspects into Him who is the head, even Christ" (Eph. 4:15).

The point is that your spiritual DNA is complete because you received the life of Christ at your conversion, and nothing can be added to Christ. Our challenge as Christians is to maximize what we already have, not run around and look for that which we don't.

Spiritual Growth Demands Relationship

As you know, a baby is dependent on other people for the nourishment needed for proper growth. This demands a relationship that begins even before birth as an unborn child draws nourishment from the mother through the umbilical cord. In this case the importance of that relationship is clear because the baby is feeding off of the mother, whose life is supplying life to the child. If that relationship is disrupted, the baby is in serious trouble.

A child in the womb is not studying a book, listening to a teacher, or following a program. He or she is simply piggybacking off of a life that is, ideally, already mature and strong. As long as the umbilical cord isn't cut or blocked—as long as the baby stays in right relationship with the mother—growth will continue to occur.

The spiritual application of this physical truth is, of course, the importance of our relationship with Jesus Christ. It's interesting that Jesus did not say, "I have come to give you My program," but rather, "I came that they may have life, and have it abundantly" (John 10:10). So if we are not growing as we should, even though Jesus came to give us not just life but abundant life, then maybe it's because we have chosen to focus on the program rather than the Person. Spiritual growth is progressively learning to let Christ live His life through us, and that only happens by relationship.

THE INGREDIENTS FOR SPIRITUAL GROWTH

Since this chapter is an overview and introduction to our subject, I'm hitting the highlights as we talk about the importance of spiritual growth. Let me give you two ingredients of this growth as found in a key verse from 2 Peter 3: "Grow in the grace and knowledge of our Lord and Savior Jesus Christ" (v. 18).

These two things work in partnership to enhance our growth, but let's be sure we understand once again that our growth is not in the grace and knowledge of a program, a denomination, or anything else. Our growth is inextricably connected to the person of Jesus Christ, the One whose life flows through our spiritual veins. The supply of grace and knowledge we need comes from Him.

The Essence of Grace

One reason the grace of God is so amazing is that it comes up no matter where we turn to talk about the Christian life. We're devoting chapter 5 to grace and its place in spiritual growth, so let me just give you the essence of grace and how it relates to spiritual growth.

Grace is all that God is free to do for you based on the work of Jesus Christ on your behalf. It is God's inexhaustible supply of goodness whereby He does for you what you could never do for yourself. This is the ABCs of the faith, but we need to review it because the truth of grace seems to get lost so often when it comes to how we grow in Christ. That may be true because growth suggests effort on our part, while grace is a gift that can only be received and enjoyed, not earned. But the Bible says we are saved by grace, and we grow by grace. Or as Paul told the Colossians, "As you have received Christ Jesus the Lord, so walk in Him" (Col. 2:6).

If I were the devil and I didn't want Christians to grow, I would keep them from drawing on God's grace and drive them back to the principle of law to keep them in bondage. Romans 6–8 contain Paul's classic contrast between the law of Moses and grace, describing in painful detail our complete inability to obey God's commands in our own power.

Now Paul made it very clear that the problem is not with God's law, which is "holy and righteous and good" (Rom. 7:12). The fault is with our sinful, fallen flesh. What happened under the Mosaic law is that when God's perfect standard, with its requirement of perfect obedience, was applied to sinful and weak human beings, something had to give—and God was not about to lower or adjust His standard to accommodate our sinfulness. And since the law carried with it a penalty for failure to obey, we fell under the sentence of death.

Paul also wrote, "The Law is spiritual, but I am of flesh, sold into bondage to sin" (Rom. 7:14). The reason this is important is that the law had no power to help anyone obey its commands. Law tells you what to do, but it doesn't hold out a hand to help you. The law reveals God's demands, which never change. But we need someone to give us the power to obey God's commands.

Living under law is like living with a perfect person who takes joy in telling you everything you are doing wrong, but never lifts a finger to help you get it right. Under these conditions you will inevitably live an unhappy, defeated, and empty life.

We can see why grace is required for spiritual growth. Spiritually dead people can't grow, but all that the law of Moses could produce was death because it was all command and penalty without the enablement to obey. That's why Peter said if we are going to grow, it has to be by grace. And not just grace as a theological concept, but as it is related to Christ.

The Knowledge of Jesus Christ

As an author, I rarely ever receive one of my books in the mail from someone I've never met with a request that I sign the book. But when I speak at a conference where books are available, a lot of people come to me and ask me to sign their copy. The difference is that they have met the author, and so the book takes on a new meaning. They have connected the content with a person.

Peter told us to grow in the knowledge of Jesus Christ. We have His book, the Word of God, to learn from, and the Holy Spirit as our Teacher. In other words, we have everything we need to put the ingredient of knowledge to work in our lives.

I have already mentioned how easy it is to get off track in this area and seek spiritual knowledge for its own sake. But that's like a young man who carries around a boxful of letters from his girlfriend, content to read them instead of using the insights they contain to deepen his relationship with her.

Our goal is to know Christ, not just know about Him. A lot of people can give you facts and details about the lives of their favorite sports star or celebrity. But there's a world of difference between that kind of knowledge and having the person invite you over for dinner because you are good friends.

You can put the Bible in an honored place in your home, post pictures of it on social media—particularly of underlined verses inside—and yet not know the Savior it speaks of. Knowledge is an ingredient of spiritual growth, but it is knowledge of a Person that we must seek.

To change the analogy, we could say that even though it's good to use a cookbook, it's even better to call Mom. Why? Because while the cookbook can give you the steps in a recipe, Mom can tell you why it didn't work or give you a secret to make it work better the next time. Mom can bring the cookbook to life by her wisdom, experience, and loving touch.

Information about the Christian faith is critical, because our faith has specific content. But it is also critical that this information gets connected to the living reality of Jesus Christ. So if you are serious about spiritual growth, the driving force must be pursuing a living relationship with Christ, which is deepened as you get to know Him better.

THE PURPOSE OF SPIRITUAL GROWTH

The ingredients in a recipe are designed to lead to a finished product, which can then be consumed to enhance someone's physical growth. The ingredients of spiritual growth are also designed to lead to a product, or an end result, which is the glory of God.

Reading further in 2 Peter 3:18, we come to a crucial phrase. After instructing us to grow in the grace and knowledge of Christ, the apostle wrote, "To Him be the glory, both now and to the day of eternity." This sounds to me as if God takes His glory very seriously. He does, which is why He wants you to seek Him, know Him, and grow in Him, not just because it's the right thing to do, but because you want to be a person through whom He can express Himself and display His magnificent glory.

I said earlier in my definition of spiritual growth that the goal is to expand and increase your capacity to bring God glory. You need to understand that God exists for His glory. Once you grasp this truth, it will revolutionize your entire approach and attitude toward spiritual growth. Many Christians are not growing, even though they desire a closer relationship with Christ and are doing things to facilitate this relationship. The problem is that their emphasis is on them and what they are doing, instead of focusing on God and His glory.

God said that He created mankind for His glory (Isa. 43:7). This issue of our bringing glory to God is so important that the Bible defines sin as a failure to bring God glory. "All have sinned and fall short of the glory of God" (Rom. 3:23). That is, we are not sinners just because we do bad things, but because in our sin we fail to live up to the purpose for which God created us, which is to glorify Him.

This is spelled out in detail in Romans 1, where Paul explains why God's wrath is being unleashed "against all ungodliness and unrighteousness of men" (v. 18). Those who practice this evil fail to honor God or give Him the glory He is due (v. 21). And it gets worse, because the ungodly have "exchanged the glory of the incorruptible God for an image in the form of corruptible man and of birds and four-footed animals and crawling creatures" (v. 23). They also "did not see fit to acknowledge God any longer" (v. 28), still another way of saying they did not give God the glory He is due.

The word *glory* means to be heavy or weighty, and it came to refer to something or someone of great worth. Those of us who grew up in the sixties used to say, "That's heavy" when we heard something that was deep or made a lot of sense to us.

When we glorify God, therefore, we are saying that He is a person of great value. We attach weight or importance to Him. Glory also has to do with the way that something attracts attention by the way it shines, so glorifying God means that we draw attention to Him and promote Him as worthy of all praise and adoration. God wants to go public, but since He is invisible, He has created people whose full-time job is to make Him visible so that the world might see and be drawn to Him. We glorify God when we reflect the light of His character the way the moon reflects the brilliance of the sun.

A company that really wants to glorify or show off its product or service will often erect a large billboard along the highway so everyone driving by will see it and get the message. A company that is intent on promoting its glory does not usually settle for a small ad buried online somewhere. The company may start that way, but the idea is to grow into something bigger so more people will be reached with the company's message.

God says that your job and mine as believers is to be billboards advertising His grace to a lost world. And He wants us to grow so that we can display Him more. As we get up in the morning our prayer should be, "Lord, grow me today so I can show You as being bigger and clearer to the people around me. I want to glorify You by advancing Your kingdom agenda on earth."

To advance God's kingdom agenda is to bring Him glory through serving His purpose and reflecting His rule through our lives. For those of you who may not know, I define the kingdom agenda as *the visible manifestation of the comprehensive rule of God over every area of life.*

The reason so many of us believers are struggling in this area of spiritual growth and having a limited impact in the world is that we want God to bless our agenda rather than us fulfilling His agenda. We want God to "okay" our plans rather than our fulfilling His plans. We want God to bring us glory rather than us bringing Him glory. But it doesn't work that way. God has only one plan—His kingdom agenda. We need to find out what that is so we can make sure we're working on God's plan, not ours.

The Greek word the Bible uses for kingdom is *basileia*, which basically means a "rule" or "authority." Included in this definition is the concept of rule. So when we talk about a kingdom, we're talking first about a king or a ruler. We are talking about someone who is in charge.

Now if there is a ruler, there also have to be "rulees," or kingdom subjects. In addition, a kingdom includes a realm; that is, a domain over which the king rules. Finally, if you're going to have a ruler, rulees, and a realm, you also need kingdom regulations—guidelines that govern the relationship between the ruler and the subjects. These are necessary so that the rulees will know whether they are doing what the ruler wants done.

God's kingdom includes all of these elements. He is the absolute Ruler of His domain, which encompasses all of creation. Likewise, His authority is total. Everything God rules, He runs—even when it doesn't look like He's running it. Even when life looks like it's out of control, God is running its "out-of-controlness."

God's kingdom also has its "rulees." Colossians 1:13 says that everybody who has trusted the Lord Jesus Christ as Savior has been transferred from the kingdom of darkness to the kingdom of light. If you are a believer in Jesus Christ, your allegiance has been changed. You no longer align yourself with Satan but with Christ.

And just in case there's any doubt, let me say right now that there are no in-between kingdoms, no gray areas here. There are only two realms in creation: the kingdom of God and the kingdom of Satan. We are subjects of one or the other. Anytime you seek to glorify anything or anyone other than God, you have aligned yourself with the kingdom of darkness. Glorifying God is our purpose as children of the King. As our purpose, it is part and parcel to our spiritual development. If we ignore it, we will not grow spiritually.

What I am talking about here is a radical decision and passion to live for God's glory. Once you decide in your heart that you are going to be consumed with God's glory, your whole life will be pointed in this direction. It's like putting on a pair of tinted glasses that color everything you see from that moment on. First Corinthians 10:31 puts it like this, "Whether, then, you eat or drink or whatever you do, do all to the glory of God." God is passionate about His glory. Spiritual growth increases your capacity to bring Him glory.

One reason this commitment is so radical is that it is diametrically opposed to the prevailing attitude toward God today, too often even in the church. What we see being promoted today is a "vending machine" God who gives us what we want when we select our choice, drop in our coins, and push the right button. In other words, too many people believe that God is here to glorify us—to make us more healthy, wealthy, and wise. It's a simple transaction. You choose what you want, and then you reach into the divine vending machine and claim it from God. He's obligated to respond.

Don't get me wrong. God is not opposed to blessing you. But this is the by-product and overflow of our decision to live for Christ and reflect His glory. Don't forget too that God's blessing may also include trials and problems we would never choose for ourselves. But growth usually comes in the heat of testing.

And by the way, if you are pursuing a relationship with Jesus Christ and are passionately committed to bringing Him glory, your spiritual life will grow at a speed you never imagined possible. The reason is that your growth will take care of itself as you feed your soul on God and His Word, the way a child's growth takes care of itself as he feeds and exercises his body.

We often say to a child or adolescent we haven't seen in a while, "Look how you've grown!" That child's growth is evident to all because his pants are suddenly too short, and his shoes no longer fit. That's what will happen to you when you are pursuing Christ and His glory. Your growth will be evident to everyone, and people will be saying to themselves, *"Look how she's grown!"* They will be attracted to the life and love you exude and discover that God is the focus and the glory of your life. Christians aren't growing as they should because God isn't getting the glory He seeks and deserves from their lives. God only expands that which brings Him praise.

THE BENEFITS OF SPIRITUAL GROWTH

So what's in this for you and me if we commit ourselves to grow God's way? That's a fair question. Spiritual growth includes God's greater good for us. Peter asked a similar question of Jesus one day as he watched a rich man go away from the Lord with his wealth intact. "Behold, we have left our own homes and followed You" (Luke 18:28). In other words, "Lord, what are we going to get for following You?"

Jesus didn't scold Peter for asking, but replied, "Truly I say to you, there is no one who has left house or wife or brothers or parents or children, for the sake of the kingdom of God, who will not receive many times as much at this time and in the age to come, eternal life" (vv. 29–30). Think about that promise for a minute! God is not a miser doling out tidbits to His children. It's just that His benefits are of His timing and His choosing. They are not ours to demand. Jesus said, "Seek first [God's] kingdom and His righteousness, and all these things will be added to you" (Matt. 6:33). God will meet the needs of His children.

Here's another benefit of growing God's way. In 2 Corinthians 3:13, Paul said that Moses had to put a veil over his face so the Israelites would not see that the glory on Moses's face from being with God on Mount Sinai was fading away. Paul concluded his discussion with this statement: "But we all, with unveiled face, beholding as in a mirror the glory of the Lord, are being transformed into the same image from glory to glory, just as from the Lord, the Spirit" (v. 18).

Paul is saying that when we stare into God's glory in the sense of focusing on Him, something amazing happens. We are changed into the image of God the way a person looking into a mirror sees the image in the mirror reflected back to him.

Did you get that? God will change you when you make Him your focus. You've been trying to change—to shed that bad habit or attitude. Your parents tried to change you when you were growing up, and your spouse has been working on you for years. But God says if you want to change, you need to stare into the mirror of His glory until you start seeing His image reflected in you. This is spiritual growth. It involves reflecting God's glory and becoming more like Him as you and I advance His kingdom agenda through our various spheres of influence during our time on earth.

Where does your greatest good come into all of this? The Bible answers this in Romans 8:28, the familiar promise that God causes all things to work for the good of those who love Him. That's the benefit, but don't miss the purpose of the benefit in verse 29: "For those whom [God] foreknew, He also predestined to become conformed to the image of His Son."

This means that even when things happen that don't seem to be good for us, God is at work shaping and growing us in the process no matter what the trial or the mess. I don't know about you, but I can't think of a greater benefit than knowing that God has a good purpose in *everything* He allows into our lives. He wants to grow us even when we are being tested and tried. If you will prioritize the pursuing and glorifying of God, He will prime you for great growth, freeing you to enjoy all the rights, privileges, peace, and power of your deepened relationship with Him.

2

Conversion:
The Foundation of
Kingdom Living

THE STORY IS TOLD of a scorpion that needed to cross a pond. He couldn't figure out a way to get across until he saw a frog sitting on the bank of the pond. The scorpion went over to the frog and said, "I need to get across this pond, but I can't swim. Can I get on your back and have you hop me across the pond?"

"Well," the frog replied, "as a matter of fact I was just about to hop across the pond. I'll be glad to give you a ride on my back if you promise not to sting me when we reach the other side."

"Oh," the scorpion promised, "I won't sting you. I just want a ride across the pond."

So the frog said, "Hop on." And then he leaped across the pond with the scorpion on his back. But as soon as they landed on the other side, the scorpion stung the frog. As the poisonous venom took effect and the frog lay dying, he looked at the scorpion in disbelief and asked, "How could you do this to me? I gave you a ride across the pond just like you asked, and you promised not to sting me. Now look at what you've done."

But the scorpion simply shrugged and said, "It's my nature to sting."

Scorpions sting because that's what they have been made to do. The only way to change this characteristic is if scorpions were to undergo a radical transformation of their nature, and that isn't going to happen. In the same way, sinners sin because it's their nature to sin, and the only way to change that is by a radical transformation of that sinner's nature.

But that's where the comparison between scorpions and human beings ends, because the transformation of a sinner's nature is not only possible but absolutely essential if spiritual growth is to take place.

Growth presupposes that a birth has taken place and a life has begun. Spiritual growth presupposes that a spiritual birth has taken place. This occurs at conversion when a sinner places his or her faith in Jesus Christ alone for the forgiveness of sin and the gift of eternal life. This results in the imparting of a new nature to replace the sinful nature that every person inherits at birth.

Conversion is the basis or foundation of kingdom living, and the better you understand what happens when a person is converted, the better you will understand the dynamic and the process of spiritual growth afterward. You can't build a solid structure on a partial or faulty foundation, so I want to lay a solid foundation for spiritual growth by discussing our complete need for conversion, the character of conversion, and the completeness of the new life and new nature that God places within us when we trust Christ for salvation.

To whet your appetite for this subject and let you know where we are heading, consider the way the apostle Peter described salvation in his second epistle. He declared that "[God's] divine power has granted to us everything pertaining to life and godliness," and further that as saved people we have "become partakers of the divine nature" (2 Peter 1:3–4).

That's a radical conversion. If you are a Christian, you have a new nature within you that is from God. And along with this new nature, you have received everything you need to live a life that pleases God. To understand and appreciate what God did for us at conversion, and its implications for our spiritual growth, we need to see it against the backdrop of the sinful nature we had before coming to Christ.

THE NECESSITY OF CONVERSION

When Adam sinned against God, his innocence was lost, and he became corrupted by sin. At the core of Adam's being there was deposited a sin nature, which became a part of his humanity and was transmitted to every one of his descendants. The Bible says, "Through one man sin entered into the world, and death through sin" (Rom. 5:12). Because Adam was acting as the representative head of the human race when he sinned, all of us are born with a sin nature, a disposition toward rebellion against God that is part of what it means to be human. This aspect of our nature is so pervasive that it makes everything we do, say, or think unacceptable in the eyes of a holy God.

The point is that sinful human beings cannot approach God in their own power, let alone grow spiritually closer to Him. When David confessed his sin after committing adultery with Bathsheba and having her husband, Uriah, positioned to be killed, he declared, "I was brought forth in iniquity, and in sin my mother conceived me" (Ps. 51:5). David was acknowledging the sin that pervades the human soul in this passage.

Isaiah recognized the same truth when he said, "All our righteous deeds are like a filthy garment" in God's sight (Isa. 64:6). These actions are unacceptable because they are filtered through and contaminated by our sin nature. It's not that sinful people don't want or don't try to do good things. But a sinner's attempts to please God are like a person with a highly contagious disease volunteering to donate blood. That may be a good gesture, but that person's blood cannot be accepted because it is contaminated by disease. In the same way, sin has contaminated and corrupted the human race.

That's why no one has to teach children how to lie or be selfish. Our problem as people born in sin is not that we have a minor flaw that needs to be ironed out, or a quirk of personality that we ought to work on. Sin sets us at complete hostility toward God and puts us under His judgment. Paul stated it succinctly: "Those who are in the flesh cannot please God" (Rom. 8:8).

The effect of the sinful nature on our lives is something like the effect that a disease known as myasthenia gravis has on the physical bodies of its victims. Myasthenia gravis occurs when a muscle does not receive a message from the brain because there is a problem with the nerve that transmits the motor impulse.

For example, the brain of a myasthenia gravis sufferer may send a signal to move the right arm, but the muscle doesn't respond to the signal because the motor implant that transfers the signal from the nerve to the muscle is defective. The brain's signals are interrupted, and the normal process of movement is short-circuited.

The Bible declares that every person is born with a short circuit in his spiritual nervous system. God is sending out His signals, but the unsaved person has no capacity to receive them. Paul said, "A natural man does not accept the things of the Spirit of God, for they are foolishness to him; and he cannot understand them, because they are spiritually appraised" (1 Cor. 2:14).

The implications of this fact for spiritual growth are tremendous. There can be no growth where a new spiritual birth has not taken place. Now that may be obvious to you, but there are numbers of people who go to church every week and consider themselves Christians, yet never exhibit any spiritual growth. They think they are doing all the right things, yet they wonder why their religion seems so empty and unsatisfying.

The answer to that problem, in many cases, is that these people have never experienced genuine conversion. Jesus told Nicodemus, one of the most religious men of His day, "You must be born again" (John 3:7). We don't know if he came to Jesus because he was dissatisfied with his religion and wanted more or because he wanted to find out more about Jesus.

But whatever his motive, Nicodemus learned that religion was not enough. He needed to be born again, and we have the same problem he had. Deeply embedded within us at birth is a sin nature that is defective and requires a spiritual rebirth.

THE CHARACTER OF CONVERSION

Now if our problem is a defective, corrupt, and ruined nature, then we need a brand-new nature implanted within us to fix that mess. That's exactly what God does for us at conversion, as we saw earlier in 2 Peter 1:4.

God Gives Us His Nature at Conversion

Conversion, or salvation, also known as the new birth, is the process whereby God deposits within every believer a new nature that is from Him and is therefore perfect. At the same time the old nature, called "our old self," is "crucified with [Christ]" (Rom. 6:6). That old sin nature that dominated us and kept the life of God from flowing through us has been put to death, and in its place is a new nature from God that the Bible says cannot sin (1 John 3:9). But hold on, because that doesn't mean we are perfect. We still bear the residue of the old sin nature, which Paul called the "sin which dwells in me" (Rom. 7:17), because these imperfect bodies have been corrupted by sin. The body contaminated by sin, or what Paul calls "the body of this death" (v. 24) is where our battle with sin exists (v. 23). It is no longer our old nature, which has been crucified. Our old nature deposited sin in our bodies so that even though it has been destroyed, the presence of sin is still with us. It is just that sin no longer is operating as the essence of who we are. This is why this body must die, so that we can receive new ones. But God is going to take care of that too someday (1 Cor. 15:53–54).

Conversion is of such a radical character that Paul wrote, "If anyone is in Christ, he is a new creature; the old things passed away; behold, new things have come" (2 Cor. 5:17). When you receive Christ, everything becomes new at the core of your being, and it is this new life or new nature that gives you the disposition and the capacity to know and serve God and others rather than serving sin and self. When Adam and Eve sinned and became infected with a sin nature, they ran away from God. But when God deposits the new nature in someone's life, it gives that person the desire and ability to run toward God, because the new nature is tuned to receive God's signals, if we can use the analogy of the brain and muscles again.

If you are a Christian, you are brand-new on the inside. Now this is where the truth of the new birth impinges on the issue of spiritual growth. A lot of Christians would respond to what I have just said by asking this question: "Tony, if I have this new nature on the inside of me that gives me a great capacity to know God, where is it?" What they are really saying is, "When I look at my life, I can't seem to locate this wonderful spiritual reality and drive you are talking about."

Our New Nature Needs to Be Nurtured

Well, if you are a genuine believer, that new nature from God is there. It has perfect DNA with all the encoding necessary for you to grow into a mature spiritual adult. This new nature may be buried under old ways of thinking and acting, but it's there and it needs to be nurtured. Spiritual growth is the process of nurturing and developing the new nature that God implanted in your human spirit, at the deepest core of your being.

Let's illustrate this by going back to the physical counterpart of spiritual birth, which is human birth. When conception occurs and a new life is created within a mother's womb, the whole package that will become a grown person is present in that fertilized egg. But that life is microscopic, not fully developed. In fact, the mother does not even detect that this life is present until a number of weeks have passed.

Since this is true, if you expect to see hands and feet appear in the first weeks of a human embryo's development, you will be disappointed. There has not been sufficient growth for these limbs to fully develop, although they are present in the embryo's genetic makeup.

Our spiritual growth follows much the same process. This is why the Bible talks about Christians who are infants, children, and mature adults. The goal is to see the life that God has implanted within us, which John calls God's "seed" (1 John 3:9), begin to grow and develop the way a baby grows in its mother's womb.

And just as a baby's earliest growth within the mother is not evident on the outside, so we may not see a lot of immediate, outward evidences of the spiritual growth taking place within us. But that will change as God does His work within us. An expectant mother soon gives evidence of the life within her as her body grows. Our growth will also become evident to others as we develop into the full-grown, mature Christians that God designed us to be.

The miracle of the new birth is that this transformation and growth occurs in the midst of, and in spite of, our flawed humanity. Christians still struggle with sin, and we will continue to struggle until Jesus comes and gives us new bodies. It's important to understand that God is not interested in just trying to knock the dents out of our old sinful self, sand down the rough places, and give our flesh a fresh coat of paint. You see, that's what a lot of people think the Christian life and spiritual growth are all about.

Not at all! God has already condemned these sinful bodies of ours to eventual decay. The problem with too many of us Christians is that we are busy trying to repair the old nature and make it look new, when God is in the business of throwing out the old and crafting something brand-new.

A person whose car has been declared a total loss in an accident receives another car. But if the car isn't totaled, then the owner has to get it repaired and hope it can be restored at least close to what it was. God has declared our old nature a total loss because we were born in sin. He wants us to concentrate on the new nature He has given us. If you have spent years trying to fix up what God says cannot be fixed up, then I hope the truth of God's Word and the message of this book will liberate you from a frustrating way of life.

Whenever I teach about the radical character of conversion, I think of caterpillars and butterflies. I'm not into insects, so caterpillars are ugly to me. But once they break free of the cocoon of their old nature and become butterflies, the transformation is incredible. What was once ugly is now beautiful. A creature that could only crawl can now soar.

This transformation requires a growth process, and that isn't always easy. There is a lot of struggle involved in changing a caterpillar into a butterfly, but the result is worth the effort. A butterfly is not just a fixed-up caterpillar, but a new creature with a new capacity for life.

THE COMPLETENESS OF CONVERSION

You may have heard the story of Mr. Yates, the man who was given a farm but couldn't afford to keep it up and was being forced to sell it. But just before he sold the farm, some men came to Mr. Yates and told him they had reason to believe there might be oil on his property. They asked for permission to drill, which Mr. Yates readily granted, and they hit a gusher. All of a sudden, the destitute farmer who was about to lose his place became a millionaire.

But in the truest sense, Mr. Yates became a millionaire the day he was given the farm. He just didn't know it, because he didn't know about the treasure that resided deep in the heart of his farm. And because he was unaware of his riches, Mr. Yates spent all of his time and energy concentrating on what was visible above the surface, struggling to maintain something that was more than capable of maintaining him.[1]

This is a picture of the way far too many Christians live. If you are struggling to keep things up, you need to see that God has deposited more in you at your salvation than you could ever imagine. You have everything you need to grow and become spiritually mature, because you have the Holy Spirit living inside of you and because of the work God has done in your heart and mind. The Holy Spirit is the subject of a future chapter, so let's talk about the work God does within you when you come to Christ. The Bible says:

> For by one offering He has perfected for all time those who are sanctified. And the Holy Spirit also testifies to us; for after saying, "This is the covenant that I will make with them after those days, says the Lord: I will put My laws upon their heart, and on their mind I will write them," He then says, "And their sins and their lawless deeds I will remember no more." (Heb. 10:14–17)

God tells us in this passage that He is doing something new with His people under the new covenant, which is described in Jeremiah 31:31–34 and from which the writer of Hebrews was quoting. Under the old covenant, the law of Moses, God wrote His laws on tablets of stone—but the people lacked the internal power to keep those laws. But under the new covenant, God writes His laws on the hearts and minds of His people, which means that He gives us both the desire

---

1. Lisa Kepner, "Ira Griffith Yates, Jr. (1859–1939)," Texas State Historical Association, February 1, 1996, https://www.tshaonline.org/handbook/entries/yates-ira-griffith-jr.

(through our hearts) and the power (through our minds) to obey and please Him (Rom. 7:22).

This is a staggering change in God's way of dealing with people. Old Testament Israelites had to go out and find God's law, so to speak, and then do their best to try to keep it. But we carry His law written on our hearts and minds, where it is always ready to instruct and correct us. This, by the way, is why Paul said the problem with the old covenant was not the law of God, which is perfect. God has always demanded holiness and faithfulness from His people, and His requirements have never changed. What has changed is the ability of believers to live up to His standards.

This new work of God within us is why spiritual growth isn't finding the latest or newest program or small group, but energizing the new life within us and allowing it to flourish. It's a matter of the heart, spirit, and mind. When God gives you a new heart and your mind is renewed by the Holy Spirit (Rom. 12:2; 1 Cor. 2:11–16), you are going to grow.

You'll Have a New Struggle

Now I have to be honest and tell you that you are also going to struggle at the same time. You see, having a new heart and mind means that you get an entirely new set of tastes, attitudes, and desires that are directed toward God. And when these new things come into contact with your old sinful flesh, conflict is inevitable.

Paul wrote very candidly about this conflict in Romans 6–8, particularly chapter 7. For example, at one point he said, "What I am doing, I do not understand; for I am not practicing what I would like to do, but I am doing the very thing I hate. But if I do the very thing I do not want to do, I agree with the Law, confessing that the Law is good. So now, no longer am I the one doing it, but sin which dwells in me" (Rom. 7:15–17).

Does this sound familiar? Paul's struggle was so intense that some

Bible commentators believe he was writing about his life before he became a Christian. But it isn't necessary to argue that Paul wasn't a Christian, because he ended this section with a declaration of victory: "Thanks be to God through Jesus Christ our Lord!" (Rom. 7:25).

What Paul discovered is that when he came to Christ, his entire orientation to life changed. Now that he had God's law written on his heart, he could not sin without feeling his new nature coming against that sin and constantly drawing him back to Christ. Paul had a new heart because God had performed a heart transplant on him.

We have undergone the same heart transplant as believers. God doesn't deal in bypass surgery, which leaves the old heart in place and simply goes around the problem. When the Bible declares in 2 Corinthians 5:17 that we are new creatures in Christ Jesus, that's exactly what it means. If you know Christ, you have a new heart, not just a patched-up, bypassed former heart.

You'll Have New Appetites

When a woman becomes pregnant, one of the most marked changes that occurs is in her appetite. In the same way, this new heart we received at salvation manifests itself in new spiritual desires or appetites (see Heb. 10:14–16). Your new nature craves intimacy and fellowship with God, and it desires to please and obey Him more than anything else. These are intense cravings, which is why you can't sin as a Christian and enjoy it or feel no remorse for it the way you did when you were an unbeliever. You'll still sin because you are still in your old flesh, but your new sensitivity to spiritual things will cause an intense struggle in your soul because now you have to try to ignore the new appetites God has placed within you.

But the flip side of this issue is the exciting reality that when you feed your new, God-given appetites, you enjoy the immense satisfaction of His blessing, and you begin to grow spiritually. God's law that is written on your heart becomes the most real and vital thing operating in your life, and you are able to bring more areas of your life under the Lordship of Christ. In the process you'll also have a new desire to glorify God, which as we learned in the first chapter is God's all-consuming desire for His people.

It's What's on the Inside That Counts

When it's all said and done, then, spiritual growth does not primarily depend on what is happening around you, but on what is happening inside of you. Growth comes from the inside out, which is the way God designed all of His creation to function. Full-grown oak trees don't just appear. Neither do full-grown Christians. But all the requirements for growth are already there.

Spiritual growth is the process of expanding and releasing what is on the inside so that it becomes visible on the outside. What God often does is apply the heat and the pressure to bring about this release. That's why our greatest times of spiritual growth are almost always our times of greatest trial.

This is the way it works with popcorn. Did you know that popcorn pops because the heat applied to the kernels causes the moisture inside of them to build up pressure? The moisture is changed to steam, and as the steam rises it presses against the shell of the kernel, which breaks under the pressure and releases the corn inside.

Popcorn kernels don't look like much before they are heated, and if you try to eat one, you may break a tooth. But put them under heat and you'll find out there is a lot more on the inside than you thought. Now the popcorn is useful and satisfying because it grew under pressure into the tasty food item it was designed to be. Delicious popcorn is the realization of the potential that was there all along.

When He saved us, God put deep within us a new nature made in His image and gave us a new heart. When the Holy Spirit begins to heat up your new nature so that the steam of your new life begins to rise and bursts through the outer shell called your body, then you will begin to explode with new growth and the good stuff on the inside will be manifested.

Lasting spiritual growth comes about through internal transformation, not just external reformation. Paul wrote, "Walk by the Spirit, and you will not carry out the desire of the flesh" (Gal. 5:16). The order is crucial here because a lot of Christians get this backward. We think that if we can just stop fulfilling the desire or lust of the flesh, then we can begin walking in the Spirit.

But it's just the opposite. The Holy Spirit working on the inside produces spiritual victory on the outside. All that we need to walk in victory and grow in Christ is already present within us.

Several years ago a TV commercial for spaghetti sauce showed a mother in the kitchen cooking the spaghetti. As the aroma fills the house, her son comes in and looks at the sauce. "Hey Mom, where are the mushrooms?"

"They're already in the sauce," she says.

"What about the sausage?"

"It's in there, too."

"And what about the tomatoes?"

Once again the mother says, "They're already in the sauce."

You get the idea. God is cooking up a batch of spiritual growth sauce for you, and it's all in there. You're looking for victory? It's in there. You're looking for strength to obey Him? It's in there. Do you need faith to trust Him more, or grace to endure a trial? They're already in the sauce! Are you ready for the meal?

3

Identity:
The Key to
Kingdom Living

IF YOU HAVE EVER BEEN to a circus, then you have probably seen the elephants. It always amazed me when I was at a circus looking at these enormous elephants weighing several tons that each of them was kept in place by a single chain wrapped around one foot and tied to a small stake. Any one of those elephants could have easily ripped that stake out of the ground and run away, but that almost never happened because circus elephants have been conditioned to forget who they are. Their identity has been taken from them.

By that I mean that these elephants have been trained since they were babies to submit when they feel the tug of that chain on their legs. The trainer has conditioned the elephants to accept their chains so they can be tamed and controlled and put on display for the entertainment of others. This system works so well that whenever a circus elephant exercises its power to throw off its chains and go on a rampage, videos of it doing so quickly go viral.

Much like elephants in the circus, a lot of Christians are being held hostage by a small chain around their ankles that holds them down and keeps them from getting anywhere. These people go to church and hear about all the power and spiritual authority that God has for them as believers in Jesus Christ, but they can't seem to kick free of the chains holding them back.

I'm convinced that what people in this condition need is not primarily a deliverance service, but an identity check. They need to understand who they are in Christ. If you are confused about your identity as a Christian, if no one has ever explained to you who you really are, I hope the Holy Spirit will use what we are going to explore in this chapter to help liberate you from any chain that is holding you down. God did not go to the trouble of saving you just so the world, the flesh, or the devil could chain you up and make you perform at their demand. God created you with a specific purpose in mind. In order to live out this purpose, it is important to understand your true identity. Your spiritual identity is the key to kingdom living.

A person's identity is a critical thing, especially in today's information-driven society. Your identity has great commercial value not only to you, but to someone else who might try to steal it and use your name and credit line to run up a stack of bills. Identity theft has become so pervasive in our digitally obsessed culture.

Having a clear identity is so important to our human makeup that some people go to great lengths to try to gain an identity they think will make them acceptable to a certain group. These people may buy designer clothes or a certain kind of car in order to appear affluent. A few years ago there was a string of cases in which several high-profile public figures were found to have lied on their résumés to help them obtain a new position. A good portion of the world's commerce, at least in the Western world, is geared toward helping people look, feel, and act as something other than what they really are, because someone has convinced them there is something wrong with their true identity.

Besides trying to buy an identity, another common mistake many people make is linking their identity with their activity. We do this when we identify ourselves by our profession or trade. Believers are especially prone to this trap because we often reduce the Christian life to a set of activities that we either perform or avoid. One of my former seminary professors once taught at a large secular university, where his unsaved colleagues had the idea that Christians were people who didn't smoke or drink or go to parties. He said he had a very hard time trying to show them that Christianity was not a performance, but a relationship with Christ.

Confusing what we do with our real identity is an easy mistake to make, but the confusion is still lethal if we want to grow and thrive in our daily walk with the Lord. I heard about a man with an extreme case of identity confusion who went to see a psychiatrist. "What's wrong?" the doctor asked him.

"I have a problem," the man answered. "I've become convinced that I'm a dog. Every time I pass the dog food section at the grocery store, I have an overwhelming urge to buy several cans and eat them. I sleep on a rug on the floor, and I turn around three times before lying down. I've also been chasing cars and barking at cats. I have really come to believe that I'm a dog."

"Well, this is certainly serious, and it's not like anything I've ever dealt with before," the psychiatrist said. "I think I can help you, but first I need to know how long you've been dealing with this problem."

The man blurted out, "Ever since I was a puppy!"

I don't know anyone with an identity crisis this severe. But I've met many Christians who are confused or basically uninformed about their true identity as children of the King. And it's clear that false identity leads to false growth.

OUR IDENTITY BEGINS AT THE CROSS

We saw in the previous chapter that the moment you placed your faith in Christ alone for salvation, God implanted a new nature deep within your being. This new nature, also called the new birth, is the reference point for your identity. But what I also want you to understand is that when God gave you this new nature, through which you are now alive spiritually, He also put to death your old nature. This death occurred on the cross of Jesus Christ when He died for the sins of the world. This is why your identity as a Christian begins at the cross.

The truth of this is expressed so clearly in Galatians 2:20, which has been my life verse for many years. This incredible verse contains all that we really need to know about our identity as believers, condensed into one power-packed capsule. If you can absorb and apply what the Bible teaches in Galatians 2:20, you are well on your way to growing spiritually, because your identity is the key to your spiritual development.

Let me give you the verse, and then we'll break it out into its component parts. The apostle Paul wrote to the church at Galatia, "I have been crucified with Christ; and it is no longer I who live, but Christ lives in me; and the life which I now live in the flesh I live by faith in the Son of God, who loved me and gave Himself up for me."

We Died with Christ

If you have heard this verse many times and maybe even memorized it, as I have, it may not sound as shocking as it really is. The first phrase alone is jarring enough to let us know that something major is going on here. "I have been crucified with Christ." You and I can put our names in there, because this is a done deal.

Now to be crucified is to die. We know that Jesus died on the cross, but His death also brought about the death of the sin nature of all those who are identified with Him. We are so completely identified with Christ that when we accept Him as our Savior, He takes up residence in our lives and puts to death the old nature within us, which is totally corrupted and ruined by sin. The death we experienced at the cross is death to sin and the old way of life we inherited from Adam. "How shall we who died to sin still live in it?" Paul asks (Rom. 6:2).

Our old self is dead and gone, crucified with Christ on the cross and buried with Him when He was buried in the tomb (Rom. 6:4). Because that's true, we had better be looking for our identity somewhere else, since dead people don't grow. A key step in spiritual growth and our identity with Christ that many Christians skip over is coming to grips with the fact of our death to sin and the old life. This spiritual death means that sin no longer is the core definition of who we are. Our problem with sin is now a problem of the flesh, which is the house we live in, not the essence of who we are.

See, too many believers aren't growing because they are still hanging out in the cemetery with the corpse of their old self, trying to resuscitate what God has put to death. They don't know that their old life, what the Bible calls the "old self" (Col. 3:9), is dead in Christ.

Paul wrote to the Romans, "If we have become united with Him in the likeness of His death, certainly we shall also be in the likeness of His resurrection, *knowing this,* that our old self was crucified with Him, in order that our body of sin might be done away with" (Rom. 6:5–6, italics added). Paul said we need to know that we've been crucified with Christ. But many Christians would have to say if they were honest, "I didn't know that."

A union with Christ occurred at the cross that is often not understood, and because it's not understood, people are oblivious to its life-changing implications. This is similar to what happens to some married couples. They stand at the altar on their wedding day and nod in agreement when the preacher talks about them no longer being two, but becoming one. They go over and light the unity candle, blowing out their individual candles to symbolize this brand-new union.

But soon after the wedding those old individual candles somehow get reignited. Why? Because it turns out that one or both of the parties was not really ready to die to singleness. That is, they are still trying to live as they did when they were single, coming and going and spending their time and money as they please, without being accountable to anyone. But any married person who has not died to his or her singleness cannot fully enjoy the marriage union. Marriage demands a totally different mindset and commitment to a new way of life.

Our Death Is Spiritual

Now even though Jesus' death on the cross was physical, the death we died in union with Him is spiritual. But that doesn't make our death any less real.

You may be saying, "But I didn't feel like I died when I got saved." It's true that the impact or the emotions surrounding a spiritual death may not be as vivid as we experience when someone dies physically. You may not have felt your spiritual crucifixion when Christ came into your life, but according to 2 Corinthians 5:17, you become a new person and the things associated with your old life passed away.

So how do you make this real in your life? Romans 6:11 says, "Consider yourselves to be dead to sin, but alive to God in Christ Jesus." *Consider* is an accounting term. It means to add up the figures and arrive at the answer. God says we died with Christ, and when He arose to new life, we were resurrected with Him to begin a new way of life. God gave us a means of demonstrating this death and resurrection through the ordinance of baptism.

Again in Romans 6 we read, "Do you not know that all of us who have been baptized into Christ Jesus have been baptized into His death? Therefore we have been buried with Him through baptism into death, so that as Christ was raised from the dead through the glory of the Father, so we too might walk in newness of life" (vv. 3–4). Baptism is not salvation, but it is a public picture of what Jesus did for us. When we go under the waters of baptism, we are picturing our identification with Christ in His death, and when we come up out of the water, we declare our identification with Christ in His resurrection.

Now if God has pronounced your old self dead, why would you want to mess around with that corpse and live in the realm of death when He has a new life for you? God wants you to leave the cemetery of the old life and take up your new identity as His child. You need to understand that once you belong to God, He no longer sees you as a sinner. He sees you as a saint and His son or daughter.

We often hear Christians say, "Well, I'm just a sinner saved by grace." No, that devalues the radically new nature of what God has done for us and helps to confuse our identity. A Christian should not say, for example, "I am a homosexual," or "I am an alcoholic," but rather "I am a new person in Jesus Christ who is struggling with the sin of homosexuality or drinking." If you define who you are by what you do, you're starting with the problem instead of the perspective that you are a blood-bought, totally purchased, absolutely forgiven child of the living God who has a problem in some area. Knowing who you are in Christ completely changes your reference point.

Are you beginning to see that this is revolutionary stuff? Let me give you two more facets of the Christian's new life that blow me away every time I read them. Paul said, "We have the mind of Christ" (1 Cor. 2:16). Did you get that? We now have the capacity to think God's thoughts after Him. This new mind also includes our emotions, desires, attitudes, and all of the other components that make up the core of our being.

We also have a new location. When Christ raised us from the dead, He raised us all the way. That is, after Christ was resurrected, He ascended back into heaven and is seated "at [God's] right hand in the heavenly places" (Eph. 1:20). So if our identity is bound up in Christ, guess where we are? We are also seated "with Him in the heavenly places" (Eph. 2:6). That's a spiritual reality, not just wishful thinking. Everything that happened to Christ in His death, burial, and resurrection happened to us spiritually.

CHRIST HAS BECOME OUR LIFE

Our identification with Christ is so complete that Paul could say, reading further in Galatians 2:20, "It is no longer I who live, but *Christ lives in me*" (italics added). That last phrase is loaded with meaning. We must come to grips with the reality that what is happening in this body, through the soul, is the very expression of the life of Christ as He lives in us.

I need to make a crucial clarification here, because most people read this and say, "I get it. Christ is in me, and I am in Him." Well, that's true. The most fundamental truth of the Christian life is that Jesus Christ takes up residence within us when we receive Him as Savior. But Galatians 2:20 is saying more than that in terms of our identity as believers. It is not just that Christ is in us, but that He is *living* in us.

Christ Wants to Be at Home in You

The difference between these two is the difference between the standing or security we enjoy in Christ, which never changes, and the state or condition of our Christian lives at any particular time, which can be very changeable. The Bible says that because we are in Christ we are "sealed in Him with the Holy Spirit of promise" (Eph. 1:13). This is His seal of security that no one can break and that guarantees us heaven.

But Christ does not just want to dwell in you. He wants to *live* in you—to move in and settle down and fully express Himself through your life. Allowing Christ to live out His life through you is the fountainhead of spiritual growth, for only God working in us by the power of the Holy Spirit can produce lasting growth and change in us.

The tragedy is that a lot of Christians who are going to heaven are not growing in Christ here on earth because they are not allowing Him to be fully at home within them. These individuals treat Christ the way we treat our guests. We invite our guests to make themselves at home when we have visitors at our houses, but we don't usually mean what we say. We don't really want them roaming around our house, looking in our closet, and helping themselves to whatever they find in our kitchen. What we mean by "Make yourself at home" is, "Make yourself at room, and only at the room I take you into!"

But in order for Jesus Christ to make Himself at home in your life, He needs to have the run of the house. Christ indwells every believer, but His presence is more alive and vital in some people than in others because they are allowing Him to live through them and take possession of the whole house.

We're talking about the contrast between just living and being alive. An electric eel and an electrician are both involved with electricity, but the difference is that the electrician simply works in the presence of electricity, while an eel *experiences* electricity in its body. A lot of us work in the presence of Jesus. We go to church, read books about Jesus, and gather information on Him.

But Jesus is saying, "No, this is not enough. I want to express the power of My resurrected life through your body and your spirit. I want to live in you." The Bible says, "We have this treasure in earthen vessels, so that the surpassing greatness of the power will be of God" (2 Cor. 4:7). The purpose of everything we experience is that "the life of Jesus also may be manifested in our body" (v. 10).

Quit Trying to Live the Christian Life

I've met many frustrated Christians over the years. And when I talk to them, more often than not I find out they are frustrated because they are trying so hard to live the Christian life, but it isn't working. If that's your problem, I want to lift a load from your shoulders. Quit trying to live the Christian life. You can't do it. It's impossible. The harder you try to do what God wants you to do, the flatter you will fall.

Jesus is the only Person who has ever lived the Christian life successfully—and the good news is that He offers to live His life in you! God never asked you to be a Christian in your own power. But He does expect you to yield your body to Christ as a living sacrifice (Rom. 12:1) so He can express His perfect love, power, and holiness through you. That's what it means to be identified with Christ. Anything less than this is like putting your car in neutral and then flooring the gas pedal. You'll make a lot of noise, but you won't get anywhere.

I love 1 Corinthians 1:30, where Paul wrote, "By [God's] doing you are in Christ Jesus, who became to us wisdom from God, and righteousness and sanctification, and redemption." In other words, when you received Christ, you got the whole package. He is your reference point and identity. Through Jesus, there is nothing you cannot do (Matt. 19:26). You can declare with Paul, "I can do all things through Him who strengthens me" (Phil. 4:13).

Give me the fingers of Mozart, and there is no musical piece I cannot play. Give me the mind of Einstein, and there is no mathematical formula I cannot unravel. Give me the arms of Hank Aaron, and there is no home run I cannot hit. Give me the life of Jesus Christ, and there is no victory I cannot achieve.

CHRIST IS LIVING THROUGH YOU

Now before you get to thinking that this matter of the Christian life is too otherworldly to be practical, I want to take you back to Galatians 2:20 once more to bring this thing home. In the last half of this great verse we read, *"And the life which I now live in the flesh* I live by faith in the Son of God, who loved me and gave Himself up for me" (italics added).

The Christian Life Is Not Passive

The Christian life is not just "Let go and let God." This is not a passive relationship in which we sit back and cruise along while Jesus Christ does all the work. He is our life, for sure, but He does not live it apart from us. The new life we received from God operates through our bodies and our personalities. God will not levitate you around so you will always go where He wants you to go. He will be with you as you speak to someone about Christ, but He will not speak through you like a puppeteer drawing the strings. He is no Puppet Master.

A lot of times we sit around saying things like, "Lord, I know You want me to read my Bible, so I'm waiting for You to give me a real desire for Your Word." There's nothing wrong with praying for a desire for the Word, but that is more likely to come when you put down your mobile device and pick up your Bible. Again, God is not going to levitate your Bible into your lap and open it to the place He wants you to read. We must work in cooperation with Christ's work in us.

A person who has been using drugs for years may be unable to stop on his own. But when that person yields the members of his body "as instruments of righteousness to God" (Rom. 6:13), he will find new power to break that destructive cycle. But the believer has to do the yielding. In fact, verse 13 is part of a command to Christians that begins, "Do not let sin reign in your mortal body" (v. 12). A drug addict's body and mind may have been trained to seek drugs for many years. But the issue now is not that training, but Christ's power. He can supply all that is needed, but not apart from our will and our mind.

Many Are Carrying a Fake ID

I'm afraid that too many of us have been carrying around fake IDs for so long we have trouble remembering who we really are. For example, some Christians get all wrapped up in legalism, which tells them that their identity is tied up in what they do or don't do. But this is not only a false source of Christian identity, it also confuses outsiders like my former professor's university colleagues, who look at us and conclude that Christians are simply people who don't smoke or drink or whatever else is on the don't-do-it list.

Now there are definitely things we should and should not be doing, and as new creations in Christ, we have the Holy Spirit within us affirming that this is true. The problem Paul struggled with in Romans 6–8 is that while he agreed that God's law was perfect and good (Rom. 7:12), he found himself unable to pull off the good things he knew he should be doing.

Paul had to come to grips with the fact that it wasn't him trying his best to obey God, but it was Christ in him that gave him power over sin. His testimony was that Jesus "condemned sin in the flesh, so that the requirement of the law might be fulfilled in us, who do not walk according to the flesh but according to the Spirit" (Rom. 8:3b–4). One reason Romans 6–8 is in the Bible is so we can see that even a great and exemplary Christian like the apostle Paul had to come to the understanding that it was not his ability, but the living Christ operating inside of him, that enabled him to walk "according to the Spirit" and please God.

You Live Your New Life by Faith

You may be saying, "Tony, I'm getting on board with the fact that Christ wants to live His life and express Himself through me. I want to get this thing working, but how do I do it?" The answer is in the phrase from Galatians 2:20 that says that we live this new life "by faith in the Son of God."

Sorry, but I don't have surprises or an "easy" button to push here. The Christian life is a life of faith from beginning to end. Faith is not simply believing *in* God, but believing God when He says we cannot live the Christian life apart from Him. I often define faith as acting like God is telling the truth. That means your actions align with a belief that what God says is true.

I like to say that faith is acting like something is so even when it is not so in order that it might be so simply because God said so.

Paul learned his lesson of aligning faith with actions when he learned to lean on Jesus to live in and through Him. That's why Paul could say that it is "Christ in you" which is "the hope of glory" (Col. 1:27).

The Christian life is lived by faith in Christ, but this faith is not a cold academic exercise. The last part of Galatians 2:20 reminds us that Christ "loved me and gave Himself up for me." That's the language of loving, intimate relationship. Jesus wants you to trust Him, but not the way you trust your bank to take care of your money or your car to get you where you're going. Living by faith is cultivating a relationship with the living Christ who wants you to identify with Him so closely that people can't tell you apart.

Have you ever seen a married couple who had been together for so long that they even began to look alike? On top of that, they had many of the same mannerisms, or could finish each other's sentences as if they were thinking the same thoughts. That's what intimacy will produce over time. Jesus wants you to abide so closely with Him that you reflect Him in all you think, say, and do.

So who are you? You are a totally forgiven, fully accepted, absolutely loved child of God. That is your identity in Jesus Christ, and once you come to grips with the reality of it you will be ready to grow like you have never grown before.

4

Sin:
The Hindrance to
Kingdom Living

ANYTIME A HUMAN BEING experiences malnutrition, doctors want to observe for signs of stunted growth. Whether it is a child or an adult, the growth and development of cells in the body will be minimized without proper and adequate nutrition.

In order for us to grow and develop as believers the way God intended, there must be an unrestricted flow of nutrition as well, which is the grace of God at work in our lives. This is the grace that saves us and releases within us the power of the Holy Spirit reproducing the life of Christ. The goal of this growth process is to produce holiness in the believer's life (1 Peter 1:14–16)—which means living in a way that glorifies God and brings good to others. We do this when we seek to advance God's kingdom agenda in all we say and do.

Jesus referred to this flow of God's grace and power when He stood up in Jerusalem one day at the climax of the Feast of Tabernacles and called out, "If anyone is thirsty, let him come to Me and drink. He who believes in Me, as the Scriptures said, 'From his innermost being will flow rivers of living water'" (John 7:37–38). John then added, "This He spoke of the Spirit, whom those who believed in Him were to receive" (v. 39).

Many people tend to think that only "super saints" ever achieve this level of spiritual growth and productivity. But what Jesus was offering is the normal Christian life. Notice that the promise is to everyone who believes in Him. God doesn't have categories of believers, with the chosen elite at the top of His list and the run-of-the-mill individuals at the bottom. The full flow of His grace is available to all of us without distinction.

However, there is a blocker called sin that can hinder the flow of grace and interfere with our spiritual growth. In fact, more than anything else that exists, sin is the biggest hindrance to kingdom living.

We seem to have a generation of spiritually malnourished people today who are failing to reach their full potential and maximum maturity in Christ. There may be many individual reasons for this, but when all is said and done, we have to come back to the fact that sin in its myriad forms and manifestations is the biggest hindrance to spiritual growth.

Sin's impact on our lives is not by accident, since we have three formidable enemies arrayed against us. These include the world (an evil system, 1 John 5:19), the flesh (our evil desires, Rom. 7:14–15), and the devil (an evil person, Rev. 12:9). They join forces in a well-planned campaign to use sin to stunt our spiritual development. But we are not alone, because Jesus has overcome the world (John 16:33; 1 John 4:4), God has given us victory over our evil desires (Rom. 7:25), and He has stripped the devil of his power through Jesus' death on the cross (Heb. 2:14).

SIN ALWAYS SEPARATES US FROM GOD

I don't want to confuse you with terminology here. The sin that hinders growth and fellowship in the life of a Christian is a different issue from the sin that separated us from God as unbelievers. The difference between these two conditions is the difference between heaven and hell, but it's also important to realize that sin separates us from God, whether we are talking about eternal separation in hell or the breaking of intimate fellowship between a believer and the Lord.

Our Relationship with God Is Eternal

The loss of *fellowship* with God is the issue for Christians, because our *relationship* with Him was eternally settled the moment we placed our faith in Christ. The Bible says, "Therefore, having been justified by faith, we have peace with God through our Lord Jesus Christ" (Rom. 5:1). Later in that same chapter, Paul said that through the "obedience" of Christ, His sacrificial death on the cross, we have been "made righteous" (v. 19).

Justification in the New Testament is a legal term that means to be made or declared righteous. When we come to Christ for the forgiveness of sin, God places our sin on Christ's account and credits His righteousness to our account. This allows God to render a legal decision, declaring us righteous because we are in Christ.

Elsewhere Paul described the transaction this way: "He made Him who knew no sin to be sin on our behalf, so that we might become the righteousness of God in Him" (2 Cor. 5:21). This is the wonderful exchange of our sin for Christ's righteousness by which we are made fit to enter heaven. If you have not trusted Christ for salvation, you have already been tried and declared guilty of sin in the courtroom of God—and there is nothing you can do to erase your guilt. No number of good deeds, church attendance, or community service is acceptable in the court of heaven as payment for sin.

No matter how much good an unbeliever does, it does not eradicate guilt in the heavenly court. Unbelievers are like cut flowers in a vase. They may be beautiful, smell good, and appear to be at the top of their form. But they are dead because they've been cut off from the source of life. And the fact that they are dead will be revealed with the passing of time as they wither.

But when lost people come to Jesus Christ and look to Him alone for the forgiveness of sins, they are forgiven and justified forever. And as part of that transaction, God imparts to the believing sinner a new nature—a new life that is in seed form and must grow, just as physical life begins in seed form and must grow.

Our Fellowship with God Must Be Maintained

So let's be clear that we are addressing the sin that contaminates the life of a believer and hinders communion with God and usefulness for Him. Those who are outside of Christ must deal with the sin that condemns a person to eternal separation from God.

How many times have you heard Christians say they wish they didn't have to continue struggling with sin? The day is coming when Jesus will deliver us not only from sin's power, but from its very presence. Until then we must deal with sin, but we have a powerful ally in the spiritual realm called God's grace. As grace flows to us and through us, it stimulates the growth of our new nature, the seed life that God placed in us.

The apostle John made a very interesting statement about this new nature. "No one who is born of God practices sin, because His seed abides in him; and he cannot sin, because he is born of God" (1 John 3:9). That's a strong statement that might throw you a little bit, because all of us sin every day in thought, word, and deed. How can John say we cannot sin when sin is a daily reality for us?

Don't misread the verse. It is "His seed," the new nature God placed in us, that cannot sin. It is impossible for anything that comes from God to be contaminated by sin in any way. His spiritual DNA has no defects. Your new nature is without flaw, so your new nature cannot sin.

But we still struggle with sin because our new nature is living in the old house of our sin-contaminated flesh. The former resident of that house, the old sinful nature, is gone. The Bible says, "Our old self was crucified with [Christ]" (Rom. 6:6). So while we still battle with sin, it is no longer in the control center of our lives. It is, however, in the brick and mortar of our bodies (Rom. 7:7). The good news is that the new nature is now in the dominant place of influence and control.

Unfortunately, as long as we are in these sin-infested bodies that someday will be consigned to the grave, sin will continue to be a problem. Our new nature exists in the old flesh, and they are diametrically opposed to each other. That's why the Bible says, "The flesh sets its desire against the Spirit, and the Spirit against the flesh" (Gal. 5:17). One proof you are saved is that you feel this battle going on inside of you. Lost people don't have this battle, because they are slaves to the flesh and do not have the Holy Spirit.

That's why it's so important that you grow in Christ. The more you grow spiritually, the more the Spirit dominates the flesh rather than the flesh defeating us and thwarting the Spirit's work in our lives. When we were kids, our parents and other adults used to warn us against smoking with this statement, "It will stunt your growth." In fact, they seemed to use that argument against any bad habit they didn't want us to pick up.

As teenagers we may not have known exactly what our parents were talking about in terms of stunted growth, but whatever it was it sure didn't sound good. And whether they were medically correct in their warning didn't matter, because we didn't want anything messing with our growth. When it comes to sin, that warning is well stated. Sin will stunt your growth by restricting the flow of the nutrients of God's grace and power to you.

WE MUST RECOGNIZE OUR SIN BEFORE GOD

If you are starting to feel that sin may have the upper hand in this battle, hang on, because we are coming to the good part. God has made a wonderful provision to remove the hindrance of sin from our lives and restore the free flow of His grace. People who would have died of heart disease earlier in human history are walking around alive and well today because a method was devised to deal with blockage in the arteries around the heart. God's method of removing sin's blockage is described in a classic passage from the first epistle of John. This is worth moving through verse by verse.

God Cannot Tolerate Sin

Let's begin in 1 John 1:5, where John had a special word from Christ to deliver. "This is the message we have heard from Him and announce to you, that God is Light, and in Him there is no darkness at all." When light is used of God in Scripture it stands for His absolute holiness and purity. No darkness, sin, or evil can exist in the perfect light of God's presence. Sin is like rotten garbage to God. It repulses Him. He places a "No Trespassing" sign around His holiness, which must be protected at all times (Ex. 19:21–24).

If you have ever stood under a blazing light, you know that it's not always a comfortable place to be. The light of God's holy presence could be a condemning and consuming place to be, except that we have been forgiven of our sins and stand in a right relationship to Him. But since no sin at all can exist in His light, we have to realize that our sin even as believers creates a barrier between us and a God who is absolutely pure.

John wanted us to understand how complete the contrast is between the God of light and the darkness of sin, so he added the phrase we read above: "In Him there is no darkness at all." God is telling us that He will never adjust to the darkness. In terms of our intimate fellowship with God, if unconfessed sin is present in our lives, His presence is minimized.

We Often Adjust to the Darkness

Now don't take that too far. God is omnipresent in His deity, which means we cannot go anyplace where He is not. But fellowship with Him is only found in the light. Our problem is that we can and do adjust to the darkness. If you step out of the light into a dark room, or go outside on a dark night, you know that if you stay there long enough your eyes will make the necessary adjustments. After a while you can begin to make out shapes and objects, and pretty soon you can actually function in the darkness.

That's often the way we deal with sin. We just stay there long enough that it doesn't look so awful anymore. But God doesn't view sin that way. If you really want to experience darkness as God's Word describes it, go down into an underground cavern and then have the guide turn the light off. You will be enveloped in darkness so thick and so complete that it chills you. You cannot see your hand directly in front of your face.

I think you get the idea that God and sin are completely separate and incompatible because sin is totally against His nature. Sin cuts us off from fellowship with God. And if fellowship with God is severed, our growth is stunted, because the seed of our new life isn't exposed to the light it needs to develop properly. God's grace is experienced in the light, and grace is where our growth is located because we are told to grow in grace. Too many of us are spiritual dwarfs because we hang out in the darkness and avoid the light of God's presence.

Sin Is a Contradiction in Our Lifestyle

Did you notice the contrast implied in 1 John 1:5? John spells it out in verse 6 just in case we missed it: "If we say that we have fellowship with Him and yet walk in the darkness, we lie and do not practice the truth." If we say we are in tight fellowship with God and yet we allow sin to exist unchecked in our lives, we are living a contradiction. That's a big word for a lie, which is what John calls it. If you are walking in the darkness—if you are practicing sin and failing to deal with it—you need to look around you, because you are walking alone. God doesn't show up when you are hanging out in the neighborhood of sin.

Verse 6 doesn't need a lot of explanation, so let's go on to the opposite of walking in the darkness and living a lie. John wrote, "But if we walk in the Light as He Himself is in the Light, we have fellowship with one another, and the blood of Jesus His Son cleanses us from all sin" (v. 7).

It's interesting that John switched the focus of our fellowship here from God to other believers. Don't say you are in close fellowship with God but somehow you can't seem to stand being with other Christians.

When we come into the light, we are going to find other believers standing there with us. The epistle of 1 John is filled with the importance of love between God's kingdom family. God wants to use other believers to help grow us up, but He can't do that the way He wants to when we are at odds with everyone around us. That's why the Bible is full of passages that focus on the "one anothers." These are things we are to do, or be, for each other.

We Need to Come into the Light

Now let me explain something in 1 John 1:7 that may cause you to pause for a moment. The verse says that Jesus' blood cleanses us from all sin as we walk in the light. But I can hear someone saying, "Wait a minute. If God is light and there is no sin in Him, and if I am walking with Him in the light, then there should be no sin, right? Why do I still need Jesus to cleanse me from sin?"

Walking in the light doesn't mean you don't sin. John must have anticipated this kind of objection, because he quickly added in verse 8, "If we say that we have no sin, we are deceiving ourselves and the truth is not in us." Don't let anyone sell you on the idea of sinless perfection. That's an old teaching that says every shred of our old sinful self was eradicated by Christ at salvation. Therefore if we sin it must mean we have lost our salvation and need to get saved again.

That teaching is not supported either by the Bible or by experience. Walking in the light means that you see your sin as God sees it so you can do something about it. One problem with the darkness is that it hides things that are obstacles to our spiritual growth. Since we can't see them in the dark, we plunge on and stub our toe on them. I'm a great one for trying to navigate through a dark room in our house, which is why I like the illustration of stubbing your toe on something.

There's an easier way to get through a room in the middle of the night without crippling yourself. Just reach over and turn on the light, and you will see the room as it really is—including whatever might have been left out on the floor, like a pair of shoes worn that day. Walking in fellowship with God means you see things as they really are.

Rather than trying to cover up or deny sin, truly spiritual people who are growing in grace are constantly becoming more aware of how unlike God they are. The darkness in us is most fully exposed when we come into the pure light of God's holy presence. One of the paradoxes of the Christian life is that the closer you draw to God, the more aware of sin you become.

Isaiah was one of the greatest prophets in the Old Testament. One day Isaiah went into the temple and began enjoying a Holy Spirit led, angelic worship service. He saw God "lofty and exalted," and he heard the holy seraphim calling out, "Holy, Holy, Holy, is the LORD of hosts, the whole earth is full of His glory" (Isa. 6:1–3). The worship was so intense the doorposts of the temple started to shake (v. 4).

This sounds like the kind of worship service we would give anything to be part of. But Isaiah was horrified by the sense of his sin in the presence of pure holiness. "Woe is me, for I am ruined! Because I am a man of unclean lips, and I live among a people of unclean lips" (v. 5).

What brought about this reaction? The rest of the verse gives us the answer: "For my eyes have seen the King, the LORD of hosts." Isaiah was walking in the light in a way we will probably never experience, and he saw his sin clearly. An angel had to come and cleanse him before he could go on (vv. 6–7).

WE NEED TO CONFESS OUR SIN TO GOD

We have two choices when it comes to the sin that cuts us off from the free flow of God's grace and stunts our spiritual growth. We can cover it or confess it. When we confess or come clean with our sin before God, we have the tremendous promise of 1 John 1:9, which most of us have memorized: "If we confess our sins, He is faithful and righteous to forgive us our sins and to cleanse us from all unrighteousness."

This is a powerful statement. Remember that John has already said if we walk in the light, Jesus' blood "cleanses us from all sin" (v. 7). This is a verb form in the original language that means to "keep on cleansing." It's a continual process. The great thing about the blood of Christ is that it is not just for heaven; it works on earth too. The blood that gives you judicial forgiveness in heaven gives you sanctifying forgiveness on earth. Jesus' blood delivers you from sin's power (which allows you growth and fellowship) as well as from sin's penalty (which guarantees you heaven).

We Give God the Right to Expose Our Sins

Walking in the light gives God the right to shine on you and expose your sins. Allowing your sin to be exposed is a good thing, even though it may feel bad for a while. When you start feeling convicted because of something that is not right in your life, it means the Holy

Spirit has shined the light on a problem so it can be corrected.

Whenever I am scheduled to go to the dentist, I spend extra time brushing and flossing my teeth to impress him. Don't tell me you don't do it too. But he doesn't buy my superficial cleaning. He x-rays my teeth, and sometimes he uses that dye that reveals plaque or some other bad news I can't see. My mouth shows up in an entirely different light when my dentist gets through with me.

We Must Agree with God

The dentist brings these problems to my attention so he can address them. I can either agree with him that the problems are there, even though I can't see them myself, or I can deny what he found. If the dentist says I have a need and I say the same thing, I am confessing that he is right, and I need help.

That's what the word *confess* means, to agree or say the same thing. When God x-rays our hearts and applies the dye of His holiness to reveal our sins, confessing those sins means we don't run from or ignore them, but we stand exposed and say, "Yes, Lord, I agree that this was sin, and I confess it to You."

Notice that the plural word *sins* occurs twice in 1 John 1:9. The emphasis is on the individual sins we commit, not sin as a general category. God doesn't want us just to bundle everything together and give it a general once-over by saying, "Dear God, forgive my sin today." That's like the college student who tied all of his laundry into a bundle and threw it into the washer without separating the clothes because he didn't want to mess with the individual pieces of clothing. The trouble is that the clothes didn't really get clean.

A lot of us treat our sins the way we treat our laundry, letting them pile up until wash day and then dealing with them all at once. But the Holy Spirit doesn't follow our schedule. His conviction of sin is often instantaneous. The minute those words went out of your mouth, you knew you shouldn't have said them. The time to confess and be cleansed of that sin is the moment you are aware of it.

We Can Keep the Alarm from Going Off

The conviction of sin works something like the alarm system in a home. When you come into the house, most systems set off a sound that reminds you the system is armed and gives you time to get to the keypad and turn off the alarm before it goes off. If you ignore the sound, the alarm will trigger, and you'll soon be dealing with a mess. When you hear the "buzz" of the Holy Spirit's conviction of sin, God is giving you time to respond before the alarm goes off.

You may be saying, "But if I deal with my sins individually, I'll be confessing all day."

That's not necessarily the idea behind 1 John 1:9. The Holy Spirit may not bring a sin to your attention until the end of the day when you are praying, or the next morning in your devotions. And He may reveal several sins to you at once. The point is to confess them as they come to mind. When you confess, the blood of Jesus cleanses your sins and fellowship with God is maintained.

Most people who offer the objection I mentioned are confusing confession with repentance. Repentance means to change your mind about something and go in the opposite direction. Genuine confession of sin certainly involves the desire to turn from it. But repentance has more to do with the entrenched patterns of sin in our lives that need sustained, maybe even long-term, attention.

All sin is serious because it disrupts fellowship with God. But confession is designed to help us keep short sin accounts with God, as someone has described it, so the sins don't accumulate over time like unpaid bills and become an entrenched pattern of spiritual debt that needs long-term attention.

When we confess, God is "faithful and righteous to forgive us our sins." Faithful means you can bank on Him, and righteous means He won't compromise His integrity. *Forgiveness* is a great word, because it means that sin is no longer charged against our account.

In terms of our eternal standing before God, our forgiveness occurred at the cross. That was a judicial act that brought us into right standing with God for eternity. Forgiving our sins as Christians is a relational act that keeps us in close fellowship with God every day.

To illustrate forgiveness, open the calculator app on your phone and pretend that you have entered the wrong numbers. For instance, let's say you needed to multiply five times five, but you accidentally entered four times five. You immediately see your mistake, but you can't just trace the wrong numbers through all of those complicated electronics to unravel your wrong entry.

But you aren't stuck with those wrong numbers forever, because calculator apps have a wonderful little button labeled "clear entry" or "C" that allows you to erase the numbers from the display and start over. That's what the blood of Christ does for us when we hit the "clear" button by confessing our sins to God. He forgives us. This is the grace of God at work. Confession allows us to override sin by triggering God's forgiveness so that the flow of grace continues. And when grace flows, growth follows. Nobody has to remain spiritually malnourished.

Carnal Christians Must Repent

While confession is necessary to forgive sins as they occur, repentance is necessary for believers who adopt a carnal (or fleshly) lifestyle. Carnality may be defined as *a spiritual state in which a believer knowingly, intentionally, and persistently lives to please and serve self rather than God.* To put it simply, carnality is adopting a sinful pattern of life, which the Bible calls "walking like mere men" (1 Cor. 3:3). In such cases, confession or agreeing with God about a sin is not enough. Getting back into a right condition with God must include repentance.

Repentance means to change your mind in order to reverse your direction. It is turning from sin back to God to prevent or bring to an end God's discipline for walking in persistent sin. Unaddressed sin becomes a spiritual cancer in the believer's life. Over time it metastasizes, spreading out to influence every aspect of life and seeking to undermine that person's spiritual growth. Repentance functions like radical surgery to remove the cancerous growth so that spiritual health can be regained and fellowship with the Father restored.

The principle here is that unconfessed sin leads to carnality, which necessitates repentance. The prodigal son of Luke 15 is a good example of this process. He was covered with the stench of sin in that pigpen. But when he agreed with God's conviction that he was in the wrong (confession), and changed his direction by getting up out of that pigpen and returning to his father in repentance, his father immediately forgave him and welcomed his son back into full and intimate fellowship. But he also replaced his son's smelly clothes with a new robe. I can imagine him saying, "Son, I'm glad to have you back, but we have got to get rid of that stench."

God is holy and will not fellowship with the stench of sin. But when we repent of our sins, Jesus Christ cleanses us from all sin with His blood so the Father can re-establish and maintain fellowship with us. Don't let grace get blocked by unconfessed or unrepented sin. Bring it into the light and let Christ cleanse you from it.

When my now-adult children were just babies they regularly "sinned" against me by dirtying their diapers. For me, there was no fellowship with a dirty diaper. The smell repulsed me and sent me in the other direction. Fellowship with my children was definitely broken, and as far as I was concerned, the whole growth process was on hold until the mess was cleaned up.

When the babies got uncomfortable with the mess they were in, they would "confess," agreeing with me that something was wrong by crying out for cleansing. At this point one of us would intervene, cleaning the baby and changing the diaper, so that cleansing occurred and fellowship with those around them could be restored.

Similarly, God is repulsed by sin in the lives of His children. But His Son, Jesus Christ, intervenes when we cry out about the mess we have made and applies His purifying blood so that fellowship with the Father is restored, resulting in continued spiritual growth.

5

Grace:
The Environment of
Kingdom Living

A MAN WHO WAS FISHING one day noticed that the fisherman next to him threw the big fish he caught back into the water, while keeping the small ones. This went on all day until the first man couldn't hold his curiosity any longer.

"I don't understand," he asked the other fisherman. "Why do you keep throwing the big fish back and keeping only the small ones?"

"It's simple," the other man answered. "My frying pan is too small to cook the big ones."

A lot of Christians are like that fisherman. They are limited in their growth and enjoyment of what God has for them—not because God doesn't want to give them the "big ones," but because their frying pans are too small. That is, their understanding of and response to God's grace are too limited, and so their growth in grace is stunted. This is a crucial issue, since the Bible commands us to grow in grace (2 Peter 3:18) precisely because grace is the environment necessary to experience true kingdom living.

We love to sing songs about God's grace, but growing in grace each day is often another story. Why is this so hard to do? One reason is that grace is a foreign environment to us. It's like an American moving to China and trying to get accustomed to the language and culture. It's hard to adjust to any culture you were not born into or in which you did not grow up. The Bible says we have to grow in grace because it is outside of our normal orientation.

A failure to understand and grow in grace inevitably results in faulty development and stunted spiritual growth. Christians who do not learn to function under grace are underdeveloped saints. This failure is the single greatest cause of spiritual regression.

We were born in sin, not in grace. No one had to show us how to act out our sinful nature, but we will spend the rest of our lives learning what it means to live by grace. Therefore, we need to learn all we can about grace, because it is the environment in which spiritual growth occurs.

The Bible never commands us, "Grow in the law." You will never read in God's Word, "Become better at keeping the rules." Now don't misunderstand me, I'm not saying that obedience to God is merely optional. Jesus said, "If you love Me, you will keep My commandments" (John 14:15). But our growth comes in response to God's grace because grace and growth are two sides of the same coin. My goal is to help you along in this process of growing in grace by taking a closer look at the Bible's teaching on the grace of God.

Probably the greatest section in the Bible having to do with grace is the first ten verses of Ephesians 2, in which Paul contrasts what we were like before God's grace reached us with the amazing change that came when grace found us.

Grace can be defined as all that God is free to do for you based on the work of Jesus Christ on your behalf. It is the inexhaustible supply of God's goodness whereby He does for you what you could never do for yourself. Grace is so wonderful because it gives you for free what you do not deserve, could not earn, and would never be able to repay.

Grace allows God to show us His kindness, as we will see in Ephesians 2. The reason is that through the death of Christ on the cross, God has gotten rid of the sin problem that kept Him from responding to us in grace.

WE WERE DEAD WITHOUT GOD'S GRACE

Sometimes we need to look back and remember where we once were before we can appreciate where we are today. One of the great problems in our culture is that people who have "arrived" forget where they started their trip from. When this happens, people begin thinking that they deserve all the stuff they have, and they stop thanking and start demanding. We call this an entitlement mindset, and our society is rampant with it these days.

God is not in favor of entitlement attitudes. In fact He had several ways to make sure His people, the Israelites, did not forget that they were once slaves in Egypt and then had wandered in the wilderness for forty years. One of these reminders was during the Feast of Tabernacles or "Booths" (Lev. 23:33–44). During the week of this festival, the Israelites left their comfortable homes and lived in booths or huts made of foliage. When their children said, "Hey Dad, why are we leaving our home to live in this old hut?" the father was to explain that this was to remind the people of God's provision in bringing Israel out of Egypt and sustaining them in the wilderness.

Setting Grace against a Dark Background

Maybe we should institute a "Feast of Grace" for the church, during which we go back to where we were before Christ and remember how hard and hopeless it was without Him, so we can teach ourselves and our children to value grace more. Your appreciation of grace will soar, and your spiritual growth will be helped, when you see where God brought you from. Paul wrote:

> You were dead in your trespasses and sins, in which you formerly walked according to the course of this world, according to the prince of the power of the air, of the spirit that is now working in the sons of disobedience. Among them we too all formerly lived in the lusts of our flesh, indulging the desires of the flesh and of the mind, and were by nature children of wrath, even as the rest. (Eph. 2:1–3)

If you have ever shopped for a diamond or other precious stone, you know that the jeweler places the stone on black velvet to make it shine more brilliantly and enhance its beauty. Verses 1–3 of Ephesians 2 are the dark background against which Paul is about to show us the grace of God.

And the background is very dark, because in our natural, unredeemed state, we were totally unacceptable to a holy God. We were alienated, or cut off, from any possibility of a relationship with God. The problem is that by nature we were disobedient sinners who invited God's wrath on ourselves. We lived in an environment of sin and breathed the air of rebellion against God.

Paul summed up our hopeless condition by saying that we were "dead" in sin. I suggested earlier that it might be a good idea for us to go back to where we were before Christ and remind ourselves from where He has brought us. If we were to do that, the place we should visit is not necessarily the old hangouts or old neighborhood. If we really want to see where we were without Christ, we should visit the cemetery.

The Heavenly Coroner's Report

What we have in Ephesians 2:1–3 is fundamentally a coroner's report. Now among dead people there are different levels of decomposition.

A person who has been dead a long time won't be looking so great, while someone else who has just died may still be looking pretty good in the casket. But pretty or ugly, long time or short time, both people are equally dead.

Before we came to Christ we were cut off from God who is the only Source of true life. So how could we have been anything but dead? The Bible is talking about spiritual death here and not necessarily physical death, although physical death is the natural consequence of sin. But since the death spoken of here is spiritual, most people don't grasp its reality as readily as they do the reality of physical death.

A lot of spiritually dead people don't feel dead. And as far as they and the people around them are concerned, they don't look dead. But those who are still in their sins are dead, according to God's Word. What people do is try to mask the reality of spiritual death with worldly activities and amusements, the same way we try to mask the reality and finality of death by making it look more attractive.

In the old days, people didn't surround death with all the finery we have today. A poor person who died was often placed in a crude wooden box with no adornments or fanfare. The box was taken out of town to the cemetery in a wagon and lowered into the grave with ropes. The gravediggers would then shovel the dirt back into the grave, and that was it.

But today, you can die in style. No more of that crude stuff. Now they have mortuaries that look like mansions. They put you in a nice bronze casket lined with satin. Professional makeup artists do their thing to get you looking nice. Some people look better dead than they did when they were alive.

And that's not all. You always wanted to be somebody and ride in a limousine? Well, now you have that too. A whole fleet of limousines, in fact, is available for you and your family. People are going to pay attention when you ride through traffic on the way to your burial. And at the gravesite, they have a nickel-plated machine to ease you down into the hole. Even the dirt they are going to use to cover you up is hidden under fresh-looking artificial grass.

We do all of these things to dress up death. But don't miss the point. Whether you go out in a pine box or a beautiful coffin, you're still dead. When we were dead in our sins, we were cut off from the eternal life that Christ gives. And the only alternative to eternal life is eternal death, which means eternal separation from God and the suffering of hell.

This was our condition prior to the arrival of God's grace in our lives. We were completely unacceptable to God. Some of us may have been attractive, educated, rich, or even nice, but we were all unacceptable to God and cut off from Him. Ephesians 2:1–3 is heaven's coroner's report on the human race apart from God's grace.

GOD'S GRACE HAS MADE US ALIVE IN CHRIST

The "before" picture of our standing before God isn't pretty, but thank God there is also an "after" picture. Verse 4 of Ephesians 2 begins with two of the most important, exciting, and life-changing words in the Bible. "But God" are words that will reverse any situation. "But God" will bring life where death existed because of what God has done for us in grace.

We need to look at verses 4–5 to get the entire thought here. Paul writes, "But God, being rich in mercy, because of His great love with which He loved us, even when we were dead in our transgressions, made us alive together with Christ (by grace you have been saved)."

That last phrase is the key here. Do you understand that if you know Christ as your Savior, you are saved not because of your decision or anything else you did, but because God took the initiative to reach down and save you by grace? Salvation is God's work from beginning to end. So the question we need to ask concerning our spiritual growth is this: "If we could not save ourselves by our own efforts, what makes us think we can grow in Christ on our own?" We've already seen that our growth is as much by grace as is our salvation.

Grace Gives You a New Relationship to God

We're contrasting the mess we were in before God reached down to us with the incredible blessing we enjoy as saved people because God decided in love to be gracious to us. An illustration may help you to picture this contrast.

If you took your children to a petting zoo and a little lamb came running toward you, you probably wouldn't be afraid at all because lambs are harmless. You might even reach out your hand and let the lamb lick it.

But let's say you are at the zoo and the alarm goes out that a lion has escaped from its cage. If you are standing there in the zoo and that lion comes running toward you, you will be terrified and start to run because you know what lions can do. Now suppose that runaway lion corners you in one part of the zoo and comes at you—but instead of attacking you, the lion simply licks your hand gently the way the lamb did.

If that happened, whose gentleness would you appreciate more, the lamb's or the lion's? I don't know about you, but I would appreciate the lion's gentleness more because I know that he could just as easily have destroyed me without violating his nature as a lion at all.

My friend, grace is God's kindness and gentleness to us when He could have backed us into a corner as guilty sinners and destroyed us without violating His holy character. But God wanted to make us His children, so instead of expressing His wrath against us, He poured it out on His own sinless Son on the cross. Jesus took our punishment so God could embrace us. We have a brand-new relationship with God through grace.

Grace Gives You a New Location in Heaven

Learning about God's grace is like opening one of those huge, cellophane-wrapped gift baskets at Christmas. Every time you think you've found all the goodies in the basket, you reach in a little deeper and find something else good just waiting to be discovered and enjoyed.

That's what we are finding in Ephesians 2. It would have been enough if God had put a period after the tremendous declaration, "By grace you have been saved." But grace doesn't stop there. After making us alive with Christ when we were dead, God took us to heaven with Jesus when He rose from the dead and ascended back to His place at God's right hand.

According to Ephesians 2:6, "[God] raised us up with Him, and seated us with Him in the heavenly places in Christ Jesus." There is a divine relocation program involved in grace, whereby God takes those people He has saved and by that same grace seats them with Christ in what the Bible calls "the heavenly places."

Now in case you think this relocation is just a figure of speech or a nice thing that we will experience someday, notice the tense of the verbs. God "raised" us up and "seated" us with Christ, past tense. It has already been done. You may be living on earth, but your true existence is in heaven, where the Bible says you are already seated with Christ.

We know that Christ is seated at the right hand of God (Heb. 10:12), which is the position of power and divine favor. That means Jesus Christ can make any request of His Father and know that it will be granted. So if you need power, wisdom, strength in temptation, victory over sin, or any other spiritual blessing, guess where you find them? At God's right hand, where Jesus is seated, and you are seated with Him.

You see, the reality of our lives as Christians is that we are seated with Christ in the heavenly places. This life on earth is just the shadow, not the reality. You have a new location in Christ where all your blessings are, and you are there by grace.

Grace Brings You God's Eternal Kindness

Now if you think the blessings God has for you today by His grace are wonderful, you haven't seen anything yet. Ephesians 2:7 is what I call the whopper. It begins with the words "So that," which are key because Paul is about to tell us why God loved us, saved us, raised us up with Christ, and seated us with Him in the heavenly places. God did all of that for this reason: "So that in the ages to come [God] might show the surpassing riches of His grace in kindness toward us in Christ Jesus" (v. 7).

In this verse Paul turns from talking about our grace blessings in this present life to those waiting for us in "the ages to come," which is another term for eternity. Do you know what God is going to spend eternity doing for you? He is going to show you how much He loves you by lavishing His "kindness," His grace, on you.

In practical terms, this means that during every minute of eternity God will reveal something new that shows us how much He loves us. There is so much God wants to reveal to us about His grace that we can't receive down here because of the limitations of time, space, and our humanity. But all of these limitations will be removed when we are with Christ, so we can receive all that He has stored up for us.

God says that during the endless ages of eternity He is going to show us the "surpassing riches of His grace." This is part of what will make heaven so glorious. Think of all that God has blessed you with on earth, and then try to imagine what His kindness will be like when all the limitations of earth—including sin—are removed. God's grace will just keep flowing in a never-ending stream, and no two gifts will be alike because He is infinite.

That's what God has waiting for us in heaven, and He has no problem telling us about it up front. And by the way, Christianity is the only religion that promises heaven up front. Other religions, and the cults that distort Christianity, generally keep their followers in the dark about their future destiny so that they can promote a lifestyle of law.

Now don't get me wrong. This doesn't mean that as Christians, we get off without doing good works. We'll deal with that later when we get to Ephesians 2:10. But there's a world of difference between serving God out of gratitude for His free grace and trying to earn His grace by our works. The moment you came to Christ, God brought you back from the dead and seated you with Jesus Christ in heaven. Your eternal future is secure because heaven is included in the package called God's grace.

GOD'S GRACE IS SUPER ABUNDANT FOR OUR NEEDS

Whenever I preach or teach the Bible, I try to anticipate questions or objections that my listeners might have. One issue that usually comes when the subject is God's grace goes something like this: "Tony, so God has all of this never-ending grace waiting for us in heaven. But how am I going to make it until I get there? How can I grab hold of the grace I need now to endure these trials and even be victorious?"

In other words, a lot of Christians are asking, "Does this super-abundant, never-ending grace of God begin only in heaven, or can I experience some of it down here?"

You Can Start Drawing on Grace Today

I want to answer this with the most powerful verse about grace in the Bible. But first, let me clarify that the grace we are talking about here is not saving grace, but grace to live the Christian life after you are saved. God's promise of abundant grace is found in a verse you ought to memorize if you haven't already: "God is able to make all grace abound to you, so that always having all sufficiency in everything, you may have an abundance for every good deed" (2 Cor. 9:8).

If you're a student of the Bible, you are saying, "But Tony, in the context this verse applies to our giving." You're right, but take another look at the occurrences of the word *all* in this passage. They are a comprehensive statement of God's grace; the ability to give flows out of this abundance. My point is that God's grace is as abundant here on earth as it is in heaven. The difference is that in heaven there are no challenges to grace, while down here there are plenty of things to distract us and keep us from taking hold of grace.

God will always relate to you in grace, and He has all the grace you need. But it is grace related to your need. You don't get tomorrow's grace today. You don't get dying grace until you're dying. You don't get grace to face temptation until you're being tempted. God has grace available for every situation that is over and above the need. Make no mistake about it. God's throne is called "the throne of grace" (Heb. 4:16).

We can even see God's abundant grace all around us in the blessings that are common to all of creation. For instance, has the atmosphere ever run out of oxygen to breathe? Has the earth ever run out of foliage for the animals to eat, or the oceans run out of water for the fish and whales to swim in? No, and the sun has never failed to appear either. These blessings are called common grace because every creature shares in them.

What God has done for His creation in common grace, He has done for His people in special grace. We're in trouble if any believer in any age can ever say, "I faced a situation that was so severe it exhausted God's grace and I was left on my own." But that is never going to happen.

Grace Doesn't Keep the Thorns from Coming

What most people really want to know is, if God is so gracious, why doesn't He just take away the trial or the suffering? Why doesn't He keep the thorns from growing in our lives instead of giving us the grace to endure them?

We can't answer that for everyone, but we know why God sent a thorn to Paul (2 Cor. 12:7–10). He called it "a thorn in the flesh, a messenger of Satan to torment me—to keep me from exalting myself!" (v. 7). Paul's thorn could have been a physical problem, a person who caused him grief, or a problem with no solution. Whatever it was, God allowed it to keep Paul humble and to teach him this valuable lesson: "My grace is sufficient for you, for power is perfected in weakness" (v. 9).

Paul had asked God three times to remove the thorn (v. 8). God's answer was sufficient grace to endure the thorn, and power to minister in spite of the human weakness caused by the problem. Paul wanted God's grace and power more than he wanted relief from the thorn, so he responded, "Therefore I am well content with weaknesses . . . for when I am weak, then I am strong" (v. 10).

So the question that needs to be asked is from God to us, not us to God. His question to us is, "Do you want to see My grace operating in super-abundant power in your life?"

If your answer is, "Yes, Lord, more than anything," then be ready to accept the thorns He puts in your path. When problems come, it means God is getting ready to show you more of His grace, because where He's taking you is greater than where you are now. All you need to know is that His grace is sufficient.

OUR RESPONSE TO GOD'S GRACE

We detoured from Ephesians 2 for a while to learn an important principle about the super-abundance of God's grace. Now we're ready to go back and look at Ephesians 2:8–10, a passage that ties in so well with what we have just been talking about. These verses teach us that anything we could possibly do for God is simply a response of gratitude to His grace, not a payment for it.

Here are two verses you may well have memorized if you have been a Christian for any length of time: "For by grace you have been saved through faith; and that not of yourselves, it is the gift of God; not as a result of works, so that no one may boast" (Eph. 2:8–9). Remember Paul saying that God left the thorn in his flesh to keep him humble? God doesn't want anyone bragging about how he or she earned His favor. You don't brag about a gift someone gave you.

Our Service Is Our "Thank You" to God

But immediately after this great statement of salvation by faith through grace alone, we read these words: "For we are His workmanship, created in Christ Jesus for good works, which God prepared beforehand so that we would walk in them" (Eph. 2:10). Grace should not lead us to try to take advantage of God's goodness by sinning all we want, or by doing nothing while soaking up His favor. God has work for us to do, but He doesn't want us serving Him because we're trying to pay Him back and earn our own way. That is working against grace. God wants us to serve Him in response to His relationship with us, which is a relationship of love and grace.

Grace shows up in our daily lives and relationships and it reflects God's great grace to us. I recall a time when a friend of mine was having trouble getting tickets to a Dallas Mavericks basketball game his son wanted to see. So my friend asked a man in his church, whose company is a Mavericks sponsor, if he could tell him where to buy a couple of tickets to the game for himself and his son.

A week later, this businessman handed my friend an envelope. My friend didn't know exactly what was in the envelope, but when he offered to pay for it the businessman just smiled and told him not to worry about it. When my friend got home and opened the envelope, he discovered not two, but four tickets to the game. And not just four tickets, but four prime seats along with a free parking pass. He took his son and two of his son's college buddies to the game, where they had a great time.

Now that was a grace gift, but it didn't end there. During the game a Mavericks front office executive walked down to where these guys were sitting and handed each of the three college students a huge bag stuffed with every kind of Mavericks souvenir and memorabilia imaginable, compliments of the businessman who had given them the tickets. My friend said he was completely stunned by the man's generosity, and he realized that he had no way of paying for this gift—and that even to try to do so would have been an insult. All that he and those boys could do was say thank you and enjoy their great gift.

Our Service Is Not a Duty to Fulfill

Paul said he "labored even more than all of them" (1 Cor. 15:10), referring to the other apostles, although he added, "Yet not I, but the grace of God with me." Paul knew that he was created in Christ for good works, but his service for the Lord was not a burdensome duty he had to carry out. His goal in everything was to know Christ more intimately (Phil. 3:10). In other words, Paul served from a position of relationship, not obligation.

Grace is cultivated and grows by relationship, not by rules or endless spiritual calisthenics. This is true because grace is not just a doctrine, but a Person (John 1:16; Titus 2:11–12). The greater our relationship with Christ, the greater the experience of grace, and therefore the greater the spiritual growth.

If you are a parent, when your child falls down and skins her knee, do you go to the medicine chest, take out a list of things to do for skinned knees, read it off to your child, and say, "This is what I am obligated to do for you"?

Of course not. When your little girl hurts herself, you take her in your arms and wipe away her tears as you apply the healing solution, because your relationship is the driving force behind your actions. And your child responds in love to your gracious act. That's the response God wants from us.

Grace doesn't mean that we sit back and do nothing while expecting God to do everything. Grace means that we make ourselves available to God for Him to do something through us.

When I think of Christians and the way we respond to God's grace, I think of watering our lawns in Texas. Trying to keep a lawn green in the heat and drought of a Texas summer is a big deal. There are three basic ways to do that. Some people do it themselves, dragging their hoses and sprinklers around and moving them constantly. It's a lot of work, and it can be costly because it's often inefficient and it uses so much water.

A second way to water a lawn is to put in an automatic sprinkler system. All you have to do is set the timer and let the system work. But it's not perfect, because there can be leaks and malfunctions in the system. If you have a sprinkler system, you know that you still have to keep your eye on it. Nothing ever works perfectly all the time, and you still have to pay the water bill.

The third way to water a lawn is the best, which is when God opens up the heavens and pours His rain on the land. The water is free, and all you can do is watch it rain, thank the Lord, and then mow the lawn in response to the rain. When heaven opens up, it rains evenly and it's all free.

Some Christians are like the do-it-yourself water-sprinkling folk. They are trying to do it all by themselves, dragging around their lists of good works and checking off when they have done each item.

Other people see how much work the first group is doing, and they decide that's too much. So they try the automatic approach to grace. They sit back and wait to grow automatically by going to church, listening to the sermon, and singing the songs. They just wait for God to move them.

But there's a third group who are ready to work. They have their lawn mowers ready to go, so to speak. But they also realize that the best growth comes when heaven opens up and rains on them. These are the people who understand that true kingdom living is all carried out by grace.

6

Faith:
The Action of
Kingdom Living

THE STORY IS TOLD OF a wealthy English baron named Fitzgerald who had an only son he loved with all his heart. Unfortunately, the young man got sick and died, and Baron Fitzgerald's heart was shattered at the loss of his beloved son.

As time went on this wealthy man passed away and left a large art collection that was extremely valuable. Baron Fitzgerald had specified in his will that his art collection be sold at auction, since he had no heir and his wife had also died. A date was set for the auction. Art collectors and dealers came from far and wide, eagerly anticipating the opportunity to bid on the baron's fabulous art collection.

But the auction began in an unusual way, for the first piece offered for sale was a portrait of the baron's late, beloved son. This portrait was clearly not of the quality and value of the other pieces being offered for sale, and the buyers seemed puzzled at this personal item from the baron's estate being offered for sale.

This was not the kind of art the buyers had come to purchase, so when the auctioneer asked for bids, none were made. Everybody was waiting for the piece to be taken away so the valuable artwork could be brought out. But the auctioneer continued to call for bids on the portrait of the baron's son, to the growing annoyance of the crowd. Finally, an old man who had been Baron Fitzgerald's servant walked down the aisle and said, "I'll take the portrait if no one else wants it."

A nominal fee was agreed upon, and the auctioneer handed the old man the painting. Then he announced, "The auction is now over."

There was a gasp from the stunned audience. Somebody said, "How can that be? You only offered one piece for sale, and it wasn't even a significant part of the collection. Nobody wanted it except this servant."

But the auctioneer repeated, "The auction is over. Baron Fitzgerald's will reads, 'Whoever buys the painting of my son receives my entire art collection at no charge, because I want to reward anybody who loves my beloved son as much as I do.' This gentleman bought the painting, so he is entitled to Baron Fitzgerald's entire art estate."

This story reminds me of all that we have because we have put our faith in Jesus Christ for salvation. God loves His only begotten Son so much that He wants to share the treasures of heaven with anyone who also loves His Son. The Bible says we are "heirs of God and fellow heirs with Christ" (Rom. 8:17). God has "blessed us with every spiritual blessing in the heavenly places in Christ" (Eph. 1:3).

Part of the inheritance we received is the new nature that God put within us, which is made in His image and gives us the ability to relate to God and grow in His grace and knowledge. My point is that when we trust Christ, God gives us the whole package with Him. All that God is ever going to do for us in terms of our new life, He has already done.

This is crucial to understand, which is why I keep emphasizing that spiritual growth is the process of discovering all that God has already given us, not running around looking for something new and different. We have learned that everything in our Christian life, including our growth, comes by grace, through the power of the indwelling Holy Spirit, who is accessed through relational prayer.

Now we need to talk about faith, which we could call the action of kingdom living.

Faith is so important to our spiritual growth because it is the mechanism God has given us by which we can tap into the spiritual realm that is above and beyond the world of our five senses. So crucial is living by faith to the process of knowing and experiencing God that without it spiritual growth is impossible, since the absence of faith means we are displeasing rather than pleasing to God (Heb. 11:6). Now don't misunderstand. When I refer to the action of faith, I don't mean the kind of kingdom life in which you have to do it all yourself. One of the messages I hope you take away from this book is the truth that the kingdom life is not a matter of self-effort.

Neither is faith a magic wand we can wave over our circumstances and manipulate God to make Him do our will. A lot of online preachers, podcasters, and influencers will make you think that all you have to do is claim something by faith and God is obligated to give it to you. If you don't get your miracle, it's because your faith is too weak. Faith does link us to the supernatural resources of God, but He provides them according to His will and plan, not ours.

So if faith is the means by which we open the door to the spiritual world, and if it is a key component in our spiritual growth that demands a response on our part, then the first question we need to ask is, what exactly is faith as the Bible defines and describes it?

THE MEANING OF FAITH

It's almost impossible to discuss the nature of faith without turning to Hebrews 11. Here we find the Bible's great "faith chapter" where faith is both defined and illustrated in powerful statements that have become a part of the church's vocabulary and memory.

But before we get there, let me show you the context of Hebrews

11 that led the writer to this great discussion of faith. One of the basic principles of Bible study is that every Bible text has a context that cannot be ignored, lest someone use that text as a pretext for teaching error.

Faith Believes God Is True

The eleventh chapter of Hebrews did not just drop out of the sky. The author was writing to a community of Jewish Christians who evidently were undergoing a severe trial of some kind—so severe that they were being tempted to turn back from following Christ. The basic message of the letter to the Hebrews is "Don't quit. Keep on going with Christ."

This theme comes through strongly in Hebrews 10, where the readers are warned not to turn back from Christ to the old way of the law, but to draw near to Him and press on. The writer concludes this discussion with a message about the importance of faith. Quoting from the prophet Habakkuk, the writer says, "My righteous one shall live by faith; and if he shrinks back, My soul has no pleasure in him" (Heb. 10:38).

Now notice the conclusion in verse 39: "But we are not of those who shrink back to destruction, but of those who have faith to the preserving of the soul." Then we read immediately, "Now faith is the assurance of things hoped for, the conviction of things not seen" (Heb. 11:1). This is all part of the same thought, since there were no chapter or verse divisions in the original text.

In other words, the writer is saying, "If you are going to avoid caving into your trial and letting your faith in God slip so that your lives become useless, then you need to exercise the faith God gave you and stand strong. And in case you wonder what faith involves, here is a definition and a list of people from your own history who exercised great faith."

Let me clarify something before we go any further. The issue in Hebrews 10–11 is not a loss of salvation. The Bible teaches very clearly that we are secure in Christ forever. Neither He nor God the Father will let any true believer slip out of His hands (John 10:27–30). Our future in heaven is secure, but our usefulness to God between here and heaven is not automatic. The writer of Hebrews wasn't warning his readers against eternal judgment in hell, but against a shipwrecked life that produces little spiritual growth or kingdom influence for the Lord.

By the way, this connection between our faith and our growth is underscored in Hebrews 5:11–6:3, another key passage in which the Hebrews are admonished for failing to grow even though they had been believers long enough to teach others. Instead they were still in spiritual kindergarten struggling to learn their ABCs. The point is that spiritual growth and faith are inextricably woven together. A life of faithfulness to God demands that we live by faith, just as we were saved by faith.

That brings us to Hebrews 11:1, where we are told that faith is "the assurance of things hoped for, the conviction of things not seen." Faith connects us with that which our senses cannot detect. Faith is a firm conviction about something we cannot see, hear, feel, taste, or touch, but which is nevertheless very real (2 Cor. 4:18; Heb. 11:3). Faith brings the invisible realm into spiritual view. Faith is acting like something is so even when it is not so in order that it might be so simply because God said so. Faith always involves your life, not just your lips. It involves your feet, not just what you say. That's why we are told to "walk by faith," not talk by faith.

In the case of saving faith, it is the conviction that God is true when He says we are sinners without any hope apart from Christ. And it is the confidence that God will keep His word when He says if we will put our complete trust in Christ alone, He will forgive our sins and make us His children. In the case of sanctifying faith for the purpose of spiritual growth, it is acting like God is telling the truth. It is believing enough to obey even in spite of how you feel. Faith is not an emotion. Faith is always an action.

Notice the strong words *assurance* and *conviction* in Hebrews 11:1. Faith is not wishing upon a star, crossing your fingers, and telling yourself just to have faith in faith itself, or hoping against hope that something is going to happen. The Bible says in Romans 4:18–20 that Abraham hoped against hope, but his faith was solid because it was in "the promise of God" (v. 20).

Biblical faith is a settled confidence in the Person and the promises of God as revealed in His Word. Faith trusts in the integrity of God because it believes that God has told the truth about unseen realities. Faith transports us to a supernatural realm that transcends our senses.

It's Foolish to Trust Your Senses Only

Now let me ask you a question. If faith transcends our five senses, then is it not a contradiction of faith to depend on our senses to guide us? If you can see it before you, you don't need faith. But the Bible says, "We walk by faith, not by sight" (2 Cor. 5:7). Paul was even more specific about the contrast between faith and sight in Romans 8: "For in hope we have been saved, but hope that is seen is not hope; for who hopes for what he already sees? But if we hope for what we do not see, with perseverance we wait eagerly for it" (vv. 24–25).

The reason many of us as Christians are not growing and seeing more of the life of Christ being expressed through us is that our faith does not reach beyond our sight, or beyond what we feel. The Bible says it is impossible to please God without faith (Heb. 11:6). Failure to believe God is the same thing as accusing Him of being a liar. When we are not pleasing God because of our refusal to trust in Him, we won't see Him at work in our lives. Faith begins where our senses end. When we can see it, we don't feel the need to trust God for it. And since we can't see very far, living by sight keeps us living small.

It reminds me of the African impala, an incredible animal that

Lois and I got to see when we took a trip to South Africa. The impala is known for its ability to soar ten feet high and thirty feet out with one jump. But we were told on our visit there that you can put an impala in a three-foot-high cage, and it will not attempt to escape, although it has more than enough jumping power to clear the cage. This is because an impala will not jump if it cannot see where its feet are going to land. The impala lives by sight. Because of that, it is easy to keep an impala caged.

The unseen element of faith is crucial if freedom is to be experienced, but that's not all there is to it. The object of our faith is all-important. There are children who have faith in Santa Claus, and who trust the tooth fairy to fly in and leave money under their pillow when they lose a tooth and put it under there.

But the problem is that this faith is illegitimate because the object is not real. Faith is only as legitimate as its object.

I was scheduled to preach in Iowa one time, and the people were going to send a twin-engine private plane to pick me up. Lois was supposed to go with me, but she made it known to me that she was not about to fly all the way to Iowa on a small airplane (not that she even liked commercial flying that much). I said to her, "Your faith is too small."

She replied, "No, your plane is too small." We wound up changing our plans and going on a full-sized commercial jet, and Lois's faith grew as the size of the plane grew.

"Your faith grew," I kidded her.

"That's because your plane grew," she replied, laughing. The object of her faith was now worthy of her trust. Biblical faith has substance because God has substance. The more you know about the character and promises of God, the more substance your faith will have. And the more faith you have, the more of God you will experience, and the more growth will take place in your life.

Faith Is Acting Like It Is So Simply Because God Said So

As I mentioned earlier, a practical definition of faith I like is that faith is acting like it is so even when it is not so in order that it might be so simply because God said so. Now you may be saying, "But that sounds like I'm supposed to pretend something is real when it isn't." Oh no, this is not pretending. We're talking about believing that what God says is true even when no evidence is available. And the way you know you believe it is when you act on it.

A good biblical example is Abraham, who had God's promise that he would be "a father of many nations" (Rom. 4:17a) even though he and Sarah were an old, childless couple. The Bible says Abraham believed in a God "who gives life to the dead and calls into being that which does not exist" (v. 17b). Abraham had no child, and his human prospects weren't looking that good at his age, but he acted like it was so even when it wasn't so in order that it might be so simply because God said so.

Faith says, "God, I know that whenever You speak, You are telling the truth and I can stake my life on it." Faith establishes what we think about God, and I'm afraid that many of us as His children act like we have more confidence in ourselves than we do in Him. If faith is the action by which we lay hold of the power and promises of God, then if our faith is lacking, we will not see the supernatural work of God at work and we will wind up living in the natural.

The faith heroes in Hebrews 11 were people who acted on what they said they believed. Noah believed and got out his hammer and saw to build the ark. Abraham believed and put a "for sale" sign in his front yard in Ur. Moses believed and left Pharaoh's palace to identify with Hebrew slaves. You cannot say you have faith and sit where you are.

Someone could argue that people like Noah, Abraham, and Moses had it easier than we do because God spoke to them directly. God did speak to them, but that didn't make their obedience any easier.

Remember, Noah worked for 120 years with no water around him. Moses didn't get to see the movie *The Ten Commandments* and find out he was going to lead a nation to freedom. They had their struggles. They had their doubts. But they chose to overcome both through kingdom actions of faith.

We actually have an advantage over earlier saints because we have God's completed Word. He speaks to us as surely as He spoke to the patriarchs. But we still have to experience the turbulence of life. Have you ever been on an airplane when it hit some sudden turbulence and started shaking or dropped? Your heart probably jumped, and your stomach sank.

But remember how you felt when the captain spoke over the intercom and calmly explained that this was no big deal, and he was going to look for an alternate path to fly around the problem? It turned out you were never in danger at all, even though all your senses told you differently. Your choice was to have faith in the captain or believe what you just saw and felt. Depending upon that choice, you either spent the rest of your flight with a white-knuckle grip on the arms of your seat and your body tensed up, or you relaxed in the seat and turned on some music or a movie and enjoyed the rest of the trip. Faith takes you beyond the limits of your senses so that you believe if God said it, it is true. Simply put, then, faith is acting as if God is telling the truth.

THE MECHANISM OF FAITH

Along with faith's meaning, it is also important to understand its mechanism, by which I mean the way faith works and what it does. This is not to suggest that faith is a mechanical process as we normally use the word, but that the Bible gives us clues into how faith operates in our lives.

One of these clues on faith is sort of buried in the middle of an extended passage in which the apostle Paul prayed that his readers would gain spiritual insight. This prayer is found in Ephesians 3:14–21, where the apostle made this request: "I bow my knees before the Father . . . that He would grant you, according to the riches of His glory, to be strengthened with power through His Spirit in the inner man, so that Christ may dwell in your hearts through faith" (vv. 14, 16–17a).

Making Christ at Home in Our Hearts

I want to stop there so we can focus in on this last phrase. Paul prayed that we as believers would experience the Holy Spirit's power in our inner being so that Christ can live in our hearts by faith. What Paul was praying for here goes beyond our salvation, although that is certainly included because it was at salvation that Christ first indwelled us.

But the word *dwell* here means more than just to move in and take up residence. It means to be at home, to make yourself comfortable, to spread out and have the run of the house. Paul was praying that the Ephesian believers would allow Christ to have complete control of their lives so that He could make Himself at home in their hearts and produce growth and kingdom influence through the power of the Holy Spirit.

In other words, faith is not only the mechanism by which Christ comes into our lives. It is also the mechanism or the means by which we give Him the freedom to enter every room and do whatever He wants to do there, including throwing out the old stuff and redecorating.

When you are given the freedom to do that in someone else's house, you are definitely being welcomed and made to feel at home! But when you don't feel at home, you aren't free to move around. Your access is restricted. If you want to grow as a Christian, Christ needs to be at home in your heart. And you make Him at home by faith.

You can see illustrations of this principle at work on those programs where people allow someone else to redo their homes or yards. These are fun shows to watch but without a doubt it takes faith in the homeowner to trust someone else to redo their home.

Giving Christ the Key to Our Hearts

Giving others the key to your house and letting them tear out your kitchen fits my definition of making yourself at home! Now if people can demonstrate that kind of faith in other people, why can't we allow Christ to make Himself at home in our hearts by faith? One thing is sure—we won't be unhappy with the results, as some people on these remodeling shows actually are when they go back and see what was done to their home.

That's not a problem when we allow Christ to make Himself at home in our hearts by an act of faith. When you give Him the keys to the home of your heart, He "decorates" it with love, joy, peace, and the other fruit of the Holy Spirit, and rewires it to tap you into Holy Spirit power. Paul went on in Ephesians 3 to pray that we might "be able to comprehend with all the saints what is the breadth and length and height and depth, and to know the love of Christ, which surpasses knowledge, that you may be filled up to all the fullness of God" (vv. 18–19). This is the kind of spiritual growth we can anticipate when we make Christ at home.

The Bible also uses the analogy of clothing ourselves with Christ. "All of you who were baptized into Christ have clothed yourselves with Christ" (Gal. 3:27). This is an accomplished fact, but we are also commanded, "Put on the Lord Jesus Christ, and make no provision for the flesh" (Rom. 13:14). This is the difference between our standing in Christ and our state or current condition. To put it in our earlier terms, Christ lives within us but also wants to be *at home* within us.

THE MEASUREMENT OF FAITH

Now that we know faith is an unshakable conviction about the unseen things of God that kicks into action as we give Christ full control of our lives, we are ready to talk about faith measurement. The question is, since faith is an action, are there ways we can tell when we are growing in the grace and knowledge of Jesus Christ (2 Peter 3:18)? There certainly are, and I want to show you several from God's Word.

Putting Feet to Our Faith

In James 2, we find a powerful and very practical method for measuring the size of our faith. James began the discussion by posing this question: "What use is it, my brethren, if someone says he has faith but he has no works? Can that faith save him?" (James 2:14).

Now let's recall up front that James is not talking about faith in terms of how we are saved and get to heaven, but in terms of how we live here on earth. That's why he gives the illustration of the brother or sister in need who is turned away by a fellow believer empty-handed with this hollow blessing: "Go in peace, be warmed and be filled" (v. 16). James then makes the poignant statement, "Even so faith, if it has no works, is dead, being by itself" (v. 17).

So if someone comes to us who is hungry, and we sit the person down and have a Bible study, showing him all of God's promises to meet our needs, then pray and send him on his way still hungry, James says we have just wasted our time. A lot of Christians are wasting their time going to church because they hear the Word with their ears, but it doesn't reach their hands or feet. They are not doing anything about what they are hearing. True faith will produce works because it is an action. If you want to measure your faith, look at the response it is producing or failing to produce.

A farming community had gone a long time without rain, and

things were getting desperate. So the ministers of the community decided to call a prayer meeting, inviting the whole town to come and bring their religious symbols. When people came to the town square for the prayer meeting, they were carrying Bibles, crosses, crucifixes, and all manner of other religious items. They all cried out to God for rain, but nothing happened, so after some time they all went home.

The next day, a young boy came to the town square by himself and prayed this simple prayer: "Dear God, we need rain. Show Your power and give us rain." As he was praying, the sky got dark, the thunder began to rumble, and it started pouring rain.

People in the town were glad for the rain, but they wondered what the little boy had done that they failed to do. After all, they had come to the square with all of their religious symbols to pray for rain. The difference, they found out, was that when the boy came to pray, he brought an umbrella. He expected God to answer prayer, and he expressed his faith in his actions as well as words.

When you ask God for rain, take an umbrella! We reach for our umbrellas when the weather reporter says it's going to rain, even though these forecasts are frequently wrong. But we often fail to act on the Word of God, which is never wrong.

Finding Out That God Is Faithful

I mentioned earlier that one way we know Abraham's faith was real was that he got up and left Ur for Canaan. As James was making his point that genuine faith produces actions that can be seen and measured, he also turned to Abraham, picking up on a different incident in his life (James 2:21–23).

This was the offering of Isaac, probably the single greatest act of faith that any human being has ever been asked to perform. You can review the story in Genesis 22. James asked, "Was not Abraham our father justified by works when he offered up Isaac his son on the altar?" (v. 21).

Abraham had believed God and been justified earlier (Gen. 15:6), but God still wanted to see Abraham demonstrate his faith. After the Lord stopped Abraham from killing Isaac, he said, "Now I know that you fear God" (Gen. 22:12).

Didn't God already know that Abraham's faith was real? Of course He did. God knows everything. But He still wanted to experience it. He also wanted Abraham to know it too, and the best way to learn that was to undergo a trial of faith. This is why God often puts us in a difficult situation. He wants to experience us trusting Him, and He also wants *us* to see if we will trust Him when what He tells us to do seems to make no sense.

God also tries our faith so we can have the experience of walking with Him through the trial and proving Him faithful. It's one thing to say we trust God, but it's another thing to be able to say, "I know God is real because I trusted Him in the fire, and He brought me through." God loves to see us trust Him over our friends, our feelings, and our finite thoughts.

One place where spiritual growth takes place is at this crossroads where we are called to put our faith into action. Do you think Abraham's faith was stronger after seeing God spare Isaac? Do you think your faith would grow if, for instance, you gave sacrificially to care for those in need, and then saw God activate His promise to supply your own needs "according to His riches in glory in Christ Jesus" (Phil. 4:19)?

If you want a balloon to go high, just fill it with helium. The balloon is simply an environment through which helium expresses itself. God's desire is to take you higher, but He can only do that if He can fill you with Himself. And He can't fill you with Himself until you trust Him. You aren't really trusting Him until you are willing to walk by faith, instead of just talk by faith. If your faith never reaches your feet, James says it is dead faith. Is there an area where you need to trust God right now? I want to encourage you to do by faith what He has asked you to do, and watch the kingdom impact take place all around you.

7

The Holy Spirit:
The Supplier
of Kingdom Living

SUPPOSE YOU GO TO THE STORE one day and see the most incredible refrigerator you can imagine. The thing is huge. It not only has all the bells and whistles you expect, it has some you've never seen before. It costs thousands more than a normal refrigerator, but you buy it anyway because you have never seen anything like this before.

While you are waiting for your new refrigerator to be delivered, in your excitement you go out and buy all the food you want to store in it. Then when the refrigerator comes you stock it with all the stuff you bought and go to bed for the evening.

The next morning you run into the kitchen excitedly, only to discover that the milk has spoiled, the ice cream is running out the bottom of the freezer, and the vegetables are changing colors. Your new refrigerator is not working. So you call the store to let the people there know that you are very upset and want your money back.

The man at the store tells you, "I don't understand what could have happened. Open the door and see if the light comes on." So you open the door, but there's no light.

Then he tells you, "Put your ear up close to the refrigerator and tell me if you can hear the hum of the motor." You do that, and there's no hum. So he says, "There's a cord at the back of the refrigerator. Please check to see whether it has been plugged in." That's when you go to the back of your new refrigerator and there the problem is. The cord has not been plugged in.

You come back to the telephone and say, "You're right. The cord was not plugged in. But for the kind of money I paid for this refrigerator, that shouldn't matter. This thing should work anyway!"

Now if you were to say this to the customer service representative at the store, you would probably receive a brief lesson in how appliances work. "No, you don't understand. Appliances are dependent in nature. Although your refrigerator has all the parts necessary to cool all the food you put in it, it was manufactured in such a way that it will not operate without an invisible power source called electricity. Unless you plug in that cord, your food will continue to spoil."

Now that's an obvious truth. No matter how much you paid for it, your refrigerator won't work the way it was designed to work unless it is plugged in to the power. Neither will your spiritual life work unless it is plugged in to Holy Spirit power. The Holy Spirit supplies all you need for kingdom living.

When God saved us, He gave us all the component parts necessary for us to experience a life of victory. We've already looked at this truth, which the Bible calls our new nature. God has given us a new mind, new heart, new conscience, and new emotions—all of this through the new covenant that was put into effect for us by the death and resurrection of Jesus Christ.

But we are dependent beings. We have not been designed to work on our own. Only as we are empowered and supplied by the indwelling Holy Spirit will we produce what our lives are supposed to produce in order to experience kingdom living at its finest. If you don't rely on that power, don't be surprised if the milk of your new nature begins to turn sour, the ice cream of your devotional life begins to melt, and the fruit of the Spirit begins to turn colors.

The Holy Spirit is God's supernatural gift to make experiential, alive, and real the new beings we have become. The Spirit is the heart and soul of a growing, flourishing Christian life, and if we don't get plugged in to Him, we will continue to stagnate and remain stunted in our spiritual development.

However, once we are plugged in to the Spirit, we will experience the supernatural wonder of a life in which the power of God's grace flows through the conduit of our new nature, keeping our spiritual lives at a temperature that, like an expensive refrigerator, preserves us from spoil and ruin.

GOD'S GIFT OF THE HOLY SPIRIT

We need to be reminded occasionally that the indwelling Holy Spirit is God's great gift to us. In John 7:37–39, Jesus stood up at the Feast of Tabernacles in Jerusalem and declared that those who believed in Him would experience a thirst-quenching flow of living water springing from their inmost being.

We're going to look at this passage in a minute, but I want to pick up on verse 39: "This He spoke of the Spirit, whom those who believed in Him were to receive; for the Spirit was not yet given, because Jesus was not yet glorified."

Something that is given is a gift. Now the Holy Spirit is a Someone, a Person—the Third Person of the Godhead, in fact—and not a something, but Jesus spoke of the Spirit and the abundant, flowing life He would bring as a gift. The Spirit had not yet been given when Jesus said this, since the Spirit's coming awaited the Day of Pentecost after Jesus' ascension.

Unfortunately, to many believers today the Holy Spirit is the forgotten member of the Trinity. They know He is there, but they don't know what He does or why He is important. Yet the Holy Spirit is the most active member of the Godhead when it comes to the matter of spiritual growth, so let's find out more about Him.

How the Spirit Will Function

As believers living on this side of the cross and the Day of Pentecost, we are accustomed to Jesus' physical absence and the Holy Spirit's invisible presence because we never knew what it was like for Jesus to walk among us. But His disciples had experienced that, so when on the night before His crucifixion Jesus announced His soon departure and the Holy Spirit's coming, it created a huge crisis in that upper room.

During the meal that night Jesus announced, "Where I am going, you cannot come" (John 13:33). That precipitated an exchange with the disciples in which they tried to come to grips with the fact that Jesus was leaving. The disciples were in a panic. They had been with Jesus and looked to Him for everything. How were they going to make it on earth if He left them and went back to heaven?

Jesus knew the disciples were deeply troubled, so He answered their questions with this promise: "I will ask the Father, and He will give you another Helper, that He may be with you forever" (John 14:16).

I want to note two key words in this verse. The word *another* in the Greek language means another of the same kind. God was not sending His people a cheap substitute for Jesus, but Someone just like Him—meaning of the same essence and character as Christ. We've already said that the Holy Spirit is God, the Third Person of the Trinity, which means He shares the same divine essence as Jesus, the Second Person of the Trinity.

The other key word in John 14:16 is *helper*, a word that means one who is called alongside to assist, to enable, to make it work. A few verses later Jesus said, "The Helper, the Holy Spirit, whom the Father will send in My name, He will teach you all things, and bring to your remembrance all that I said to you" (v. 26).

Jesus' promise of the Holy Spirit's coming was fulfilled on the Day of Pentecost (Acts 2), when the Spirit came to indwell the followers of Christ and empower them to do the work of Christ. This promise is made real to each believer since Pentecost at the moment of our salvation, when the Bible says we are baptized by the Spirit into Christ's body (1 Cor. 12:13).

Now let me clarify right here that this baptism is not some special emotional or spiritual experience that we have to seek after conversion, but the act by which we are placed into Christ. All believers are Spirit-baptized and Spirit-indwelt. In fact, the Bible says, "If anyone does not have the Spirit of Christ, he does not belong to Him" (Rom. 8:9).

If you know Christ as your Savior, the Holy Spirit lives within you at the very depths of your inner being. And according to Jesus, the Spirit wants to flow through you and out from you to others in a mighty stream of power, blessing, and refreshment. In John 7:37–38, Jesus said, "If anyone is thirsty, let him come to Me and drink. He who believes in Me, as the Scriptures said, 'From his innermost being will flow rivers of living water.'"

We saw earlier that Jesus was speaking of the Holy Spirit, the power supply of the Christian life—the pump, if you will, that makes sure the water of new life within us does not stagnate but continues to flow. Stagnant Christians don't grow, but Christians in whom the Holy Spirit is allowed to flow freely will grow and flourish in ways they never thought possible.

Getting Rid of Our "DIY" Approach

Before we talk about how to get that flow going and keep it going, we need to address what I call the "DIY" approach to the Christian life, otherwise known as "do-it-yourself." This is important because we need to learn that the Holy Spirit only enables us when we give up our own efforts and realize how *dis*abled we are without Him.

I hate going to the local home improvement store. The reason I hate to go is that it's a store for do-it-yourselfers, and having to go there usually means I am messing with something around the house that would be better left to the professionals.

This do-it-yourself approach may be okay for taking care of your lawn or making minor house repairs, but it doesn't work in the kingdom life. If you could make your own inner being flow with living water, you wouldn't need the Holy Spirit. His energy would not be necessary. But Jesus said, "Apart from Me you can do nothing" (John 15:5). When Christ saved us, He gave us Someone to lean on who has the strength to hold us up. He gave us the Holy Spirit because He knows the number that sin has done on us. The Spirit is the divine enabler for spiritual growth.

No number of programs or religious activities can substitute for the filling of the Holy Spirit. In fact, the more of His filling you have, the fewer programs you need. So if you're tired of trying to make your spiritual life work, if you are weary of trying to grow and gain victory only to keep tasting defeat, your problem may be a power shortage. The Holy Spirit lives in every believer, but not every believer allows Him to express the fullness of His power. This comes through the Spirit's filling, which opens up the fountain of living water that He wants to send flowing through us.

OUR NEED OF THE SPIRIT'S FILLING

The Bible makes it very clear that even though every Christian possesses the Holy Spirit, it is possible to experience very little of His power and influence in our day-to-day lives. The issue is not how much of the Spirit we have, but how much He has of us. Verses 14–17 of Ephesians 5 tell us that it is possible to be a Christian, and yet be asleep spiritually as well as unwise and foolish.

This is why Paul issued the familiar command of Scripture: "Do not get drunk with wine, for that is dissipation, but be filled with the Spirit" (Eph. 5:18). There is so much in this verse and its surrounding context that we need to spend some time understanding what God is saying to us and how it should affect the way we live. This is important, because the more consistently you and I are filled with the Holy Spirit, the faster we will grow in our faith. But the less filled we are, the slower will be our growth. In order to see what Spirit-filled people should look, act, and think like, I want to show you what's behind the concept of being filled with the Spirit.

What It Means to Be Filled

The basic meaning of the command "be filled with" is not hard to grasp. It means to be controlled by. When you are filled in the New Testament sense, it means that somebody or something else has taken over the command center of your life and is calling the shots. You are no longer in control of yourself because this person or thing has overwhelmed you and taken over.

The purpose of the Holy Spirit's filling is that He might control our lives. We know from Scripture and from experience that Satan also wants to control us. Jesus said to Peter during the Last Supper, "Simon, Simon, behold, Satan has demanded permission to sift you like wheat" (Luke 22:31). The devil wants to rule our emotions and our passions, just as he wanted to dominate Peter and turn his betrayal of Christ into a permanent failure. Satan wants to set the agenda for our attitudes and actions, so we have to replace the wrong control with the right control. Don't ever buy into the illusion that you are in total control of your own life. If you aren't yielding to God, you are giving Satan permission to influence you.

This command is in a form in the original language that means "keep on being filled" as a continuous process. Just as you don't resist Satan once and then you are done with him for the rest of your life, so the filling of the Spirit is not a one-time event that sets you up from then on. The filling must be constantly and continuously renewed day by day.

The illustration of control that Paul gives us here is that of a person who is drunk on alcohol. Even if we didn't know what it means to be filled with the Spirit, we know what it means for someone to be drunk. A drunken person doesn't get that way by looking at advertisements for liquor. He gets drunk by drinking. And the more he drinks, the more completely the alcohol inside of him is controlling him.

When a man becomes drunk, another power takes over his life. We say he is under the influence of alcohol. This substance transforms him into someone he was not before. One minute he may be nice and quiet. But when the juice takes over, he may become loud and boisterous. People who are normally passive may become aggressive when alcohol is controlling them. A drunk may think he is Pavarotti and start to sing.

When a police officer stops someone who is driving under the influence of alcohol and tells him to walk a straight line, he can't do it. No matter what the officer tells him to do, he can't do what he used to do the way he used to do it because something else is running the show.

What alcohol is to the body negatively, the Holy Spirit is to the new nature positively. When you are under His control, He makes you walk in ways you would not normally walk and talk in ways you would not normally talk. When the Spirit takes over, a lot of our excuses are nullified because the Spirit can change our personality. The Spirit transforms us supernaturally.

That's why rather than spending our time, energy, and effort trying to change, we need to spend our time getting filled. A sober man doesn't have to try to stagger. All he has to do is get drunk. The alcohol will take care of the staggering. He doesn't have to try to change his personality. He just has to get drunk. Now you can see why Paul drew the analogy between someone who is drunk and someone under the Spirit's control.

The New Power of the Spirit's Filling

I wish I could help more Christians understand that the filling of the Holy Spirit brings power for kingdom living that is beyond anything many of us have ever experienced. When people become intoxicated with the Spirit, men or women who verbally abuse their spouse through insults and vulgar speech when they got angry will find the ability to tame their tongues. When the Spirit takes control, people who had no control over their passions will be able to say no to immorality. When our lives are filled with the Spirit, we can witness to that unsaved friend or neighbor, and spending time with the Lord in His Word and in prayer becomes a delight instead of a duty.

Too many believers who are saying, "I am going to try hard and do my best to grow as a kingdom disciple of Christ" need to quit trying so hard and become intoxicated with the Holy Spirit. Why exhaust yourself with a rowboat when you have a high-powered speedboat at your fingertips? When we yield control to the Spirit, He takes care of the transformation and releases His power and influence in our lives.

When people get indigestion, sometimes they reach for a little packet containing two tablets and drop them in a glass of water. Those tablets start to fizz because they are releasing power to solve the sufferer's problem. The power in those tablets is in concentrated form, so it has to be released by coming in contact with the water. When that happens an explosion occurs in the glass and that plain glass of water is now loaded with power to cure an upset stomach.

When you were indwelt by the Holy Spirit at your salvation, you received "Holy Spirit concentrate." The Spirit was placed in you in concentrated form. But when His power comes in contact with your surrender to Him and willingness to be filled, an explosion occurs that cures your spiritual indigestion and empowers you to pull off great things.

THE PROCESS OF BEING FILLED

If being filled with the Holy Spirit is the key to our growth and power as kingdom disciples, we need to ask how a person experiences the Spirit's filling. This crucial question is answered in the verses that follow the command of Ephesians 5:18:

> Speaking to one another in psalms and hymns and spiritual songs, singing and making melody with your heart to the Lord; always giving thanks for all things in the name of our Lord Jesus Christ to God, even the Father; and be subject to one another in the fear of Christ. (vv. 19–21)

I believe these verses address the means to being Spirit-filled rather than the results of being filled. Paul's concern here is to tell us how to be filled and keep being filled with—controlled by—the Holy Spirit. The short answer is that the Holy Spirit's filling is made real when we make worship our lifestyle.

Making Worship a Lifestyle

Remember those wonderful times when you left church on Sunday morning on "cloud nine"? You were spiritually full. What filled you when you came to church that Sunday? It was being in the environment of the redeemed, the holy presence of the family of God.

What did you do in that environment? You got filled up on God's Word. You were inspired and lifted up to heaven by the music. You poured out your heart to God and you were filled with a sense of His holy presence as you communed with Him in the quietness and celebration of that hour.

All of those things add up to a worship service. For a couple of hours every Sunday, God's people gather in a worship service where we minister to one another and to Him. We hear His Word and we talk to Him. We worship and adore Him.

Well, who said that had to end at noon on Sunday? The way you learn to live a Spirit-filled life is to learn to do Monday through Saturday what you did on Sunday.

Taking Sunday Home

So you left church on Sunday full of the Spirit because you were in God's presence with God's people, communing with Him. But when you go home Sunday afternoon or even into the workplace or elsewhere in the week and start experiencing the impatience, demands, or vitriol of our current culture, your experience of the Spirit's filling can get depleted in a hurry. If He is going to continue ministering to and through you, you need to refuel.

If you pull into a gas station and fill your tank with gas, what is going to happen the minute you pull away and start driving down the road? The tankful of gas in your car will begin to be depleted. If you could just stay at the station all the time, your tank would stay full. But I don't know anyone who lives at a gas station, and I know for a fact that you can't hang around church all the time. Some people just want to stay on the mountaintop at church and not come down.

But it doesn't work that way. The only reason you fill your car's gas tank is so you can go somewhere and get something done. You come to church on Sunday and get full spiritually as the choir and worship leaders and pastor pump God's Word into your tank. However, you don't have to go far before your mate, children, coworkers, news anchors, talking heads, or other people begin drawing on that filling and deplete you. You may feel drained by evening.

That means you are going to have a very long and hard week if you wait until the next Sunday to get refilled. I don't know about you, but if I only filled my car once a week, I would be doing a lot of walking with a gas can in my hand. We need to learn to draw on the Spirit's filling as a day by day way of life, and my contention is that we do this as we learn how to come into God's presence in worship on a day by day basis. According to Ephesians 5:19–21, we do this as we commune with God by making decisions in accordance with His Word, with a song in our hearts, a spirit of thanksgiving to Him, and an attitude of humble submission toward other believers.

Now I want to make a crucial distinction between the Spirit's filling and illustrations like gasoline. When your gas tank gets depleted, you are empty and have to replace the loss with another round of fuel. But don't ever think that if you are not Holy Spirit-filled it's because He leaves you empty. He doesn't leave you, period. The depletion of the Spirit's filling that we're talking about is the loss of the experience and enjoyment of His full benefits in your daily life. The Spirit's filling is not perpetual and must be renewed.

THE IMPORTANCE OF WALKING BY THE SPIRIT

I want to change the analogy as I talk about the Holy Spirit as the enabler of our spiritual growth. In Galatians 5:16–17, Paul stated the case this way: "But I say, walk by the Spirit, and you will not carry out the desire of the flesh. For the flesh sets its desire against the Spirit, and the Spirit against the flesh; for these are in opposition to one another, so that you may not do the things that you please."

While the issue in Ephesians 5 is who will be in control, the issue in Galatians 5 is who will win the battle. One way you know you are a

Christian is that you feel a battle raging within you between your sinful flesh and the Holy Spirit. If you don't feel the struggle, you had better check your spiritual pulse, because the only people who don't have the Spirit warring against their flesh are lost or spiritually stagnant people.

The Bible tells us again and again that God and the flesh will never get along because they are diametrically opposed to each other. That was the whole point Paul made in Romans 6–8 when he finally cried out, "Wretched man that I am! Who will set me free from the body of this death?" (Rom. 7:24). His answer was that victory is found in being "in Christ Jesus" (Rom. 8:1). That's where the Holy Spirit wants to keep us.

But the struggle comes because we are still in our sinful flesh, and we will be until Christ returns and gives us new bodies. That's why Paul had to exhort us to walk by the Spirit so we won't fulfill the flesh's wrong desires. It's easy to misread Galatians 5:16 as saying, "Walk by the Spirit and you will not have the desires of the flesh." As much as we might wish that were true, it's simply not so.

Our human flesh will never behave itself. That's why Paul went on to say in verse 24, "Those who belong to Christ Jesus have crucified the flesh with its passions and desires." It's not that if we are filled with the Holy Spirit, we will never have the desires of the flesh. It's that when the Spirit is in control, the flesh won't have the last word in our lives.

It's easy to reverse the order of verse 24 by seeking to put the flesh to death so that we may walk in the Spirit. But the order is just the opposite. We walk in the Spirit, which gives us power to have victory over the desires of the flesh.

WALKING BY THE SPIRIT IS A DAILY PROCESS

The concept of walking by the Holy Spirit is similar to being filled with the Spirit, but the imagery of walking may make it easier to picture the ongoing nature of the Spirit's work. Walking is something we do every day, and we do it continually. Walking has three components we don't usually think about, but it is helpful to consider them when we're talking about our spiritual walk.

First of all, walking involves a destination. When you walk, you're going somewhere, even if it's just across the room. Walking by the Spirit involves a destination too, because He is ever and always moving us toward a destination, which is God's glory. Jesus described the Holy Spirit's destination when He said of the Spirit, "He will glorify Me" (John 16:14). When you walk by the Spirit, you're going somewhere. The flesh is always seeking to move us in the other direction, toward that which pleases self in opposition to that which glorifies God, so it's important that we watch where we're walking.

Second, walking also requires dedication. Most people don't just take a few steps and then quit for the day. Anyone who does that won't get very far, because walking must continue if we are to make progress. It's like the Holy Spirit's filling, which must be renewed regularly. It must be ongoing.

A third component of walking is dependence. You have to put your weight down on one leg and then another to walk. Or if your legs aren't working properly, you have to depend on something or someone else to get you where you're going. Either way demands dependence.

When I broke my leg playing football in high school, the ambulance came onto the field, picked me up, and took me to the hospital. I was taken immediately into surgery and a steel plate, which I still have, was inserted in my leg. The doctor gave me crutches to walk with because I was too weak to stand up on my own.

Now suppose my pride had reared up and said, "This is embarrassing having to lean on these sticks. They make me look weak and helpless. I'm a football player. I can walk on my own. I don't need these crutches." My recovery would have been slowed down a lot, and I might have done more damage to my leg.

Pride will keep you from leaning on the Holy Spirit, because pride says, "I can do it myself." Now if I had tried to walk out of the hospital after surgery on my broken leg, I would have fallen on my face and discovered how weak I was. Sometimes God has to let us fall on our faces before we will look up to Him and say, "I see, Lord. This isn't going to work. I'm ready to lean on Your Spirit and walk Your way." When you come to that place of recognizing your dependence, you are ready to learn what it means to walk by the Spirit.

The exciting thing is that when you come to this point and learn to depend on God, you get stronger and not weaker. The Holy Spirit gives you the power to say no to Satan and the flesh when they try to trip you up or lead you astray. You discover that you don't have to carry out the desires of the flesh and the devil because you are strengthened by the Holy Spirit's power.

Your Growth Will Show When You Walk by the Spirit

We all know what happens when a baby in its mother's womb grows to the point that its location can no longer contain its growth. That baby decides it is time to make an appearance in the world, and there is no stopping a baby when it is ready to exit the womb and go public with its growth. The mother and the rest of the world have to adjust to the baby, not vice versa.

That's what happens in the spiritual realm when we learn to walk by the Spirit. It's no accident that Galatians 5:16–17 about walking by the Spirit instead of the flesh is followed by verses 22–23, which describe the fruit of the Spirit. When some fruit is in the early stages of development, you may not know what it is. But once the full fruit comes on the tree or vine, there is no question what has happened. Luscious, ripe fruit is not only visible to all; it can be eaten and enjoyed by all. The fruit of the Spirit is not just for us to enjoy ourselves, but to give to others.

The Faster You Walk, the Faster You Will Grow

One of the wonderful things about spiritual growth is that there is no restriction on how fast you can grow or how far you can go in the Christian life. Let me close with an illustration of what I mean.

Some time ago my late wife, Lois, and I were at the airport, and we had a long way to go to change planes. I decided to have a little fun with her, so I got on one of those automated walkways while Lois kept walking. I was walking "by the Spirit," resting my weight on the walkway, while she was "walking in the flesh" by her own effort. So I was covering a lot more ground in a lot less time (I didn't say this was a deeply spiritual illustration). I was chilling, while she was huffing and puffing.

As I rode along I decided to turn and wave to Lois—but lo and behold, she wasn't back there behind me. She had disappeared. I remember thinking *I couldn't have left her that far behind.* I looked back again, but I didn't see her anywhere.

About that time I heard a voice calling my name from in front of me, "Tony, Tony!" I looked around and it was Lois, only she was ahead of me! It turned out that she had flagged down an airport cart and breezed right past me.

I think you can make your own application here. The Holy Spirit will take you as far and as fast as you are willing to depend on Him and willing to give up trying to live the Christian life on your own.

8

Scripture: The Food of Kingdom Living

ANOREXIA IS A PREVALENT eating disorder among people who develop an all-consuming desire to be thin. Anorexia sufferers will starve themselves, ignoring their bodies' cravings for food, because they have chosen to put their physical appearance above their health. Many will put their lives at risk to avoid taking even the basic nourishment they need to live.

Many Christians are suffering from spiritual anorexia, starving themselves even though God has provided rich spiritual nourishment in His Word. Because of a desire to appear attractive to the world, these believers avoid the food necessary for spiritual growth. The Bible is food for the soul.

Jesus Christ explicitly stated the connection between spiritual health and the Word of God when He said, "Man shall not live on bread alone, but on every word that proceeds out of the mouth of God" (Matt. 4:4). Given the essential part the Word plays in kingdom living, it is unfortunate today that the Bible has been reduced to a menu to be studied rather than a nourishing meal to be enjoyed.

When learning the Scriptures becomes merely an academic

exercise, we can actually increase in biblical knowledge while regressing in spiritual understanding. Jesus told the people of His day that while they were diligent to search the Scriptures, their study didn't do them any good because it did not lead them to believe in Him (John 5:39–40).

We need to be absolutely clear that the Bible is the inspired, inerrant revelation of God (2 Tim. 3:16; Matt. 5:17–18; Isa. 55:8–9). But its purpose is not just to give us information for our heads, but food for the new nature to feed upon so that our kingdom lives can be maximized. The Bible is a book to be eaten and digested, not just read and understood (Ezek. 3:1–3).

THE IMPORTANCE OF SPIRITUAL MILK

The apostle Peter certainly knew what picture to grab onto when he wanted to urge believers to long for God's Word. In 1 Peter 2:2, we read these familiar words: "Like newborn babies, long for the pure milk of the word, so that by it you may grow in respect to salvation." What milk is to a baby's body, the Word of God is to the soul. It is the food that fuels healthy spiritual growth—and just like your parents used to tell you, if you want to grow you need to eat.

I love Peter's imagery because he is not talking about having an occasional snack on God's Word. A baby pursues milk with a passion that will not rest until his hunger is satisfied. And if that means other people have to lay aside their comfort and agenda, then so be it. It is irrelevant to a newborn baby that mom has been up all day and is tired. Three o'clock in the morning means nothing to a newborn. When a baby is ready to eat, the world stops.

Almost every time I preach at our church, at least one mother has to slip out with her baby for a feeding lest the baby bring the house down. We have rooms around the back of the sanctuary, called "cry rooms," where mothers can go for privacy to feed their babies while still being able to hear and participate in the service.

Sometimes I see a mother in a pew holding her baby who is quiet because he or she is sucking on a pacifier. You know that a pacifier is basically fake food, designed to trick a baby into thinking something is really happening. Some babies will suck on a pacifier for quite a while, but there comes a point when the baby wises up to the trick, spits out the pacifier, and announces with a loud cry, "I want the real thing." When this happens, it isn't long before that mother is getting up to leave the service. The cry rooms in our church are well named, because a baby will announce his hunger with loud cries if satisfaction is not fast in coming.

The Importance of Its Purity

Peter referred to the Word as "pure" milk, which means undiluted, the real stuff. Pure milk is the opposite of a pacifier, which looks real but provides no nourishment. I'm told that in the old days mothers would wrap sugar in a cloth and let babies suck on it as a substitute to keep them quiet in places like church where it wasn't possible to feed them.

Too many Christians are undernourished today because they are feeding on substitutes. They are teething on pacifiers instead of drinking in the pure milk of the Word. No baby ever grew feeding on a pacifier or a sugar substitute. I can really get into this sugar deal, because I like to go to the Texas State Fair, and when I go I always see candy apples.

Candy apples are a contradiction in terms, because they feature a piece of fruit that's good for you, buried under a coating of pure sugar that negates all the health benefits.

Once you dip an apple in that sugar coating, you have basically canceled out the nutrition of the apple by putting two things together that were never meant to be together. The sugar coating is all for looks, taste, and momentary pleasure, and it blunts the healthy impact of the apple.

This happens not only at the fair with apples, but in many churches around this country with the Word of God. The result is underfed saints who don't even know they're underfed because the sugar coating they're getting tastes so good. Too many churches are giving out sugar sermons and feel-good information. But God warns us not to get fooled into accepting anything but the authentic, undiluted truth of Scripture. This truth of Scripture is diluted when it is allowed to go unaddressed in our lives. The truth of God can't nourish us because of the contamination it must pass through.

The Importance of a Feeding Schedule

Other believers aren't benefiting from the Word the way they should, not because they are feeding on substitutes, but because they aren't longing for the Word the way newborns long for milk—which is every day, day in and day out. These Christians have forgotten the importance of a regular feeding schedule for their spiritual growth. Scripture is the nourishment we need on a regular basis in order to experience kingdom living.

The last time I checked, babies don't drink all the milk they can in two hours on Sunday so they can go the rest of the week without eating. Babies want to eat every few hours. Why? Because their bodies can only store and use so much food at one time. That's also true of us, which is why we need to eat regularly. We can't stuff ourselves on Sunday and live off that until the next Sunday. But that's what many Christians try to do spiritually, and then they wonder why they are not growing.

Babies eat regularly for the simple reason that they are hungry. Why don't we feed on God's Word more than we do? The answer is simple: either because we aren't hungry for it, or because we have been trying to satisfy our hunger with pacifiers and sugar substitutes. We think we are full, but all we have done is camouflage our real need. The patriarch Job said, "I have treasured the words of His mouth more than my necessary food" (Job 23:12).

Believers who aren't regularly feeding on God's Word are malnourished. It's not enough just to be under the teaching of the Bible weekly in church. We also need to be in the Word daily for ourselves. When you and I want to hear from God in His Word more than we want to eat, we are on the way to developing a healthy hunger for the Scriptures.

The Importance of Its Content

Maybe the question has occurred to you by now, "What exactly is the milk of the Word that Peter tells Christians to seek?" The comparison to baby's milk lets us know that it is the basics of the Christian faith. The best description of this is in Hebrews 5, in the middle of the writer's rebuke to the Hebrews for their failure to grow in their faith.

Although these individuals had been Christians long enough that they should have been teaching others, they still needed instruction in "the elementary principles of the oracles of God" (Heb. 5:12), which the text goes on to call "milk" that is appropriate for "an infant" (v. 13).

Milk in reference to Scripture is what has often been called the ABCs of the faith. In fact, we have a good summary of these truths in the next chapter of Hebrews: "Repentance from dead works and of faith toward God, of instruction about washings and laying on of hands, and the resurrection of the dead and eternal judgment" (Heb. 6:1–2).

Now there is nothing wrong with this list. We all need to know these basic, foundational doctrines upon which our faith is built. You can't go to high school and on to college until you have completed elementary school, or at least have mastered the elementary principles of the academic disciplines.

You learn your ABCs in elementary school, but the goal is not simply to be able to recognize those twenty-six letters when you see them. You learn the alphabet in order to construct words and sentences through which you can communicate with others, learn from them, and express your ideas.

I don't see any adults strutting around bragging, "I know the letter *A*." It's good to know the letter *A*. It's an important building block in the learning process that leads to sophisticated, adult communication. The Bible never chides new believers for needing milk, the ABCs of the faith. These things are needed to give us something to build on. Fail to teach a child the alphabet, and he will be terribly disadvantaged when it comes to the later stages of learning. Babies don't begin with solid food. They need milk until their digestive systems are ready for something more. Milk is crucial for a new Christian to feed on, but it is not the whole meal. There is much more, what the Bible calls "meat" or "solid food."

SAVORING THE MEAT OF THE WORD

Now this is where things get interesting. I want to show you that the Bible not only makes a distinction between the milk and the meat, or solid food, of God's Word in terms of content and level of difficulty. God also tells us what this more advanced diet should be producing within us. A steak-and-potatoes meal is designed to facilitate our growth and maturity in the things of God.

Adults Who Are Still Drinking Milk

Before we get to the Bible's discussion of its deeper truths as the meat of the Word, we need to recognize a spiritual malfunction concerning Christians and their appetite for Scripture that is not only possible, but I would have to say far too prevalent. This is the malady of adults who are still feeding on spiritual milk.

Peter addressed his plea to baby Christians, those who were new enough in the faith that their spiritual digestive systems were too immature to handle solid food. There's nothing wrong with a three-month-old infant feeding on milk. But when you see a thirty-year-old with a bottle hanging out of his mouth, you can be sure something is wrong. Adults who are still on an infant diet either have a serious emotional problem, or there is something wrong with their ability to digest solid food.

The Bible contains several examples of Christians who were not infants in terms of their years in the faith, but were still feeding on the milk of the Word because they had failed to grow. The first example is the Hebrews themselves. The writer was grilling up a nice, thick spiritual steak for them in Hebrews 5, teaching them about the high priesthood of Jesus Christ in relation to the Old Testament priesthood of Melchizedek.

But suddenly the writer realized that his readers weren't mature enough to enjoy this meal, so stopped teaching and wrote: "Concerning him [Melchizedek] we have much to say, and it is hard to explain, since you have become dull of hearing" (v. 11). At the risk of introducing another idea here, note that "dull of hearing" means "mule-headed" in the original language. In other words, these individuals were immature because of their stubborn refusal to learn and grow, not because they were baby Christians who needed milk. These Hebrew Christians were like thirty-year-olds drinking from a bottle, or adults scrunched into those little desks in elementary school because they were still trying to learn the alphabet.

The Corinthians were another bunch who were acting immaturely far beyond the appropriate time for infancy. Paul had to tell them, "And I, brethren, could not speak to you as to spiritual men, but as to men of flesh, as to infants in Christ. I gave you milk to drink, not solid food; for you were not yet able to receive it. Indeed, even now you are not yet able" (1 Cor. 3:1–2). These verses don't need a lot of amplification. The Corinthians' hunger for God and His truth was evidently lacking, and their spiritual digestive systems were seriously underdeveloped.

Having a Desire for Solid Food

I am making an assumption as I write this chapter, and this whole book for that matter. I am assuming that you want to move beyond the milk of the Christian life and enjoy the meat of God's holy Word so that you will continue to grow into a regular habit of kingdom living. So let's find out what it takes to move on from drinking milk to desiring and digesting the meat of Scripture that God the Holy Spirit wants to feed us on.

The Bible does not present a list of doctrines that constitute meat or solid food. Doctrine is only milk, biblical information for the mind so that the believer has the basic biblical truth to build on. That's because solid food is more than doctrine. Solid food refers to the spiritual understanding and application to the experience of truth operating in the believer's life. That's why Hebrews 5:14 makes this crucial statement: "Solid food is for the mature, who because of practice have their senses trained to discern good and evil." Mature believers have the capacity to perceive the spiritual nature of things and then function and make choices based on this spiritual insight. The more consistently you connect doctrine (milk) with spiritual discernment and life application (meat), the more mature you are. With maturity comes the increased capacity to experientially perceive things from a divine perspective.

How to Know When You're Ready for Solid Food

The last half of this verse gives us the key to knowing when we have grown spiritually to the point that we are ready to lay aside the milk bottle and dig into the meat of God's Word. The answer is not just when we have memorized enough verses or amassed a certain amount of Bible knowledge, although knowledge of Scripture is definitely a component of our spiritual growth. There's more to this than knowing the Bible.

According to Hebrews 5:14, we know we are mature enough to partake of solid food when we can take the truth of God's Word (doctrine) and use it skillfully to live our lives and make our decisions from a biblical perspective. When you and I can filter everything that comes our way through the grid of God's Word and discern His will and desire for us, and then obey what God tells us, we are evidencing a deeper, more mature hunger for the food of spiritual growth. Mature believers can pick up on spiritual signals that an immature Christian doesn't yet have the capacity to receive, grasp, and interpret, even though the immature person may possess and even be able to communicate doctrinal facts.

Here's an illustration from everyday life. Let's say you are a parent with a young daughter. You want to show her how much you love her, and one way you do this is by giving her good things. You want your daughter to respond with love and trust and come running to you when you have something to give her. But you also have to teach her not to come running trustfully when a stranger offers her a handful of candy or some other goodie through a car window.

Why? Because you know her reasoning powers aren't mature enough to automatically distinguish between someone who loves her and someone who may want to harm her. Your daughter may be able to repeat the information you teach her, but without maturity she is unable to apply it correctly in a real-life situation.

So you take great pains to teach your little girl not to approach strangers, while also being careful not to alarm her unduly or make her afraid of adults in general. Again, you have to do this, and keep reinforcing it, because your child can't always discern a good from a bad situation. Some schools even have police officers come and teach children about what to do when a stranger tries to approach them and offer them something.

But you don't see police officers going out into the community to warn adults against accepting candy from a stranger. Why? Because our senses should be trained enough in discerning good from evil that we aren't normally susceptible to situations like this.

What I'm saying is that mature people can process data and put it through the right grid to come up with the right conclusion. When it comes to God's Word, meat-eaters are those who can digest the truth so that they have a heavenly rather than an earthly response to the issues they face in life. They can turn that nourishment into solid spiritual growth.

The question isn't whether milk or solid food is more important to our growth and development. Both are important at the proper time, even though they are different. The milk stage of our growth has more to do with the doctrinal truth we take in, the basics that we need to have to lay a good foundation for later growth. Our church has a basic curriculum that every new Christian can go through to get the essentials of kingdom living, including all the major topics and doctrines in Scripture.

But once people have fed on the milk of God's Word, we want them to go on. The goal is to reach spiritual maturity so that it can be said of us, "He who is spiritual appraises all things" (1 Cor. 2:15). We want the people in our church to develop spiritual discernment.

This was the hope the writer of Hebrews expressed for his readers: "Therefore leaving the elementary teaching about the Christ, let us press on to maturity" (Heb. 6:1). Until we make that jump from milk to meat, we have not matured in the faith. And let me tell you something about the Bible. It can take you to that level because it is "living and active and sharper than any two-edged sword, and piercing as far as the division of soul and spirit, of both joints and marrow, and able to judge the thoughts and intentions of the heart" (Heb. 4:12).

A two-edged sword cuts on both sides, which means it cuts coming and going. The Word of God is so sharp and incisive that it can pierce to the deepest part of our being. The soul is your personality, the part of you that makes you who you are. Your spirit refers to the new nature that God placed in you at the point of salvation. The Word can sort things out in our lives even when we are so involved or so confused that our senses can't discern good or evil. In other words, the Holy Spirit can use the Bible to help separate the stuff you can't separate. If you are ready to cultivate an intense hunger for Scripture, you'll find all the nourishment you will ever need.

GRADUATING FROM MILK TO MEAT

Let's talk about how God's Word can become the spiritual food we need to grow from being milk Christians to those who can handle solid food. God uses trials to force us to utilize the doctrine (milk) we have learned in order to deepen our relationship with Him which automatically enhances our spiritual perceptions, resulting in greater maturity. The way we grow from milk to meat is by applying the truths in God's Word to cultivate our relationship with Jesus Christ. This intimacy when applied, especially during times of trials, produces great growth. There is a strong link between food and relationship both in the natural and the spiritual world.

The Key: Our Relationship with Christ

This connection is most easily seen in the way God designed a baby to be fed and nurtured. For most of human history breastfeeding has been the only method available to feed a baby. Many mothers still prefer it not only for nutritional reasons, but for the bond it gives them with their babies. It's a baby's cry and tears that alerts the mother to pain from hunger the baby is experiencing. While the baby is taking milk, she is being held, cuddled, rocked, and talked to with loving words.

When a mother nurses her baby, because of her need for food, it is an experience of closeness and intimacy for both of them. The baby is not only getting milk, but drawing close to her mother in the warmth of a loving relationship. We could say that the baby is eating relationally as well as nutritionally in the midst of a painful situation of hunger.

And lest we think this is just sentimentalism, recall the sobering studies done some years ago to determine why babies in orphanages who were being fed regularly were dying. It was discovered that they were dying from a lack of being held and caressed because the attendants were too busy to give the babies the individual attention they needed. In other words, these infants were dying from lack of relationship.

Even when children move beyond infancy, the family is still designed to function in such a way that eating is done relationally as the family gathers for meals. Many families could testify that the meals they share together prove to be some of their most important family times. In our home, Lois and I intentionally raised our kids around the "table." We used mealtime for devotional time, hearing about the kids' days and just general bonding. The most intimate time Jesus had with His disciples was around a meal known as the Last Supper.

I have heard of people falling in love over the internet before they ever meet. Now that seems a little strange to me, but it raises an interesting question. If two people who have never seen each other can fall so deeply in love through the written word that they wind up getting married, how much more should we be able to develop a love relationship with the unseen God using His living Word that is written to our hearts?

A long-distance love relationship doesn't depend on sight, but on the impact of words. When two people are relating this way, they are going beyond the mere passing of information to the meaning behind the information. Too many Christians view the Bible as a library of information to be studied and learned. I'm a big believer in Bible study, but when you feed on God's Word with the purpose in mind of getting to know the Person behind the page, it changes everything.

I can read the words in a medical book, but when I'm sick I want a doctor there to tell me what those words mean and what it will take to make me well. And when I'm hungry, it's nice to have a menu to choose from. But I want a waiter standing there to tell me what is in the various meals and what he has tasted and found to be good from the menu.

In other words, I want to relate to someone who embodies the information I am receiving. That's because the goal of medical treatment is health, not being able to pronounce the words of your illness. The goal of going to a restaurant is the meal, not the menu. When we move from information to personal intimacy, especially during times of spiritual need, we are on the road to spiritual maturity.

I had the model of my car I drive for several years before ever reading the owner's manual. That changed one day when my car broke down and I had to take it in for service. The store manager began showing me all that my car was equipped to do. I didn't even know half of that stuff was available because I had never cracked the book. He told me, for instance, that the car had a built-in speaker for telephone conversations.

I listened in amazement to all of this, and quickly decided that it would be in my best interest to read the owner's manual that came with my car. But I am not reading that manual just to check off how many chapters I read or memorize various passages. I am reading it so I can enjoy all the good gifts that the car manufacturer gave me when I purchased my car. My relationship with the dealer during a time of crisis brought my car manual to life, and I am not only driving more safely but enjoying other benefits too.

The depth of your relationship with another person changes the depth of the information you receive. Jesus had many people around Him who were called His followers at one point or another. For a while large crowds followed Him, but He knew that most of them were following for the wrong reasons, so He only taught them in large groups rather than spending a lot of time with them individually.

On one occasion Jesus sent out seventy disciples (Luke 10:1), but He was not on an intimate relationship basis with all of them. He was closest to the twelve apostles, and even in this group He drew closest to Peter, James, and John. And even among these three, only John enjoyed the kind of close relationship with Christ that allowed him to recline on Jesus' chest during the Last Supper (John 13:23–26). It was from this position of intimate communion that John asked Jesus who the betrayer was. Peter gestured to John to ask this hard question, because even Peter realized that John was in the best position to ask Jesus. Jesus could simply have whispered the answer in John's ear, because they were close.

The Test: Being Able to Feed Yourself and Others

You may have heard the familiar story about the weary young mother with little ones tugging at her who was asked what she wanted most. She didn't hesitate a minute. "I want to go to lunch with people who don't call me 'mother' and can cut their own meat." That statement has a ring of truth to it, because we want our kids to advance from the bottle to utensils. It's nice when the baby starts holding the bottle, then reaches for the spoon. Teaching children to feed themselves can be a messy process that takes a lot of patience, but the payoff is worth the effort—unless you want a thirty-year-old child sucking on a bottle!

In large families it helps when the older children can help feed the little ones as well as feed themselves. That's what God wants for His family too. The Bible says one mark of growing and maturing Christians is their ability to teach others (Heb. 5:12). You know you are getting somewhere in your spiritual growth when you can feed yourself from God's Word, instead of having to have it all chopped up and prepared and spooned into your mouth. And when you can help feed someone else on the Word, you are showing the marks of a mature believer.

To develop spiritual maturity requires that you read God's Word so you know what it says (Rev. 1:3), study the Word so you know what it means (2 Tim. 2:15), memorize the Word so you can use it when you need it (Ps. 119:11), and take every opportunity to hear the Word of God proclaimed and taught so we can learn to live life and make decisions based on it (Heb. 5:13–14). When you give this kind of serious attention to the Scriptures, spiritual growth is inevitable. (Jesus called the Word "food to eat" in John 4:32.)

Let me leave you with one other important word. Feeding on the Word doesn't mean that everything you consume will fit your taste. Sometimes the Word is sweet as honey, and sometimes it is an unpleasant dose of much-needed medicine.

My mother believed castor oil was the cure for everything.

"Mama, my stomach hurts."

"Bring the castor oil."

"Mama, I have a headache."

"Go get the castor oil."

It didn't matter what was wrong, we got castor oil. I didn't like the way it tasted. It was nasty stuff to me. But my mother was not interested in my opinion or my preferences. She was seeking my health, so her answer was always, "Open your mouth and take this. It's good for you."

Friend, God's Word is good for you. If you're in good shape right now, it will be sweet honey to nourish your soul. If you have a messed up heart, a confused mind, or damaged relationships, take the Word because it's good for whatever ails you. Sometimes you're going to like it, and sometimes you won't, because it's not what you want to hear at the time.

But if you will drink the pure milk of God's infallible Word and graduate to its solid food, you will discover that it's good for you because you will grow in grace and the knowledge of our Lord Jesus Christ. Then you will be able to say with the prophet Jeremiah, "Your words were found and I ate them, and Your words became for me a joy and the delight of my heart; for I have been called by Your name, O LORD God of hosts" (Jer. 15:16).

9

Prayer:
The Access of
Kingdom Living

I WANT TO BEGIN OUR DISCUSSION of prayer by expanding on the opening illustration from a previous chapter. That is, if the new nature that God placed in us at salvation is like an expensive refrigerator that has all the necessary parts to function properly, and if the indwelling Holy Spirit is the power source that makes this new "appliance" work the way it was designed to work, then prayer is like the wires and connectors through which this power flows and reaches the component parts of our new nature.

Or I can say it this way: prayer is that which causes all the parts of the Christian life to relate properly to one another, because prayer is the primary means by which we relate to God. I define kingdom prayer as *relational communication with God* and it serves as the access point for kingdom living.

The key word here is *relational*, by which I mean that prayer is a dialogue between two people who are intimately related, not a monologue in which one person does all the talking and the other does all the listening. Prayer is not a ritual of words that we must say in the right order, or a chore to get out of the way before the day is over, the way we brush our teeth before going to bed. Jesus clearly rejects this external, performance based understanding of prayer (Matt. 6:5–7). Prayer is part of a relationship with God to be cultivated.

We often use a lot of flowery words when we start talking about prayer, but the fact is that for many people prayer has little to do with the realities of life. Some people think of prayer as they do the national anthem at a game: a nice opening ritual that has nothing to do with what happens on the field. Other people treat prayer as a good luck charm, like a rabbit's foot to pull out and rub when things are tough. They believe a prayer a day will keep the devil away.

It's possible even for believers to approach prayer in such superficial ways, which may help to explain why many of us are not growing more in our walk with the Lord. God has made us in such a way that the power of the Holy Spirit flows along the wires of prayer, which makes prayer absolutely vital and central to all of life—including our spiritual growth. Prayer is so important that the Bible tells us, "Pray without ceasing" (1 Thess. 5:17).

This doesn't sound to me like an event you do just once in a while, or a flare you shoot up during a crisis. We could illustrate the centrality of prayer for the Christian by substituting the word *breathe* for *pray* in the verse above: "Breathe without ceasing." Does that sound like a good idea to you? It does to me too!

We don't breathe only when we feel like it. We don't say, "I'm not into oxygen today," and stop breathing. We don't get frustrated with breathing and say, "This isn't getting me anywhere. I'm not going to do this anymore." Oh no, we cling to the breath in our bodies as if it were life, because breathing is essential to our functioning in this world. God wants prayer to be that essential in our lives, for just as the process of breathing is the contact point, the link, to our earthly existence, so prayer is the link to our heavenly existence because it engages the Holy Spirit's power for our growth and maturity in Christ.

PRAYER GIVES US ACCESS TO HEAVEN

We know that we live "in the heavenly places in Christ" because God says so (Eph. 1:3). More than that, we are seated with Christ in those same heavenly places (Eph. 2:6). Heaven is where our Father lives, and prayer is the means by which we relate to and communicate with Him. The goal in prayer is to enter our Father's presence the way a child comes trustingly to a father that he knows loves him.

Prayer as relational communication with God is a wonderful concept, but if we are honest, we would also have to admit that sometimes the spiritual world feels like a foreign land to us.

We Are Entering a Different World

When you go to a foreign land, you can feel uncomfortable and a little bit lost because you don't speak the language and everything is different from what you are accustomed to. The language of the heavenly world is prayer, and since the heavenly world is the source of our power, victory, peace, joy, and everything else we need to grow, it is essential that we learn to speak the language of prayer. Prayer gives us access to this new land that we are now a part of.

The good news is that we have the perfect Teacher for that task, the Holy Spirit Himself. One of the Spirit's jobs is to teach us the language of prayer and guide us in learning how to pray. He is so good at this job that the Bible says the Holy Spirit can translate our prayers to God even when we don't know what to say.

Paul writes, "We do not know how to pray as we should, but the Spirit Himself intercedes for us with groanings too deep for words" (Rom. 8:26). The Holy Spirit understands prayers that we can't express adequately, and makes sense of thoughts that we don't even understand ourselves, because He knows the language of prayer and can interpret it to us. We need to pray without ceasing because prayer is the link between the physical and the spiritual worlds—and since the spiritual world controls the physical world, getting connected to the world above affects your functioning in the world below.

Because prayer is relational, the Holy Spirit will communicate God's heart back to us by connecting with our human spirit so that we will hear God talk with us in the deepest part of our being. This is why prayer cannot just be a rush job, and it is also why meditation is so important. It allows the Holy Spirit to share God's thoughts with us so that we begin thinking God's own thoughts in our minds (1 Cor. 2:12–13).

Prayer Changes Our Perception

This spiritual communication with God helps to turn what was a strange and foreign land into a wonderful new world. Prayer changes our perception of the heavenly realm, in other words. Let me give you an example that may sound a little way-out at first, but stay with me because we are going somewhere.

If you have ever been to an amusement park with your family, you know how these parks are designed to transport you to another world entirely apart from your everyday life. Every detail in the park reminds you of the theme being communicated. Everything is bright and sparkling, and many of the people are dressed in costumes appropriate to the park's theme. And all those wonderful characters you and your children read about in books are there before you, in full life size. The goal of the entire experience is to help you lose yourself in the joy and wonder of this magical world.

The illustration isn't perfect, but that's what the Holy Spirit wants to do for us, and the link in the process is prayer. When we pray we are transported to another world that is completely different from our everyday world. Now a theme park is all illusion and make-believe, and after a day or two you have to leave this pretend world and come back to the real world.

But there is no make-believe with prayer. It takes us to the real world of the spiritual realm, where Jesus is sitting at the right hand of God and we are seated with Him. Prayer positions us to hear from God, so that our new spiritual nature is ready to be spoken to by the Holy Spirit. Then we are ready to hear God's voice applying His Word to our specific needs and circumstances.

The devil doesn't want you to understand how potent prayer is, because once you do he loses his ability to throw you off track. Satan can't keep you from praying, but what he does is try to make you feel awkward, frustrated, and powerless in prayer so that you will give up more easily.

And let's admit it, real prayer takes hard work. I'm not here to tell you that effective praying is as easy as running around having fun at an amusement park. All of us know what it is like to get down on our knees with the best of intentions, but either fall asleep, run out of things to say, or find our minds wandering after just a few minutes. Prayer changes things, as the old saying goes, but it has to change us first by reorienting our perception of the world we live in. Prayer helps to turn us from a self-focus to a God-focus so we can do His will.

Jesus Taught Us How to Pray

Jesus had a lot to say about prayer during His ministry on earth. One of those occasions was during the Sermon on the Mount, when Jesus taught some very crucial principles of prayer. These principles help us move prayer from the realm of a foreign land to the intimate world of children relating to their father. Jesus said:

When you pray, you are not to be like the hypocrites; for they love to stand and pray in the synagogues and on the street corners so that they may be seen by men. Truly I say to you, they have their reward in full.

But you, when you pray, go into your inner room, close your door, and pray to your Father who is in secret, and your Father who sees what is done in secret will reward you. And when you are praying, do not use meaningless repetition as the Gentiles, for they suppose that they will be heard for their many words. (Matt. 6:5–7)

These few words set the common perception of prayer in Jesus' day on its ear. He said prayer was not to be a public demonstration of our piety, nor was it a matter of saying all the right words in the right order. The intimate nature of our communication with God is illustrated by going into a closet and closing the door behind us to pray. Why shut the door? Because it's just you and your Father in a family discussion.

Now this doesn't mean we can never pray in public. The kind of prayer Jesus condemned was that done to impress other people and elicit their admiration or awe. Jesus also condemned "meaningless repetition" (v. 7), the ritualistic formula of certain words spoken in a certain order without any sincere meaning. Even if we don't read formula prayers from a book, we can still fall into our own prayer jargon. I find that when some people say they don't know how to pray, what they really mean is they don't know how to pray the way they hear other people pray. They don't know all the "Christianese" that we who are older in the spiritual system often use.

Jesus said you don't need to worry about getting all the words right because "your Father knows what you need before you ask Him" (Matt. 6:8). Now God still wants you to ask, but because He is your Father He is listening to your heart as much as or more than your words. We'll see later that the author of Hebrews described prayer as drawing near to God, which suggests intimacy and relationship. We don't have to be self-conscious about praying to our Father, because He isn't grading us on how well we express ourselves.

Earlier we compared prayer to breathing because the Bible tells us to pray without ceasing. Most of the time our breathing is done without our conscious attention to it, or even an awareness that we are doing it. It is the natural expression of our moment by moment dependence on oxygen. That's how God wants us to treat our communication with Him. He wants prayer to be the air we breathe, the environment in which we live.

Our Prayers Can Take Many Forms

The Bible contains examples of all kinds of prayer, both formal and informal. When Solomon dedicated the temple he had built, he called the nation of Israel together and held a formal service of dedication during which he knelt and offered one of the most powerful formal prayers in the Bible (1 Kings 8:1–54). But when Peter tried to walk to Jesus on the water and began to sink, he cried out, "Lord, save me!" (Matt. 14:30). It wasn't a formal prayer, but it met the need of the moment.

Prayer can take a lot of forms, including prayers where no words are uttered. Once you realize that you can pray in your mind and spirit without having to speak out loud, then you can begin to understand how it is possible to pray without ceasing.

All of us know the power of unspoken communication. Many of us grew up in homes where our mother and father didn't have to say a word to make themselves heard loud and clear. It may have been the way they tilted their heads, the look in their eyes, or some other signal. But whatever it was, we knew exactly what was being communicated and how we were expected to respond.

That is an example of close, intimate two-way conversation. Now this is what makes prayer as relational communication with God so important. The goal in prayer is to maintain such a close relationship with the Lord that we can communicate back and forth no matter what the situation, the time of day, or anything else. We don't have to shout, and we don't have to use the right words in the right order, because our hearts are in tune with God's heart.

This relationship takes us a long way from the kind of thinking we can fall into if we're not careful. I'm reminded of the little boy who wanted a bicycle for Christmas. He was praying one night at the top of his voice, loudly telling God the kind and color of bicycle he wanted, and the features he hoped it would have.

His mother heard him praying and said, "Son, why are you talking so loud? You don't need to scream for God to hear you."

"I know, Mom," he said. "But I need to pray loud if Grandma is going to hear me and buy me that bike for Christmas."

We don't need to shout for God to hear us, and we don't need to try to make our own answers to prayer happen. Jesus said our Father knows what we need before we ask. He gives to us because of our relationship with Him, not just because we say it loud enough to be heard.

EFFECTIVE PRAYER IS POSSIBLE
BECAUSE OF CHRIST

I want to leave you with an encouraging word on prayer that I hope will spur you on to greater growth not only in your prayer life, but in every area of your Christian experience. I can't think of a better passage to accomplish this than Hebrews 4:14–16, three power-packed verses on prayer that, ironically, were written to a group of Christians who had stopped growing and were actually regressing in their spiritual experience.

You can read Hebrews 4:1–13 to see how the author of this book warns against the dangers of unbelief and turning away from the Lord. The Hebrews were about ready to give up, but the message of the book is don't quit, press on, and instead of drawing back in unbelief, draw near to God. It is in this context that we read:

Therefore, since we have a great high priest who has passed through the heavens, Jesus the Son of God, let us hold fast our confession. For we do not have a high priest who cannot sympathize with our weaknesses, but One who has been tempted in all things as we are, yet without sin. Therefore let us draw near with confidence to the throne of grace, so that we may receive mercy and find grace to help in time of need. (Heb. 4:14–16)

I want to show you four great truths from this passage that can turn anyone's prayer life from dormant to dynamic. All of these truths center on the Person and work of Christ as our great High Priest who helps us in our prayers.

We Have an Intercessor in the Person of Christ

The writer of Hebrews tells us right up front the most important fact about our High Priest, which is His identity. "Jesus the Son of God" is a great title for our Lord, indicating both His humanity as Jesus and His deity as God's Son. Jesus is unique in eternity and in history because He is the God-man. As man, He can feel what we feel, and as God, He can fix what's wrong that makes us feel that way.

I like what the patriarch Job said. As he was being accused by his friends and trying to defend himself, Job said, "For [God] is not a man as I am that I may answer Him, that we may go to court together. There is no umpire between us, who may lay his hand upon us both" (Job 9:32–33). Job was looking for somebody who would take his hand and identify with him. But he also needed somebody who could take God's hand and identify with Him, and bring the two of them together.

Job felt that God was out there beyond his reach. We don't have to feel that way because Jesus has bridged the gap between man and God. He can understand what you are going through when you cry out to Him, and He has the power of God to act. A priest represents the people to God and God to the people, and we have a High Priest who understands both sides perfectly. Jesus is unique in His Person.

We Have Access to God through the Position of Christ

Jesus is also unique in the position He holds. He has "passed through the heavens" (Heb. 4:14). Once a year under the old covenant, Israel's high priest would pass through the two outer areas of the temple and go behind the curtain into the holy of holies on the Day of Atonement to atone for the people's sins. There were many priests, but only the high priest could do this.

The Bible says that Jesus passed through the heavens and entered the holy place in the heavenly temple to offer one sacrifice forever for our sins (Heb. 9:24–26). He passed through the earthly heavens, or the atmosphere, which is the first heaven; through the starry heavens or space, which is the second heaven; and into the presence of God in glory, or the third heaven.

Now if you're living on earth, what you want to do in prayer is go to the third heaven, where God's throne is. The problem is that you and I can't get there unless someone takes us. Why? Because no one has ever gone from earth all the way to the third heaven—except Jesus our High Priest, who has passed through the heavens and is now praying for us in the third heaven, the very temple and throne room of God.

So when we pray in the power of the Holy Spirit, Jesus Christ as our Priest and Intercessor makes sure our prayer gets to the proper location, the presence of God, where our needs and concerns can be addressed. Because Jesus, the Son of God, is related to the Father, He can bypass all the stuff that blocks you and me. That's why when we pray, we pray in Jesus' name.

We Have a Sympathetic Priest through the Passion of Christ

A third aspect of Jesus' high priestly ministry that we find in Hebrews 4 is what I call His passion, or feelings of sympathy for us. We read earlier in verse 15 that He sympathizes with our weaknesses because He has experienced every temptation we will ever face, except that Jesus never sinned.

Why do we need a High Priest who knows what it's like to be tempted, to be tired and hungry and sad, and all the other feelings and emotions we feel? So He can represent and interpret these feelings to God the Father. Stay with me here, because this is important.

God the Father knows everything actual and potential. There are no facts of which He is not fully aware. His knowledge is complete, period. But although God the Father has full knowledge of everything, He does not have full experience of everything. For example, God the Father has never been tempted to sin the way we are tempted. He knows all there is to know about sin, but He has never experienced the temptation to yield to Satan.

But God the Father wanted to relate to you and me on the feeling level. So He sent His precious Son to earth and gave Him a human body and emotions like ours so the Son could live among us and feel everything we feel. And because Jesus did that, He can interpret our feelings and our needs to His Father.

No matter what temptation or trial you may face, Jesus knows what you are feeling because He went through it as the God-man. So when you pray and pour out your heart to God, Jesus acts as your great High Priest before His Father and says, "Father, I know what this person is feeling. I know what it is like to be under pressure to sin. I know the pain of loss and hunger. I sympathize with this child of Yours who needs Our help." We have a High Priest who understands our weaknesses. He sees the tears and the struggle.

Now you may say, "Yes, but Jesus was without sin, so He can't really feel my sin the way I feel it." Oh, but He can. In fact, because of His purity He actually feels the pain of sin even more.

An illustration will help explain what I mean. In the ordinary, everyday world, you and I live with germs all around us and even on us all the time. Because we aren't in a sterile environment, we don't notice the germs, and we learn to live with germs overall. Of course, that changes in the midst of a pandemic but the overall point stays the same.

It's an entirely different story in a hospital operating room. There, any contamination from germs or bacteria is a major problem that merits the attention of the entire staff. So they sterilize everything in the room because bacteria in an operating room is a major issue. The purity of the room demands close attention to the presence of even the slightest impurity that could lead to a life-threatening infection for the patient. Jesus' separateness from sin does not diminish His ability to sympathize with us.

We Can Draw Near through the Provision of Christ

Finally, Hebrews 4:16 says we can "draw near with confidence to the throne of grace, so that we may receive mercy and find grace to help in time of need." We don't have to hold anything back in prayer. We don't have to wonder if we are wasting our time or if this is doing any good.

Do you understand what it means to be invited to draw near to God, to go right up to His throne? God's people couldn't do this in the Old Testament days. Only the high priest could draw near once a year. Everybody else had to draw back and wait to see if God would accept the high priest's sacrifice and cover their sins for another year. But Jesus has satisfied the demands of God so that we can have direct access to Him.

Years ago during the college football season, I went to see my son Jonathan play for the Baylor University Bears. Jonathan threw for a touchdown and also caught a twenty-five-yard pass, so it was a great game. I was scheduled to speak to the Baylor team before the game, and I had two friends with me. They did not have authorization to go into the locker room, which is very restricted these days with all of the extra security.

But when we walked through the door and I identified myself, I told the security people that these men were with me. Their names were not on the list, but they gained access on my authorization. They walked into the locker room with the same confidence as me because they were connected with me. When I entered the team's meeting room, they entered with me. And when I walked into the coaches' office, they walked in with me. My friends were able to move about freely because someone who was duly authorized to enter went ahead of them and opened the way.

God says you have been duly authorized to enter His throne room by virtue of your connection with Christ. And please notice that it is a throne of grace. This is not the throne where you find judgment, but mercy and grace. It is a throne because the One who sits on it is the Sovereign of the universe. This is where all the power and authority you will ever need reside. This is where God gives His sons and daughters what we could never give ourselves. All of this has been provided to you by Jesus Christ, who invites you to draw near with confidence.

God gives us what we don't deserve and could never earn from a throne that never runs low on its provision—and it is all tied to our drawing near in prayer. God has all the grace we need to help us, but we have to go before the throne to ask for this grace. Therefore, a prayer-less Christian is a grace-less Christian. Christians who are not praying as a way of life are not growing in their spiritual life because they are not hanging around the throne that dispenses grace. They are denying their new nature access to the realm where it feels most at home.

The grace we receive at God's throne is designed to help us "in time of need." We've said it before, but it needs to be said again that grace is given based on the need of the moment. God will not give you tomorrow's grace until tomorrow. But don't worry, because the provision of grace we have in Christ will not run out tomorrow, or ever. You can't go to God too often. Jesus went through all that He went through on earth so you and I can know Him as Savior and draw near to Him as our great High Priest.

The grace we need to help us reminds me of an ambulance coming to a location to treat someone with a medical emergency. The paramedics come and offer assistance to the victim on the spot, often right where he or she is lying. The paramedics will dispense immediate grace to address the most serious symptoms. Then they put the patient on a gurney and slide him into the ambulance, which is equipped with more grace—more medical facilities—to deal with the problem. And as the paramedics are administering more grace to the patient, the ambulance races to the hospital where even more grace awaits. And once the patient is admitted, the hospital keeps dispensing grace to meet the need until the problem has been addressed and the patient can go home again.

One day Jesus Christ heard our emergency call to Him: "I am a sinner and I need a Savior." He came down to earth, found us dying with sin, and reached down to save us. And as our High Priest, He also transported us from where we were to a place that has all the grace we will need for as long as we live, until we are finally and fully restored at the resurrection and go home with Him.

How can you have a Savior and High Priest like this and not draw near to Him in prayer? When you tap into the power of prayer, you will start to grow in leaps and bounds as your new nature grows stronger in the spiritual environment it was made to inhabit.

You say, "But I'm tired."

That's okay. Just draw near.

"But you don't understand. I'm hurting and I feel like quitting."

I may not understand, but Jesus does. Draw near to Him. He will meet you where you are and take you where He is before the throne that dispenses grace.

One day during the Civil War, a soldier sat on a bench outside the White House looking distressed. A little boy came by and asked him what was wrong. The soldier said he needed to see President Lincoln, but the guards wouldn't let him in.

Hearing this, the little boy took the soldier by the hand and led him past the guards directly into the president's office. "Father," he said, "this soldier really needs to speak with you." That boy was the president's son, who had direct and continuous access to his father.

No matter what may be happening in your life, Jesus, the Son of God, stands ready to lead you directly into His Father's presence, where there is grace unlimited to meet your needs.

10

The Church:
The Context of
Kingdom Living

BECAUSE OF ALL THE NATURE and animal programs on TV, we can now observe the animal world up close and personal in a way that was not possible before. What's interesting is that a lot of these shows confirm what we already knew about the way many animals live.

For instance, God has designed most animals to live in a community, either for procreation, protection, raising their young, or some combination of all three. These animals seldom reach their maximum potential if they are separated from the group. They also become easier prey for predators like lions, who try to panic and scatter the herd and then pick off the straggler or the baby animal that is out there alone and vulnerable to attack.

The concept of community is an important principle both in the physical and the spiritual worlds. God designed Christians to be born, protected, and raised in the context of a community known as the church. The Bible says that our enemy, the devil, "prowls around like a roaring lion, seeking someone to devour" (1 Peter 5:8). One of the easiest people to devour is the Christian who is no longer functioning within the nurturing context of the church.

The church is the most exciting entity that God has placed on this earth, precisely because it is the life-support system for individual Christians. It is critical that we come to understand the role the church plays in our lives because God has given us the church to serve as the context for kingdom living.

Just as no one expects a baby to grow on its own, God never meant for us to grow and develop spiritually in isolation from other believers. Spiritual growth is a group endeavor, which should be good news to you because it means you don't have to do it all yourself. Christians grow best in a healthy family context where they are surrounded by spiritual fathers, mothers, brothers, and sisters to help them.

Adam's aloneness was the only part of creation that God said was "not good" (Gen. 2:18). Eve's creation had implications beyond marriage. By giving Eve to Adam, God was stating a fundamental principle that He created human beings to exist in community. This principle reaches its highest expression in the church.

The Bible uses a number of terms to illustrate this community or corporate aspect of the church. One of these terms, of course, is the family. In fact, one of Paul's synonyms for salvation is adoption, the act by which God places all believers into His family (Gal. 4:5; Eph. 1:5). The great thing about God's adoption program is that no believer is left out. There may be tens of thousands of children waiting to be adopted around the world, but no child of God is left behind without a family.

I am often asked, "Why do I have to go to church and be part of the family of God?" In reality, if you are a Christian you *are* a part of God's family. That is a biblical and theological truth. But practically speaking, a lot of God's children are trying to live as if they don't need anyone else. Believers who are not functioning as part of a local church are living selfishly and sinfully. They are outside of God's will, which means they are undermining their own spiritual development.

The answer to the question of why we need to be functioning members of the church is not just so we can come and listen to sermons. We need to be part of the church because it is the environment God has created for our maximum spiritual growth. The church is the community of the redeemed that collectively partakes of the benefits and blessings of the new covenant (2 Cor. 3:5–8). Apart from the church, our spiritual growth is stunted. I want to show you how closely and completely God has linked our growth as individual Christians with the ministry of the larger body of Christ in the church.

The truths we are going to consider are true both for the universal church that is made up of all believers everywhere, and the local church that is made up of some believers somewhere. The local church is simply the expression and manifestation of the universal body of Christ in one particular community.

Some people will tell you they believe in the church as a concept, but they aren't interested in plugging in to a local body of believers. Sorry, but Christianity doesn't work that way. That's like the guy who said, "I love humanity. It's people I can't stand."[2] Jesus Christ is so committed to this family called the church that He died and rose again to redeem us, and He has invested all of heaven's resources in the church's life. Our relationship to the corporate body of believers is so vital that there is no such thing as maximum growth and development for you and me as Christians apart from the church. Let me be clear about this. Christians who refuse to become functioning members of a local church are living in sin and are out of fellowship with God because they are living in disobedience (Heb. 10:24).

---

2. Linus Van Pelt says this line in the November 12, 1959 comic strip of *Peanuts*, by Charles Schulz.

THE CHURCH'S VITAL ROLE IN SPIRITUAL GROWTH

The church is not just a classroom for spiritual instruction, but a living and growing organism to enhance our spiritual development. No portion of Scripture teaches the importance of the church to the spiritual development of its members better than the book of Ephesians. Paul made a foundational statement about the church when he wrote:

> So then you are no longer strangers and aliens, but you are fellow citizens with the saints, and are of God's household, having been built on the foundation of the apostles and prophets, Christ Jesus Himself being the corner stone, in whom the whole building, being fitted together, is growing into a holy temple in the Lord, in whom you also are being built together into a dwelling of God in the Spirit. (Eph. 2:19–22)

These words tell us that we are part of something bigger than any one of us. And when Paul comes to wrap up this passage, he says the household of God of which we are all members is "growing." I see no mention here of individual growth apart from the church. The pronouns are all plural. We grow as we are connected because it is the church together, not great believers individually, that experiences the unique presence of God (Eph. 3:10, 17–21).

Blessings You Can't Get Anywhere Else

There are some things God will do for you just because you are one of His children. Every believer is saved, sealed with the Holy Spirit, and assured of heaven. Every believer has been baptized by the Holy Spirit into the body of Christ (1 Cor. 12:13). But there are many other things God will only do for you when you are a functioning member of His body and not going your own way. Spiritual growth is one of those blessings that can only be fully realized in the context of the church.

When movies first became available for rent on videos, there was a deep concern in Hollywood that this new business would hurt attendance at theaters. After all, the reasoning went, when a family could pay a few dollars and watch a movie in the comfort of their own home, why would they drive to a theater to pay many times more for movie tickets, let alone popcorn?

Those fears proved to be unfounded. Even though people began lining up in droves to rent movies, the movie industry made an amazing discovery. Far from declining, movie attendance actually went up even as video rentals and sales went up. An analysis of this surprising trend showed that one reason people still attended movies was that things happen in a theater full of people that don't happen in the living room.

What the theater offered was the group dynamic of a bunch of people laughing or being scared or crying together. You know that it's easier and more enjoyable to laugh at a funny performance when everyone around you is laughing too. You almost can't help yourself because the environment affects you.

There are times when we need to go into the privacy of our prayer closet. But there are other things we can only experience in the ambiance of God's people gathered in the church. The church is the corporate dwelling place of the Holy Spirit, according to Ephesians 2:22. When people who are individually indwelled by the Spirit come together for worship, praise, instruction, encouragement, and service, the Holy Spirit shows up in a powerful way, and we grow as we experience His presence.

Christ's Commitment to the Church

In Ephesians 4, Paul goes deep into the vital connection between growth and the church as Christ's body. He sets the context in the early verses by talking about "the unity of the Spirit" (v. 3) and the oneness of our faith and our Lord (vv. 4–6).

Then he discusses the unique work of Christ by which He gave spiritual gifts to His people and gifted people to His church (vv. 7–11). We will deal with spiritual gifts in the next chapter as they relate to your calling. What I want you to see here is that Jesus Christ went from the cross to the depths of hell to bring the church into being, and we cannot ignore what it cost Him to purchase His body the church.

Christ died on the cross on Good Friday to pay for our sins. He rose from the dead on Easter Sunday, and in between He descended in His spirit into Hades to declare His victory and take the righteous souls from the paradise side of Hades to heaven. He led these people right through the domain of Satan, and there wasn't anything Satan could do about it. That's what Ephesians 4:9–10 is all about.

One reason we come to church is to celebrate Christ's victory. The world and circumstances may beat us up all week and make us feel like less than, but when we gather with other members of Christ's body, we are reminded that we are on the winning side. It's hard to celebrate all by yourself. When you have something worth celebrating, you call people together so you can share the joy. Jesus Christ is so excited about His victory that He has called together His church to celebrate what He achieved on the cross. Celebration, like spiritual growth, is a group project.

A story is told of an incident in the Special Olympics that beautifully illustrates the way the church is designed to function. The competitors lined up to run the hundred-meter dash as best they could with their limitations. Everyone took off, but one of the runners fell and began to cry. All of the other runners stopped, came back and helped the fallen runner get up, then locked arms with him as everyone walked across the finish line together.

Now I can pretty well guarantee you that nothing like this is going to happen in the regular Olympics. Some years ago, a sports magazine carried the photo of a famous woman runner, the favorite to win her race, holding her leg in agony after falling on the track, as the other competitors raced past her.

What made the Special Olympics runners turn back and help the person who had fallen? Because they realized that they all had weaknesses and shortcomings, and they knew it could have been any one of them lying there on the track. So they reached out to him, and in a very real sense all the runners won the race that day.

If the other runners in the regular Olympics had gone back to the woman who fell, helped her up, and then crossed the finish line together, they may not have won individual medals, but it's safe to say that they would have grown as human beings that day. God is more interested in our growth than in the medals we can win for ourselves.

The gifted servants Paul mentions in Ephesians 4:11 are given to the church to equip us for service "to the building up of the body of Christ" (v. 12). This is growth language, where Paul ties Christ's victory to the church and the growth of its members. To build up is to grow and develop, which is what Christ wants the church to do until we reach the stature of "a mature man" (v. 13). The goal of this maturity is Christlikeness (v. 15).

ATTACHMENT BEFORE GROWTH

Someone may say, "But I thought we were talking about my individual growth as a Christian." We are, but we are talking about attached as opposed to unattached growth. That's why the use of the human body as a symbol for the church is so crucial. The body is all about working and growing together. The only place detached body parts grow and thrive is in horror movies.

We're Meant to Grow as Part of the Body

The church as a concept may be ethereal and hard to grasp because our connection to other believers is invisible. But we can get hold of the concept of a body, because we all have one and we can see how it works. The human body is not an inanimate object, but a living, growing, changing organism. The parts of our bodies have to stay connected to the body in order to function and grow. Many of us are stymied in our spiritual growth because we have cut ourselves off from the body.

This happened years ago but you may remember the incredible story (which they later turned into a movie) out of Utah of the young mountain climber who amputated his own arm to free himself after falling among the rocks. One amazing part of the story is that searchers went to the area where he had been trapped to see if they could locate the severed arm and bring it back so it could be reattached. That attempt failed, but reattaching limbs has been done enough times to prove that the human body has unbelievable powers to supply blood flow and restore life to a part that has been severed. The body of Christ has the same power to restore its severed members.

As the body of Christ all of us are to stay connected and keep building each other up "until we all attain to the unity of the faith" and to "a mature man" (v. 13). The idea is to not let anyone become disconnected so that he or she fails to grow.

The Church Provides the Fire We Need

The writer of Hebrews had this important word for the church: "Let us consider how to stimulate one another to love and good deeds, not forsaking our own assembling together, as is the habit of some, but encouraging one another; and all the more as you see the day drawing near" (Heb. 10:24–25). Nothing will stimulate spiritual growth faster than when we experience the love of God's people, join other believers in serving the Lord, and draw on Christ and each other for regular encouragement.

So we ought not to forsake the assembly, the church, because it provides the environment that stimulates our spiritual growth and development. I don't know about you, but I have days when I need to be encouraged. Life has a way of deflating and discouraging us, and we need a place where we can be built up. The word used for "stimulate" in Hebrews 10:24 means to incite or create heat. It's the picture of a fire that burns brighter and longer, and puts out more heat, when many logs are stacked together as opposed to a single log that will soon burn out. A Christian cannot stay hot for God while staying away from His family.

The Growth Needs to Be Mutual

If you said to someone, "Would you like to come to a place where you will be loved, nurtured, encouraged, ministered to, and treasured as a valuable person?" most people would take you up on the deal. That's the way the church is supposed to treat its members. But don't miss something important here. Symbiotic growth is that which occurs between two organisms when both benefit by the relationship. Parasitic growth occurs when one organism feeds off another without giving anything back.

I'm afraid the church has too many people who only want to feed and grow and give nothing back. The only part of the body they are concerned about is themselves. So if they are a toe, for instance, and they stub themselves on life, they want the whole body to react and jump in there to relieve their pain. But when a finger is hurting and the toe is called on to help, these people don't have the time or energy to care for someone else.

The Bible addresses that problem in 1 Corinthians 12:12–31, another classic passage about the body of Christ. After discussing how all the parts of Christ's body need each other, Paul said God's goal was that "there may be no division in the body, but that the members may have the same care for one another" (v. 25). Spiritual growth is mutual, although there are certainly times when a person needs to be ministered to and grow before he or she can help others grow.

WHAT WE NEED TO GROW

When Paul described the goal or result of spiritual growth as being mature, he gave us the standard. We should grow "to the measure of the stature which belongs to the fullness of Christ" (Eph. 4:13).

We Need the Right Standard

If you want to know where our spiritual growth is to lead, just look at Jesus Christ. Paul's all-consuming goal was to know Christ (Phil. 3:10).

This is a lifelong process because we will never perfectly attain this goal until we are face-to-face with Christ. But growth should be evident in our lives as we move from infancy to adulthood. One way you'll know you are growing is when your life takes on spiritual stability, as described in Ephesians 4:14: "As a result, we are no longer to be children, tossed here and there" by everything that blows in on the wind. One trait of children is the way they bounce from this to that and change from minute to minute. It doesn't take much to distract children or get them upset. They are easily fooled and misled.

If you saw a five-year-old who was jumping around in church and couldn't sit still, you might not think too much about it. But if you saw a forty-five-year-old having the same problem, you would think something was wrong. That's how a lot of Christians are living. Every little struggle wipes them out. But God wants us to grow past this stage on our way to maturity in Christ.

We Need Truth and Love to Grow Properly

For this growth to happen, at least two things need to be present in our lives—and both are supplied in the context of the church. Instead of being unstable children, Paul says in verse 15: "We are to grow up in all aspects into Him who is the head, even Christ." The elements that produce this kind of maturity are found at the beginning of the verse: "speaking the truth in love." Truth and love must be present for real growth to occur.

We have discussed the importance of truth, a fixed standard by which everything else is measured. The Holy Spirit's ministry in the church is key to the body's growth, but the Holy Spirit only works in the environment of truth. Jesus called Him "the Spirit of truth" (John 14:17). The Spirit's job is to reveal the truth of God's Word and confirm it in our hearts, and the church is the center for promoting, proclaiming, and protecting God's truth (1 Tim. 3:15).

But truth must operate in concert with love, for the church is to be "rooted and grounded in love" (Eph. 3:17). It's not either-or, but both-and. A lot of Christians are like cars whose tires are wearing unevenly because they are out of alignment. Some churches and some Christians emphasize only truth, the doctrinal content of our faith. This is vital, but we need more than knowledge—even Bible knowledge—to grow in Christ. Others focus on love to the exclusion of truth, which leads to a mushy, "anything goes" atmosphere that undercuts the church's ministry as a beacon of God's truth.

Neither extreme is healthy, as we can see by looking at a human family. Just because parents tell their children the truth doesn't mean the home is going to be a happy place to live. Just because a husband tells his wife the truth doesn't mean they are happily married. Information applied without love can be harsh and restrictive. A person can grow in knowledge while shriveling in terms of spiritual growth.

The reverse is also true, because a family in which the parents focus solely on love without content wind up raising self-centered, undisciplined kids who have little or no framework for making sound moral judgments.

Paul said that knowledge without love "makes [us] arrogant," or puffs us up, while "love edifies" or builds us up (1 Cor. 8:1). Love sacrifices to seek the well-being and meet the needs of others (1 John 4:7–12). Such love and building up of each other is specifically designed to occur in the context of the local church (Eph. 4:15).

A person can use the Bible like a hammer to break other people or a whip to keep them in line. That's not because there is something wrong with the Bible, but the problem is with the hand holding it. In order for truth to stimulate growth, it must be handled and applied with a spirit of love and concern for the people to whom it is being communicated.

This explains why there is such a major emphasis in the Epistles on the "one another," or relational, aspect of the church's ministry. Romans 12:4–16 is one great example, as Paul urged the believers at Rome to care deeply for each other. The church's indispensable role in this work is evident by the fact that the New Testament Epistles were written either to local churches or to individuals who had oversight of local churches. What that says to us is that God works with us individually as we are part of His spiritual community called the church.

This is why I tell the people in our church that no matter where I travel, there is no place I would rather be than in Dallas with the body of Christ at Oak Cliff Bible Fellowship. That's not just because I love to preach, because I get many invitations to preach. I can preach anywhere, but I love our church family and doing what God has called me to do as their pastor to teach and encourage and stimulate them to grow in Christ. That requires time and involvement in their lives, which is what the ministry of the church is all about. It's easy to preach to people you will probably never see again, but it's another thing to speak the truth in love among people you live with every day in order to help them grow up in Christ in all aspects of their lives.

We Need Every Member of the Body

I love the last verse in this section of Ephesians 4 dealing with spiritual growth, because it really nails down the truth that spiritual growth is not a solo act but a group project requiring every part of the body.

The verse continues the sentence begun in verse 15 as Paul spoke of Christ, "from whom the whole body, being fitted and held together by what every joint supplies, according to the proper working of each individual part, causes the growth of the body for the building up of itself in love" (v. 16).

It's impossible to miss the point. The church as the body of Christ grows when each and every individual part is doing its job and contributing to the whole. The growth of the church is nothing more than the growth of its members, since the church is a living organism made up of living parts. In the same way, the lack of growth by some members affects the entire body.

When your stomach is really upset, you may take something and go lie down to help get rid of the pain. Your stomach doesn't lie down by itself. It takes the whole body with it, and nothing happens until your stomach is better.

Our church sanctuary has hundreds of lights in the ceiling, and for a while some of them were burned out. I used this to point out to our congregation that because each light in the church was designed and put in place by the builders to illuminate a particular area, it wouldn't take many burned-out lights to make part of the sanctuary dark and affect the people sitting there.

A lot of Christians are like burned-out light bulbs. They like to hang out in the church and give the impression that they are making a contribution because they are filling a place. But unless we are allowing God's Spirit to use us to illuminate the body of Christ, we need to be changed. Your individual part is critical to the whole, and when you are fulfilling your part, God will make sure you grow.

Nothing on earth can compare to a group of believers in a local church who are under the control of the Holy Spirit and using their divinely given gifts to minister to the body. When this happens, the body builds itself up in love, as the last part of Ephesians 4:16 says. When believers are growing together in unity and love, a lot of problems are taken care of before they become big because the body is healing itself. A healthy body that is working the way it was designed to work will grow, and every member of that body will benefit.

The church doesn't exist solely for the benefit of the church. Rather, the church is the *ecclesia* (the original term given to it in Scripture). An ecclesia is a body of people who have been vested with governing authorities. We as the church of Jesus Christ are to be about the advancement of His kingdom agenda on earth. We are to legislate heaven's authority into the history of humanity. We can only do this when we work together to enact positive kingdom influence on our culture.

When God put together the human body, He did it so that every part would be vital for the working of every other part. The church functions the same way. If you are not in a church where God's Word is being taught in an atmosphere of love, you need to find a place where the body is functioning as God intended. You need it for the contribution you make to advancing His kingdom, and you need it for your own growth in Christ.

FINDING A LOCAL CHURCH

Since involvement in a local church is vital to your spiritual health and development, you need to find and identify with an assembly of believers, if you are not already part of a Bible teaching church. God has a church for you since "God has placed the members, each one of them, in the body, just as He desired" (1 Cor. 12:18). He desires to place you in a church that can meet your spiritual needs while you contribute to its development as well. Let me give you some guidelines for finding such a church in your community. There are four key characteristics you want to look for in finding a good church home, based on Acts 2:42–47 where we see the church at Jerusalem engaged in life-changing ministry.

The first is God-honoring worship, the celebration of God for who He is and what He has done. A biblically sound church places a high priority on praising God.

Second is quality biblical instruction. Does the church you are considering believe, honor, and teach God's Word in such a way that you understand the Bible and see how it applies to your life? Remember, you can't grow beyond what you know.

A third characteristic of a good church is fellowship, the sharing of the life of Christ among the members. This goes beyond coffee in the fellowship hall or attending church dinners. Biblical fellowship occurs when the members are involved in each other's lives—caring, encouraging, correcting, loving, and sharing with one another. The church should provide each member with a meaningful sense of belonging.

Fourth and finally is the church's ministry of outreach. A church that wants to grow cannot be ingrown. The church you identify with should provide you with opportunities to use your gifts and talents to touch other lives, while also emphasizing the importance of sharing your faith in word and good deeds with the world around you. In other words, the church's influence should extend beyond its walls. The church should be intentionally engaged in kingdom impact.

When you find a church where these priorities and experiences are regularly offered in an environment that is saturated in grace, you know you have found a solid New Testament church.

11

Giving:
The Generosity of
Kingdom Living

A MAN WHO WAS WELL-TO-DO enjoyed buying his father unusual and exotic presents for Christmas. Since cost was no object, the man would go all out to get his father the right gift. One year he bought his dad an antique car, and another Christmas he gave him hang gliding equipment.

But one particular Christmas this man found a gift for his father that was truly unique: a talking bird that could speak five languages and sing "The Yellow Rose of Texas" standing on one foot. This bird was so unusual and talented that it cost the man ten thousand dollars, but he didn't mind because he felt that his father was worthy of such a rare gift. So he purchased the bird and had it sent to his father for Christmas.

A few days later, the man went over to his father's house to see if he was enjoying his unique and expensive gift. He knocked on the door and said, "Dad, did you get my present?"

"I sure did," his father said.

"How'd you like it?"

"It was delicious!" Dad had obviously missed the point of his son's special gift, and so he treated as ordinary something that was very special.

Too often, that's how we treat the gifts God gives us. Paul asked this rhetorical question: "What do you have that you did not receive?" (1 Cor. 4:7). The answer: nothing. Everything we have, including the breath in our lungs, is a gift from God. Just to make sure we don't miss the point, James wrote: "Every good thing given and every perfect gift is from above, coming down from the Father of lights" (James 1:17). We can't talk about stewardship without first being reminded that we have *been given* everything, including the money God entrusted to us. So anything we give back to God is just returning to Him a small part of what He has given to us and opening the doors for generosity to serve as the conduit for kingdom living.

We live as stewards in God's kingdom. A kingdom always has three distinct aspects: a King, His rules, and those He rules. We have been placed under God to carry out His kingdom agenda (the advancement of His glory through the proclamation and application of His rules) in our lives. Much of this is done through how we steward, or manage, what He has given to us.

A steward is a manager, not an owner. He oversees the property of another. God owns everything (Ps. 24:1), yet He has given each of us time, talents, and treasures to manage for Him until He returns (Matt. 25:14–30). In this chapter, I want to specifically address the stewardship of our resources since we have addressed the other areas elsewhere.

I'm convinced that far too many Christians not only miss the point that our giving is simply a response to what God has given us. They also fail to make a vital connection that the Bible makes time and time again, which is that our attitude toward money and possessions in general, and giving in particular, is portrayed in Scripture as the single biggest indicator of our spiritual temperature.

Throughout the Gospels, Jesus turned to money more than to any other subject when He wanted to teach us about the Christian life and illustrate what it means to follow Him. And some of the highest praise the apostle Paul had for the believers he ministered to was related to their giving. Someone has said that the last part of us to get saved is our bank account, and the extent to which this is true helps explain why more Christians are not growing in grace faster than they are. My goal in this chapter is to help you make the connection between the ministry of giving and your spiritual growth.

A POWERFUL INDICATOR OF SPIRITUAL GROWTH

Our attitude toward giving is much like the lights on a car's dashboard. When an indicator light comes on, it's pointing to something happening under the hood that needs attention before there's a breakdown. When God turns on the indicator light of money and giving in our lives, it's not because He is hurting for cash. He is looking at something deep in the heart that we cannot afford to ignore because He wants to deal with it.

Something Is Wrong Down Deep

Today many Christians suffer from a disease we might call "cirrhosis of the giver." This is a debilitating spiritual malady that has been around since the earliest days of the church, first being clearly diagnosed around AD 34 in a couple named Ananias and Sapphira, who became greedy with God's gifts and suffered the consequences (Acts 5:1–11).

Cirrhosis of the giver is an acute condition. Those who have it show symptoms that include a sudden paralysis and inability to reach for their wallet or purse when the offering plate comes by at church. This strange symptom often disappears in stores, on the golf course, or when dining in fine restaurants. But it regularly shows up in church.

Some have attempted to treat this condition by offering tax

deductions for charitable giving, but judging from the prevalence of the problem this incentive has not had a great effect. The disease of shriveled giving continues to plague the family of God. I say that based on the most recent figures that show the average Christian in America gives only 2.5 percent of his or her income to the kingdom of God.[3] This includes evangelicals too, those of us who claim that we believe the Bible from cover to cover. As a whole, we are barely giving a decent down payment on our tithe to God's work. This is an indicator that something is wrong "under the hood" of the church in America. Our spiritual priorities are out of place.

To help us get those priorities in order, we need to spend some time in 2 Corinthians 8–9, two of the most important chapters in the Bible on the subject of money and giving. I want you to see the connection between your giving and your spiritual growth, which will be evident as Paul wrote to urge the Corinthians to finish the collection for a special gift they had promised to send to the saints in Jerusalem who were in deep financial need.

Giving Is Our Response to God's Grace

To urge and encourage the Corinthians in their giving, Paul brought up the example of the Macedonian believers. Notice the connection Paul made between "the grace of God which has been given in the churches of Macedonia" (2 Cor. 8:1) and the "liberality" of their giving despite "deep poverty" (v. 2). These people not only "gave of their own accord," but "beg[ged] us with much urging for the favor of participation in the support of the saints" (vv. 3–4). And then comes the clincher in verse 5: "And this, not as we had expected, but they first gave themselves to the Lord and to us by the will of God."

---

3. Mike Holmes, "What Would Happen If the Church Tithed?," *Relevant Magazine*, June 15, 2021, https://relevantmagazine.com/faith/church/what-would-happen-if-church-tithed/.

The Macedonians couldn't wait to give because they understood that they belonged to the Lord and whatever they had was a gift of His grace. They had their giving priorities in order because they first gave themselves to the Lord, including their billfolds. Paul said the way he knew the Macedonians had given themselves to the Lord was that they begged him for the offering plate.

That's a real challenge to us. When was the last time you sat in church and got anxious waiting for the offering to be taken because you couldn't wait to give? A person in our church told me recently how exciting it was to give. When I asked why, the response was, "Because God has been so good."

Once you connect your giving with God's grace, then you give not because the preacher was begging, you feel guilty, or you're trying to cut a deal with God. You give out of the overflow of God's goodness. Despite their poverty and afflictions, the Macedonians were experiencing an "abundance of joy" (v. 2) in the Lord that showed up in their attitude toward giving. That's key to remember, because in the Bible giving is connected to our spiritual life, not merely to our money—and the more that connection is made, the more spiritual growth will occur.

God's grace and giving are so closely linked that the words *grace* or *gracious work* are used at least five times in 2 Corinthians 8. Repeatedly, the Bible connects our giving with the flow of God's grace to us. Paul even linked giving with Christ's sacrifice on the cross, pointing out that even though Christ had the riches of heaven at His disposal, He left it all and impoverished Himself by taking on human flesh and dying for us (2 Cor. 8:9).

Understanding how gracious God is to us is important because many people give to Him from their leftovers. If they have anything left after they've paid the bills and done everything they wanted to do, they'll give. But we need to know that even if we give God a million dollars, if it's out of our leftovers, we have insulted Him (Mal. 1:6–9).

Many people are what I call "re-givers." Re-givers are people who receive a present they don't want, so they wrap it up again and give it to someone else. Some people have whole closets full of gifts they don't want, and when they need something they rummage around in that closet for an item. They haven't really given anything, but simply passed on a leftover gift they didn't plan to use anyway. This is how some believers approach their giving to God, and it's an insult.

In the New Testament you don't see begging, sales, or other gimmicks to raise money for God's work. What you see is people like the Macedonians responding to grace, because they understood the God they served. Everything God created was meant to give. He created the sun to give light during the day, the moon and the stars during the night. He created flowers to give seeds. Even Adam and Eve taught their sons to give, because the Bible says that Abel gave of the first of his flock to God (Gen. 4:4).

God is a giver: "For God so loved the world, that He gave" (John 3:16). When you understand grace, circumstances take a backseat. Our giving is not determined by debt-to-income ratios, financial indices, leading economic indicators, or tax brackets. Rather, it is governed by grace.

THE PRINCIPLES OF SOWING AND REAPING

After laying the foundation for giving in God's grace, Paul went on in 2 Corinthians 9 to urge that the church in Corinth get its offering ready before he arrived, so that when Paul came, he and the church wouldn't be embarrassed if the gift wasn't there (vv. 1–5). Then in verse 6 the apostle began another key discussion on the principle of generosity in giving.

We Must Sow to Reap a Harvest

To illustrate his point Paul used the example of a farmer, which his readers could readily identify with. "Now this I say, he who sows sparingly will also reap sparingly, and he who sows bountifully will also reap bountifully" (2 Cor. 9:6). In other words, the person who gives little will receive little, and the person who gives generously will receive much.

I'm not a farmer, but I know that a farmer's harvest depends on what he sows. You will never see a farmer who refuses to plant seeds sitting around expecting a bountiful harvest. That farmer may be a Christian who goes to church faithfully, has his devotions every day, and witnesses to lost people. But he is not going to get a crop without planting first. The law of sowing and reaping is built into creation.

There is something else a farmer won't do if he expects a harvest. He will not eat the seed that he should be planting. In other words, a farmer must start with his seed, not his need, if he has any hope of reaping a harvest. This basic fact is critical to the ministry of giving, because most people approach it from a need standpoint. Their reasoning is "I can't give to the Lord because I need to pay these bills," or whatever the case may be. Put in farming terms, what they are saying is "I can't plant this seed, even though it will yield a good crop, because I'm hungry right now."

Now this is precisely the point at which faith must kick in. When a farmer plants his seed instead of eating it, it is an act of faith that the sun will shine and the rains will come and turn the seed into a harvest. A farmer who plants is counting on nature to back him up, because all his planting does is position the seed for growth. Without proper sunlight and rain, nothing is going to happen, which means a lot of faith goes into farming.

Giving is also an act of faith in our great God. When He tells us to sow bountifully so we can reap bountifully, our willingness or reluctance to do that says a lot about whether we hold God and His promises in high esteem.

We Reap What We Have Sown

Another self-evident principle of sowing and reaping is that we will reap what we sow. We can't get apples if we sow oranges. Our harvest will be of the same nature as our seed.

This principle not only refers to our financial giving, but to our attitudes as well. If you're looking for love, how much love are you sowing? If you expect to receive a helping hand when you are in need, how are you doing in planting the seed of kindness and help in other people's lives? Jesus said, "Blessed are the merciful, for they shall receive mercy" (Matt. 5:7). The thing you want to reap must be the thing you plant, because the seeds you plant will faithfully reproduce after their kind, whether for good or bad (Gal. 6:7–9).

It's amazing how many people want to plant weeds and get roses in terms of their approach to life. So often the person who is quick to judge others is the first to plead for mercy and understanding when he messes up. A farmer doesn't shake his head in amazement if he gets a crop of corn from corn seed. But so often we shake our heads and wonder why God isn't blessing us with a harvest, forgetting that we haven't sown the right seed in the first place.

We Reap More than We Sow

There is one more principle of sowing and reaping we can draw from 2 Corinthians 9. We not only reap what we sow, but we always reap more than we sow. We read in verses 7–11 that God will bless our giving by multiplying it into a great harvest—and even give us more seed to sow. Jesus said in Luke 6:38, "Give, and it will be given to you. They will pour into your lap a good measure—pressed down, shaken together, and running over."

A farmer who eats his seed instead of planting it may have a few days' meals, but he will miss an entire season's worth of food he would have had from a harvest.

GOD'S EXPECTATIONS OF HIS PEOPLE

Before we continue in 2 Corinthians 9, we need to understand exactly what God expects of us in this matter of giving. We have the law of sowing and reaping under our belts, so let's discuss what the seed of our giving should consist of. The Bible has two words to express what God expects of us: tithes and offerings.

Giving the Tithe

Now I know that a lot of Christians get bent out of shape when the tithe is mentioned, because they believe it was limited to the Old Testament law. It's true that the concept of tithing was prescribed in the Mosaic law (Lev. 27:30), and it's true that we are not under the law. But tithing actually predates the law, because Abraham gave a tithe to Melchizedek (Gen. 14:20), and the book of Hebrews says Jesus Christ is a high priest after the order of Melchizedek. In fact, Hebrews 7:8 indicates that Melchizedek's priestly line continues to receive tithes, which means we are to pay tithes to Jesus Christ. So the tithe continues in the New Testament, not as a commandment of law but as our proper response to God's grace shown to us in His Son.

The word *tithe* means "tenth." The Israelites were to tithe of all their animals and produce, and it couldn't just be any old tenth, either. They were to give the tithe to God first, which is why it is called the "first fruits" (Lev. 23:17). This made it an act of faith instead of an afterthought or something out of the people's leftovers. Giving God the first 10 percent of your goods means you trust Him to stretch the other 90 percent to meet your needs (Prov. 3:9–10).

The tithe was prescribed in the Old Testament, but the offering was a voluntary donation above and beyond the tithe. It was given out of gratitude to God for His bounty and blessing, and it was a further expression of love for and trust in Him (there are some great examples in 1 Chron. 29:6, 9, 14, 17). If God's people in Old Testament days gave Him offerings of gratitude for His blessings, how much more should we as believers on this side of the cross open our hearts and give to Him in overflowing generosity because of His overflowing grace?

Some people say, "I gave God an offering," when all they have done is contributed toward their tithe. You have not given an offering until you've completed your tithe. The offering is in addition to the tithe, not a replacement for it.

Robbing God of His Due

How serious is God about this matter of our honoring Him with our tithes and offerings? We find out in Malachi 3, where God, through the prophet, rebukes His people for their greed and neglect of Him.

When it came to the nation's giving, God had a question. "Will a *man* rob *God?*" (v. 8, italics added). The idea is "Do you not realize from whom you are stealing? Do you really think you can get away with robbing Me? Did you think I would not see you or know about it? Who do you think you are?" In other words, do we think we can walk into God's bank, rip Him off, and not be picked up on the video?

The people of Malachi's day played dumb and asked, "How have we robbed You?" (v. 8). God answered in the same verse: "In tithes and offerings." That is, they were using the portion that belonged to God for their own ends.

Let me bring the concept of robbing God to today. Some Christians are wearing clothes, driving cars, and going on vacations with God's tithes and offerings. Some of us are living in homes we can only afford by robbing from God's portion to pay the note each month. But God says we are stealing from Him.

And lest we think the problem is just financial, consider what God said to Israel: "You are cursed with a curse, for you are robbing Me, the whole nation of you!" (Mal. 3:9). This brings in the spiritual dimension because God has attached a curse to those who try to rob Him. We live under grace and not law, but God will not allow His grace to be trampled on and abused without calling us to account. That means a lot of us today are living in a curse, driving a curse, and wearing a curse. God says if we are robbing Him of His tithes and offerings, we should not think we are being blessed or getting away with it. On the contrary, we are under a curse.

When we hear the word *curse*, we tend to think of voodoo dolls and magic spells. That's not what God means. His curse is the cloud of His displeasure. That might be why that new house isn't really a home, but a place of constant turmoil and strife. Essentially God says, "I will keep your house stirred up because you wanted to upgrade your living while downgrading My kingdom."

No parent I know will pat a child on the back when the child has just stolen something and say, "That's okay, Mommy understands." No, when your child is stealing, you address the problem. That's what God was doing with the people of Israel in Malachi's day.

I want to be very clear on this. Christians have to understand that having a lot of stuff doesn't mean we're not cursed. Just because you got that promotion and more money with it doesn't automatically mean God is rewarding you. The issue is what you are doing with what He has given you.

A curse is having stuff without the ability to enjoy it. A curse is always having something break down or some catastrophe occur to keep the bank account drained so you never seem to catch up.

How do you know when something is from God? The Bible says,

"It is the blessing of the LORD that makes rich, and He adds no sorrow to it" (Prov. 10:22). That doesn't mean you won't ever have repair bills or be hard-pressed at times to make ends meet. But it means that even in the hard times, you will enjoy a sense of God's favor and blessing. "No sorrow" is another way of saying that God gives you a sense of contentment, whether you have a little or a lot (see Phil. 4:11 for a great statement of this truth).

Realizing God's Blessing

You say, "Tony, I want God's blessing. How do I get it?" The answer is in Malachi 3:10—"'Bring the whole tithe into the storehouse, so that there may be food in My house, and test Me now in this,' says the LORD of hosts, 'if I will not open for you the windows of heaven and pour out for you a blessing until it overflows.'"

God is saying, "If you are afraid, test Me in this now." In other words, don't wait until you've paid your taxes or the Christmas shopping is done. Bring your fears to the Lord and test Him by giving Him your tithes and offerings even when you don't see how you are going to make it. When you take that step of faith, God will open the windows of heaven, another way of saying He will pour out His blessings, which are now behind closed and locked windows.

Don't miss the point here. We don't throw open our windows when we know that a thief is roaming the neighborhood. Neither does God open the windows of heaven for those who ignore or abuse His grace. You can't grow spiritually and be a thief at the same time.

Let's clarify something right here so we don't get mixed up. A blessing is more than having more stuff. The "name it and claim it" crowd may teach that you should come to God, demand what you need from Him, and He is obligated to give it to you because you asked "in faith." But He never promised that.

I'd love to be able to tell you that if you start giving to God the way

He prescribes, He'll give you a new house or car. I would love to tell you that if you give faithfully, all of your problems will disappear. But I can't make that promise, and anyone who thinks he can is mistaken.

But what I can tell you is that God will give you a blessing, the capacity to enjoy, benefit from, and grow through what God gives you (Prov. 10:22). A blessing is the presence of God in the midst of whatever He has provided. The story is told of a poor Christian in a humble cottage who looked at his meal of bread and water and exclaimed, "All this, and Christ too!" That's the blessing.

Rebuking the Devourer

There is another aspect to the blessing that comes when we bring God what He deserves in our tithes and offerings. According to Malachi 3:11, "'Then I will rebuke the devourer for you, so that it will not destroy the fruits of the ground; nor will your vine in the field cast its grapes,' says the LORD of hosts."

When you are faithful to God, He tells the devourer to leave you alone. The farmers in Israel would get their crops up and refuse to give God the firstfruits, keeping it all for themselves. They would look over their fields and think they had it made, and then across the fields would come locusts to devour and destroy their crops.

As we said earlier, sometimes we think we are blessed because we have more. But if we withhold God's tithes from Him and He sends the devourer, as soon as we get a little savings, the devourer takes it. We think we have finally found happiness, but the devourer sweeps across our lives and destroys that too. Unless God rebukes the devourer, we will not be able to hold on to anything—and the way we escape the devourer is by testing and proving God in the matter of our giving.

THE IMPORTANCE OF OUR ATTITUDE

Now I know what you may be thinking at this point. Talking about God's expectations and the curse of the devourer makes giving sound like a pretty grim business. No, that's not it at all. God does have expectations of His people, but He is more interested in the attitude of your heart in giving than He is in calculating percentages. We're going back to a familiar verse that I want you to see in a new light.

God Loves Our Cheerful Giving

Continuing his instruction on giving, Paul wrote, "Each one must do just as he has purposed in his heart, not grudgingly or under compulsion, for God loves a cheerful giver" (2 Cor. 9:7). If the only way we'll give is when someone twists our arm behind our back or makes us feel guilty, God says He would just as soon we forget it because He is unhappy with a grudging giver.

That shouldn't surprise us, because most of us don't want a grudging gift either. Imagine someone coming to your birthday dinner, throwing a gift your way, and saying, "Here, take it. I really didn't want to get you this; I only did it because I had to." That will take the joy out of any gift.

You and I can be joyful in our giving when we understand that the only reason we have anything to give in the first place is that God gave to us. "The earth is the LORD's, and all it contains, the world, and those who dwell in it," the psalmist declared (Ps. 24:1). Deuteronomy 8:18 says it is God who gives us the power to make wealth. When you understand that God is the source of everything, you won't have any trouble being cheerful as you give to Him. And the more you grow in grace, the more cheerful a giver you'll be.

The Exciting Link between Giving and Grace

Now I said I wanted to connect 2 Corinthians 9:7 to its context. So let me help you make a connection that will revolutionize your giving and take you to a whole new level of kingdom living.

Let's say you have become the kind of cheerful giver that the Bible says God loves. In other words, He is pleased with your giving and the attitude of heart behind it. You are so excited about the opportunity and privilege you have to show God how much you love Him and how grateful you are that you can't wait for the offering plate to come by or you set up recurring giving online. You do your giving with joy because you know that without God's goodness to you, you wouldn't even have the opportunity to return to Him your tithes and offerings.

If this is your attitude, the next verse in this chapter applies to you—and it just happens to be the greatest verse on grace in the Bible. "And God is able to make all grace abound to you, so that always having all sufficiency in everything, you may have an abundance for every good deed" (v. 8).

God says that when He sees a cheerful giver, He opens the floodgates of His grace and lets it flow unhindered. We've learned that grace is everything God does for us that we cannot do for ourselves. We can't earn or add to God's grace, but we can restrict its flow by our sinful attitudes, which in this case is an unwillingness to give. God's grace flows freely in the context of cheerful giving. That's why Jesus said, "It is more blessed to give than to receive" (Acts 20:35).

This is more than just a slogan to use at Christmas. It is true in every instance, because when all you do is receive, all you get is what you get. But when you give, you open a channel of grace that flows to and through you to bless you and others.

And don't ever think that your giving will outstrip God's grace. Paul goes on to say, "Now He who supplies seed to the sower and bread for food will supply and multiply your seed for sowing and increase the harvest of your righteousness" (2 Cor. 9:10). God's grace is always bigger than your gift. Isn't that true about farming? A farmer plants a corn seed, but he doesn't reap one kernel or even one ear. He reaps an entire stalk of corn from that one little seed. And that stalk not only supplies him with food, but it also provides him with more seeds to plant so he can repeat the process. In other words, God's grace just keeps on coming.

When my children were small, I would bring them a little toy or something when I came home from a speaking engagement. At first they were extremely grateful and would say, "Oh Daddy, thank you" with hugs and kisses. But after a while they came to expect the gifts, and they wanted to know when I was going away again so I could bring them something.

That's often the way we treat our heavenly Father. "God, hurry up and give me something so I can have a new toy." But when it comes time to give something to Him, we are suddenly tapped out. What God is after is people who love and value Him and give out of that affection.

Giving is a spiritual act and a key ingredient in our kingdom life. Paul told the Corinthians to lay aside their gifts "on the first day of every week" (1 Cor. 16:2). That's Sunday, the Lord's Day. In other words, giving is part of our worship. It's to be systematic, and "as [God] may prosper," which means our giving should reflect His bounty to us. Giving has to become a way of life for us as believers, and we never have to worry that God is going to slip up or forget about us.

Here's a challenge I gave to the people in our church. The next time the offering is taken at your church, imagine the usher as Jesus, and imagine that as He offers you the plate, you can see the nail scars in His hand that He got when He died for you. Would that affect your giving, or would it be business as usual?

Jesus Christ deserves your gifts, but He doesn't want you to give just because of what it does for Him. The important thing is what it does for you in terms of your spiritual growth and blessing. I love the way Paul expressed it when he thanked the Philippians for their gifts: "Not that I seek the gift itself, but I seek for the profit which increases to your account" (Phil. 4:17).

The amazing thing about the ministry of biblical giving is that the primary beneficiary is not the receiver but the giver, who lays up eternal treasure in heaven with each gift. When you give generously from the heart, you store up eternal reward while simultaneously accelerating your spiritual growth on earth. This growth comes about because according to Jesus, "Where your treasure is, there your heart will be also" (Matt. 6:21).

Are you afraid to test God in the area of giving, and afraid to trust Him to meet your needs if you give to Him first? Then I urge you to begin giving now, because your fear will only dissolve when you replace it with faith. And you have the promise of God that He will care for you when you respond to His love through giving of your time, talents, and treasures.

12

Trials:
The Test of
Kingdom Living

WHEN I WAS A CHILD, I used to get irritated whenever my favorite TV program was interrupted by a test of the emergency broadcast system. Those tests always seemed to come at the worst time, during the best part of the program.

The announcer would tell me what I already knew was about to happen, which was that "normal programming" would be temporarily suspended for a test of the emergency system. Then my show would disappear and a test pattern picture would appear on the TV screen, along with those ear splitting sounds that went on for about thirty seconds or so. But when the test was finally over, my program would come back on and life was good once again.

Those emergency system tests are a lot like the trials that come into our lives. Trials are unscheduled, and usually unwelcome, interruptions in the normal pattern of life that always seem to come at the worst possible time. You're going about your business, doing the best you can, when your life is suddenly interrupted by a test that pops up on the screen.

But unlike the test patterns on TV, life's trials don't last for thirty or forty seconds and then disappear. They may last for days, weeks, or even years, and the exact reason for them may never be made completely clear to us. Trials can make us feel helpless, but we do have control over one vital element of a trial—how we respond to it.

That's what I want to focus on, because, as the title of this chapter suggests, trials are often used as tests when it comes to kingdom living. In fact, we cannot grow as we should without trials, as much as we might wish we could. Trials test our spiritual mettle and reveal what we are made of.

THE NECESSITY OF TRIALS TO OUR GROWTH

I know a lot of people don't want to hear that trials are necessary for kingdom living, but it's true. I'm not the one who said that. I'm just the messenger here. The Bible says the hard times we face in life are so important to our growth that we should actually welcome them.

Let's define our terms before we move on. Biblically, a trial can be defined *as an adverse set of circumstances in your life, either permitted or created by God, to develop you spiritually*. Each part of this definition is important, because we don't want to gloss over or deny that a trial is an adversity. Trials are not easy to handle. They hurt, and they can be costly. But God is behind our trials, which means we are not the victims of random fate. And because God is in control, our trials have a good purpose, which is to grow and mature us spiritually.

This is a perspective the world doesn't have, which helps explain why some people's main goal in life is the avoidance of all pain and unpleasantness. But the message for us as Christians is this: "Consider it all joy, my brethren, when you encounter various trials" (James 1:2).

Now, be honest. You have probably read this verse and wondered at times if James was living on the same planet you live on. James 1:2 may just be one of the hardest commands to obey in all of Scripture.

We could handle it better if he told us to find joy in trials without using any modifier. But he said to respond to trials with "all joy." This means joy that is pure and unadulterated. In other words, get your praise on when your life is interrupted by a problem or circumstance you didn't plan on or see coming.

We Will Definitely Encounter Trials

We tend to think of trials as the exception rather than the rule in life. But the reality is that we are either in a trial right now, coming out of a trial, or heading toward our next one. Trials are so common the Bible calls them "various," which is a picturesque Greek word meaning multicolored or multifaceted. You won't get bored by the trials you face because they will come in every variety you can imagine.

Trials are like some of the mail we receive at our homes, which is simply addressed to "Occupant." All you have to do to undergo trials is to be alive and occupy a space on this planet.

We know that trials are inescapable because James used "when" and not "if" when it comes to encountering hard times. You don't have to do anything to meet with a trial.

I like the word *encounter* in James 1:2, because it suggests these trials are not of our own making. The Bible doesn't tell us to rejoice when we mess up and get ourselves in trouble. God can use our failures to grow us, but this is not the kind of trial James had in mind.

The trials we encounter come in all varieties. Some are circumstantial in the sense that things just aren't going right. We've all had those times when nothing seems to work out. Usually it's not one big thing, but a lot of little things that are going wrong. We may also encounter physical, financial, relational, or emotional trials that knock us for a loop and interrupt our lives.

Whatever the color or shape of our trials, there is nowhere we can go to escape the trial of our faith. Trying to avoid trials is like changing schools in hopes of escaping a test. The new school will also have tests, and they may even be harder than the tests in the school we just left.

Job said, "Man is born for trouble, as sparks fly upward" (Job 5:7). Jesus said, "In the world you have tribulation" (John 16:33). We have a natural desire as human beings to escape trouble, but we can't run from our God-ordained trials. He knows where to find us.

Our Trials Always Have a Purpose

Christians aren't the only people who have problems, but there is a great difference between the trials we experience as believers and the troubles of a non-Christian. For the Christian, there is no such thing as a purposeless trial. Every difficulty that comes our way as believers in Jesus Christ, no matter how severe or painful, has a reason attached to it. Trials are pain with a purpose, designed to launch us to the next spiritual level.

This is because no trial hits your life without passing through the hands of God first. Job is a perfect example. The devil had to run everything by God first before being allowed to afflict Job (Job 1–2). God either sends us our trials directly or allows them to come—all for His reason.

THE REASON WE ENCOUNTER TRIALS

I am using the singular word *reason* here on purpose. There may be a myriad of individual reasons for the trials we undergo, but all of these come under the umbrella reason given in James 1:3–4. The apostle says we can rejoice in our trials because we know something important: "Knowing that the testing of your faith produces endurance. And let endurance have its perfect result, so that you may be perfect and complete, lacking in nothing."

God Wants Us to Be Mature

The reason for our trials is to grow us into spiritual maturity, as reflected in the word *perfect*, which is used twice in verse 4 for emphasis. This word means to become mature, to grow up. Spiritual maturity is the process of our becoming more like Jesus Christ, letting more of His life show through our lives. Paul called it "Christ [being] formed in you" (Gal. 4:19). It's like the goldsmith who was asked by an observer as he refined gold, "How do you know when the gold has been refined and is ready?"

"When I can see my reflection in it," the goldsmith replied. Trials are meant to refine us so that Christ may be reflected in us.

Now you may be saying, "I don't know, Tony. The trial I'm in right now feels like it's tearing me down instead of building me up." I'm not here to tell you the pain isn't real. The statement James makes about the purpose of trials is one we have to take by faith sometimes, but it is also a promise from the God whose Word never fails. We also have the testimony of countless saints who have emerged victoriously from countless trials over the centuries to tell us that God is faithful to bring good from even our hardest times.

The interesting thing about our trials is that they are custom-made. Your trials have your name on them. One of the hardest things Paul had to handle was his "thorn in the flesh" (2 Cor. 12:7)—which he called both a messenger from Satan and something sent from God, by the way.

Why did God custom-make this affliction that apparently was very humbling to Paul? He says it was "to keep me from exalting myself" (v. 7) because of the incredible vision he was given of heaven (vv. 2–4). But don't stop there, because Paul said rather than tearing him down, his trial became something he was "well content with" (v. 10). Why? "For when I am weak, then I am strong."

God knew what Paul needed, and He knows what you need. You

say you want the power of God to rest upon your life. The path to real spiritual power lies through trials. Like a skilled tailor measuring a customer for a handmade suit that will fit perfectly, God the Holy Spirit is tailoring the trials we encounter to fit our spiritual need.

Trials Test Our Readiness for Life

I remember once telling a teacher, "I am ready for this test."

Her answer was "We'll see." She knew me pretty well!

It's one thing to sit in a pew at church and sing about God's ability to see you through any trial. It's another thing to sit down at exam time and pass the test. James says that trials are "the testing of your faith." Trials call your faith to the witness stand, to see if you really believe what you affirmed when you sang that song and said "Amen" to the sermon last Sunday. All of us want to grow, but we don't always want to take the test.

I used to hate it when the teacher said, "Clear your desk and take out a pencil and paper." That meant we were going to have a pop quiz, which I always dreaded because I didn't have a chance to get ready for them. I just had to *be* ready every class, and there is a big difference between the two. At least the midterm and final exams had definite dates so I could spend the night before cramming for them. But those pop quizzes were hard to handle because they tested what I actually knew, not what I could stuff in my brain the night before.

We Must Not Quit on Our Trials

The testing of our faith produces endurance, according to James 1:3. Endurance is the ability to hang in there until the trial is over and we have passed the test on our way to the next level of spiritual maturity. But this means we can't quit halfway through the test. That's a temptation, especially if the test is extremely hard.

It's safe to say that for most of the students at Dallas Theological

Seminary, including me, Hebrew exams were the hardest tests we had to take. I heard of guys who would become so frustrated they would just give up and turn in their exam partially completed. There were students at seminary still hanging around for a fifth and sixth year trying to get a four-year master's degree, because they couldn't pass Hebrew. I have no doubt that some simply quit and went home.

The problem with quitting on an exam is that you will just have to go back and face it again at some point if you want to get anywhere. And exams usually cost more the second time around because you're paying tuition again.

Some of us have been seated at the same desk, spiritually speaking, taking the same test for years, because we keep quitting before the test is over. In the words of James 1, we are not letting endurance have its perfect work so that we might become perfect or mature.

If you are dropping out of a trial that God has sent for your spiritual growth, He will retest you until you pass. And He has a lot more time than you have.

When we quit in the middle of a trial that is designed for our growth, it delays our advancement. When I was in eighth grade, we had a nineteen-year-old student in our class because he could never pass the class. He was basically an adult sitting kind of scrunched up in desks made for skinny little thirteen-year-olds, which was a pretty sad picture.

When you fail a grade in school, you have to repeat it, no matter what your age—and when you fail to let endurance have its perfect result in your trials, you can wind up as an adult still sitting in eighth grade. Remember that God has His hand on the process and knows when to discontinue a trial because its purpose has been realized. In the meantime, He gives us a great promise: His comforting presence in the trial (Isa. 43:2–5).

WHAT IT TAKES TO ENDURE TRIALS VICTORIOUSLY

Now if God allows trials to grow us, this raises a very practical question: How can we endure these hard and often painful times so we can reap the blessing of spiritual maturity? In his masterful treatment of trials in James 1:2–12, the apostle included several important factors that will help us handle trials to experience the victorious outcome God wants for us. These truths work no matter what the nature of any particular trial may be. The first thing that will help determine how you make it through a trial is how you look at it.

Our Attitude Decides Our Altitude

I want to back up to James 1:2 and the command, "Consider it all joy . . . when you encounter various trials." This verse is similar to Romans 8:28 in that what the verse doesn't say is as important as what it does say. Romans 8:28 doesn't say that everything that happens to us is good, but that God works in all things for the good of His children. James doesn't say that trials are joyful things in themselves, but that we can be joyful in them because of what God is going to do through them.

It is also clear that the joy James has in mind here is not circumstantial. Someone has said that happiness is based on what happens. It is elation over our circumstances. Most people would be happy if they got a raise or promotion or won a lot of money. But if their world revolves around these things, they would be *un*happy if the job was lost or the bank account went south. Happiness fluctuates based on circumstances.

In contrast, joy has to do with our internal well-being regardless of what is happening externally. The joy we can have in the heat of trials is stability of spirit that comes from God and is based on the truth revealed in His Word.

We Know Something Very Important

What God has revealed to us is the purpose behind our trials. We touched on this earlier, but I want you to see the statement of James 1:3 again. Continuing the thought from verse 2, he writes: "Knowing that the testing of your faith produces endurance." In order to have joy in our trials, we need to see where God is taking us in them. The devil doesn't want you to know that God can use your times of testing to birth something wonderful in you, which is the endurance that leads to the growth and maturity that both God and you desire.

The problem is that birth involves pain. When a woman goes into labor she will feel extreme pain. But what she won't do is quit in the middle of the process. The reason she won't quit is because she knows something. She knows that when the pain is over, however long it takes, her child will be born. And the anticipation of that wonderful outcome gives her joy even in the pain.

The pain itself wasn't joyful, but when the new mom held her new baby, she would be the first to tell you it was worth all the pain and the pushing to bring the baby into the world. In fact, the joy of having a child so outweighs the pain that many women decide to have several children despite the pain of the birth process.

Now I know that you may have been pushing against your trial, not just for hours, but for days or weeks or maybe even months. Keep pushing, because you're going to give birth. Joy comes from knowing that God is using the trial to grow you. Peter came to learn the truth about trials, and he shared his wisdom in these magnificent verses from his first letter: "In this [the assurance of our future with God] you greatly rejoice, even though now for a little while, if necessary, you have been distressed by various trials" (1 Peter 1:6).

Peter didn't deny that trials are stressful. He even called them a "fiery ordeal" (1 Peter 4:12). But notice the emphasis on joy and rejoicing despite the fire. Back in chapter 1, he said that the purpose of trials is to test and prove the value of our faith. That's why we can "greatly rejoice with joy inexpressible and full of glory" (v. 8). Peter added to this later when he said of our fiery trials, "To the degree that you share the sufferings of Christ, keep on rejoicing" (4:13).

Our example of patient endurance in trials is Jesus Himself. I love Hebrews 12:2, where the writer says of Jesus, "Who for the joy set before Him endured the cross." Joy and death on a cross are two concepts that don't go together in most people's minds. But Jesus was able to look past the cross because He knew that glory awaited Him when He went back to His Father and delivered those whom He had redeemed.

Now don't miss something crucial here. Jesus still felt the agony of His trial. He prayed in the garden, "My Father, if it is possible, let this cup pass from Me" (Matt. 26:39). But the Bible also says He kept His eyes fixed on the outcome of the cross, which was redemption for us and resurrection and glory for Him. Jesus knew that God was going to use Good Friday to bring about Resurrection Sunday, and He endured the trial.

The word *consider* in James 1:2 is an accounting term. It means to add everything up and come to the right conclusion, which is that God is using our trials to give us the growth of endurance that leads to the good result of spiritual maturity (v. 4).

God Has Wisdom for Our Trials

I am so glad that James included verse 5 in his discussion of trials. One reason I am glad is that people tend to come to their pastor after a sermon on passages like James 1 and say, "Pastor, I hear what you've been saying. Now tell me exactly what I need to do to grow in my trials."

The problem is that I don't have all the answers for these individuals, and neither does anyone else. The wisdom we need to handle our trials in a godly way comes from God alone. That's why I love this promise: "But if any of you lacks wisdom, let him ask of God, who gives to all generously and without reproach, and it will be given to him" (James 1:5).

Since we have been talking about what these familiar verses don't mean, let me tell you what I believe James 1:5 is not saying. This is not an invitation for us to quiz God about the why of our trials. That is information you and I may never know this side of heaven. If God never told Job the full reason for his incredible trials, chances are He is not going to drop a special revelation on us. Asking why is another one of our natural human responses, but it is usually not very productive.

Instead of asking why, we need to ask God how and what, as in, "Dear Lord, how do You want to use this trial in my life to grow me spiritually, and what do You want me to do to cooperate with You in this trial so I can reap the benefits?" These are the kinds of questions God will answer every time, and do so without making you feel foolish for asking.

But it's not enough to ask the right questions. We also need to ask with the right spirit. According to James 1:6–8, it is possible to ask God for wisdom and then mess around trying to decide whether we intend to obey Him or not. James calls this being "double-minded," and he is straight about the result: "That man ought not to expect that he will receive anything from the Lord, being a double-minded man, unstable in all his ways" (vv. 7–8). When you ask God for wisdom, your response needs to be, "Speak, Lord, for Your servant is listening."

We Shouldn't Waste Our Trials

The reason we need wisdom from God to handle our trials is to keep from wasting these opportunities for spiritual growth. When we get double-minded on God and start vacillating between the divine and human perspectives, we don't get anywhere.

When you look at your trials through human eyes only, you'll react humanly by getting bitter instead of better. You'll be mad at the world and take out your frustration on those around you. Eventually you'll get mad at God, too, and start throwing temper tantrums. Then you'll really be in a mess, because a tantrum will only get you deeper in trouble.

Too many of us want to view our trials the way we watch TV or digital media. Maybe you have seen those TV or phone apps that have a picture within a picture, a feature that gives you a second visual in the corner of the channel you're watching, so you can divide your focus and watch two programs or ball games at once.

A lot of us Christians want to keep superimposing our human viewpoint on the screen of God's work in our lives. We come to church to get a divine perspective, but then we go home and open up that second screen so we can try to figure it all out. Don't waste your trials by trying to fit them into your limited vision and understanding.

Wisdom Will Keep Us from Losing Heart

I can't think of anything that will discourage you faster in the midst of a trial than trying to come at it from the human perspective. In fact, you will not only become discouraged, but it will drive you crazy. How much better to rest in God's wisdom and take Him at His word. Let me give you a spiritual perspective on trials that will keep you from buckling under your circumstances when times are hard. This is not from James 1, but it fits here:

> Therefore we do not lose heart, but though our outer man is decaying, yet our inner man is being renewed day by day. For momentary, light affliction is producing for us an eternal weight of glory far beyond all comparison, while we look not at the things which are seen, but at the things which are not seen; for the things which are seen are temporal, but the things which are not seen are eternal. (2 Cor. 4:16–18)

Did you catch Paul's perspective? It's when we look at our afflictions, another word for trials, from the eternal angle that we find our spirits being renewed so we can press on to receive what God has waiting for us. The opposite of this is to take the human view, focusing on the fact that our "outer man" is decaying. That's a perfect formula for discouragement.

When my son Anthony was young, he suffered from asthma, and I would have to take him to the doctor for a shot. Those needles hurt, so before the doctor gave Anthony a shot, he would give him a lollipop. Anthony would be licking on his lollipop and life was good, until the doctor gave him the shot. Anthony would cry out in pain, and the tears would start.

The pain made Anthony forget about his lollipop for a minute, but pretty soon he would be holding it tight and licking it again as the tears ran down his cheeks. Now stay with me here. Jesus is sweet and satisfying, and if you will hold tight to Him and feed on Him, the pain of your trial will be overridden by the joy of His presence.

HOW TO WIN THE CROWN OF LIFE

At this point you may be wishing you could see what it looks like when someone is joyful and wise while undergoing a trial. This is important, because there is a great reward, a wonderful payoff, for being faithful in trials. I think James was giving us these examples when he wrote verses 9–11 of chapter 1. They involve two people, a poor person and a rich person, which pretty well covers both ends of the human experience and also speaks to everyone between these two poles. James is about to tell us what a godly reaction to trials looks like.

Two Godly Ways to Handle Trials

The first person is the poor man, or the person of "humble circumstances," who is told to "glory in his high position" (v. 9). In our setting today, this person may have humble means because he has been laid off from his job, the money is tight, and he's tired of being broke. There doesn't seem to be any way out financially, and in this setting it is easy for a believer to become angry at God because He is not coming through and the savings are gone.

Why would James tell a person in this situation to "glory" or rejoice, and what is his high position? We've already learned that even when things are tough, we can find joy knowing that God has allowed these things to help grow us up in Him, and when the trial is over and we have been faithful, He has something glorious for us.

Perhaps God allowed the money to get tight because He wants us to focus on our riches in Christ, which is a high position. If you are in this predicament right now, don't get mad at God. Let your trial draw you closer to Him as you learn to take your eyes off the physical and focus on the spiritual.

What about rich people? They also have a lesson to learn. "The rich man is to glory in his humiliation, because like flowering grass he will pass away. For the sun rises with a scorching wind and withers the grass; and its flower falls off and the beauty of its appearance is destroyed; so too the rich man in the midst of his pursuits will fade away" (James 1:10–11).

If "rich" describes you, it could be that you've never really had to trust God because you've always had American Express. But then the Dow Jones slumps, the NASDAQ nosedives, inflation soars, and you see your riches fading away. Why? Because God wants you to understand that riches are like a fading flower that is beautiful today and gone tomorrow. God may put you in a place of dependency not so you can panic, but so you can learn where your true riches lie and learn to trust God in a way you have never understood before.

In other words, both the poor and the rich need to learn that God, and not anything else, is the source of their security. The poor can rejoice that they are rich in Christ, and the rich can rejoice that they have learned not to trust in the stock market or their retirement account. When these lessons are learned, spiritual growth takes place.

Just as an oyster that is irritated by a grain of sand continues to surround it with a secretion that becomes a valuable pearl, so we need to surround the irritation of our trials with a secretion of praise and worship. When we do, we will see God turn those trials into something valuable.

We'll Enjoy a New Experience of God

The payoff for being faithful under fire is found in James 1:12. "Blessed is a man who perseveres under trial; for once he has been approved, he will receive the crown of life which the Lord has promised to those who love Him."

The crown of life sounds like something you will receive later on in heaven. But this is a reward you can enjoy today, because the crown James is talking about is life itself. When God crowns us with life, it's not just physical life, although that is certainly a gift from Him. But the crown of life is a glorious new experience of God and His glory that can change the way we live today, as well as "an eternal weight of glory" when we are with the Lord in glory (2 Cor. 4:17–18).

When God gives you the crown of life, He is saying that you passed the test and now He is going to invade your circumstances with a new level of His power and glory that will make you feel more alive than you have ever felt in your life.

Remember that wonderful feeling when you took the hardest test of your life and walked out knowing that you had aced it because you worked hard and paid the price to prepare? That's something of the experience we're talking about, except raised to a much higher power. I want the crown of life, and I believe you do too. Well, the path to the crown is lined with trials that can be irritating and painful. But God is always up to something good when He places a trial in our lives.

Most of us are like some baby birds, who would never leave the nest if they had their own way. Sometimes the mother bird has to let them get a little bit hungry, then she comes near the nest with tempting tidbits of food. When the time comes for them to fly and they hesitate too long, the mother wants them to forget their fear of flying in their desire for the good food.

God wants us to soar spiritually, but to do so He needs to get us out of the comfortable nest. Are you feeling the hunger and discomfort of your circumstances? That must mean it's time for you to move and learn to fly.

13

Temptation: The Battle of Kingdom Living

THE STORY IS TOLD of an overweight man who decided to shed his excess pounds. So he made a radical decision to change his route to work so he would not pass by his favorite doughnut shop that had contributed greatly to his excess weight. He was so determined to lose weight that he told his coworkers about his commitment to swear off doughnuts.

Not long after this, however, he arrived at work one morning with a huge bag of doughnuts. When his coworkers asked him what was going on, he said, "These are not ordinary doughnuts. They're from the Lord."

"What in the world are you talking about?" they asked.

"Well, it's simple. Today on my way to work I accidentally drove by my favorite doughnut shop and saw all the doughnuts and pastries sitting in the window. I knew I had to pray for strength, so I said, 'Lord, if You want me to have any of these delicious doughnuts, You are going to have to give me a parking place right in front of the doughnut shop. If You do this, I'll know that You want me to have some doughnuts.'

"And sure enough, after eight trips around the block, there was a parking space right in front of the doughnut shop!"

It's easy to come up with spiritual reasons for succumbing to temptation. Temptation is so pervasive that it comes in all shapes, sizes, colors, and forms. You and I will face temptation as long as we are alive. It is part of the spiritual battle we must wage if we are going to grow in the grace and knowledge of Jesus Christ and experience the kingdom life. Unbelievers are tempted too, but they are basically defenseless because they have no spiritual weapons to fight with. Christians are far from defenseless against temptation, but we need to understand what it is and how it works in order to deal with it successfully.

THE REALITY OF TEMPTATION

The Bible is very clear about the nature of temptation and the way it functions, and we are going to tap into that wisdom. A good place to start is with the apostle James's discussion, which he introduces this way: "Let no one say when he is tempted, 'I am being tempted by God'; for God cannot be tempted by evil, and He Himself does not tempt anyone. But each one is tempted when he is carried away and enticed by his own lust" (James 1:13–14).

These verses come immediately after James's teaching about trials, which we studied in the previous chapter. The connection is important, because the same basic Greek word translated "trials" in James 1:2 is used in the verb form for "tempted" in verse 13. In fact, this is the case throughout the New Testament, which tells us that the same event can be either a trial or a temptation, depending on its purpose and how we respond to it.

The difference is that a trial is created or allowed by God to strengthen us in faith and advance our spiritual growth, while a temptation is a solicitation or enticement to evil that comes from the devil and his demons. It's an invitation to disobey or rebel against God with the goal of stifling our spiritual growth and limiting our capacity to bring greater glory to God. A trial is designed to develop you; a temptation is designed to defeat you.

Satan Wants to Defeat You

You need to understand that Satan can turn a trial into a temptation to defeat you and drag you down. We can see how this works in the garden of Eden, when God put a tree in the midst of the garden and told Adam and Eve, "From the tree of the knowledge of good and evil you shall not eat, for in the day that you eat from it you will surely die" (Gen. 2:17). This was a trial, a test of their willingness to obey God.

But Satan came along and turned that trial into an opportunity for evil by tempting Eve with a desire to be like God and planting the thought in her mind that God was holding out on her. God designed the trial, but Satan twisted it into a temptation to evil.

There are many other examples we could draw from daily life. If you are experiencing financial hardships, for example, they could be a trial sent from God. If you are playing the lottery in an attempt to hit it big and wipe out your debts, you have allowed Satan to turn your God-ordained trial into a temptation to find a quick and easy fix.

At other times trials and temptations are very different. There is no way that a temptation to sexual sin can be called a trial sent from God. He doesn't test our faith by setting us up for sin. Just because your phone is an easy access point to pornographic movies doesn't mean it must be okay with God if you watch them or He wouldn't have allowed you to get your phone.

It's like the little girl whose mother found her up on the stool, eating the chocolate chip cookies that the mother had told her not to eat. "What are you doing up there?" the mother said. "I told you not to eat those cookies."

"I know, Mama, but let me explain. I got up on the stool to smell the cookies, and my teeth got caught." That's the kind of rationalization Christians sometimes use, even if unconsciously, but it doesn't fly. Temptation is different from trials in its source, its purpose, and its outcome. Temptation is a work of the enemy from beginning to end.

God Does Not Tempt You

James knew we would be tempted to blame God for our temptations, but he nixed that idea with the statement we read in chapter 1, verse 13. God does not tempt us, period. He tests and tries us so that we will endure and come out stronger, and He may even allow Satan to tempt us as part of our spiritual development. But any invitation to do wrong does not come from our God.

The reason is that God is perfectly holy and separate from sin. Jesus said, "The ruler of the world is coming, and he has nothing in Me" (John 14:30). There is nothing in God that can respond to evil at all, and therefore He cannot be the source of bringing evil to anyone else. God is the source of everything good in our lives (James 1:17). We'll see later that the source of temptation and sin is located elsewhere.

God won't cause you to sin—and the devil can't make you sin, by the way. He can offer you a temptation and make it look inviting, but he cannot force you to sin. You have to cooperate. The devil's power is influence and deception, not coercion.

THE PROGRESS OF TEMPTATION

James 1:14–15 are two verses you ought to know by heart and keep close at hand, because they spell out clearly the way temptation progresses in a downward direction from an idea or a thought to an action and its consequences.

It Begins with a Desire

A temptation begins when a person is "carried away and enticed by his own lust" (v. 14). The word *lust* means a strong desire. There are legitimate desires that can be turned to illegitimate ends when they begin to dominate your thinking and actions. You can desire food to nourish your body, or you can lust for food to the point that you live only to eat, which is the sin of gluttony.

It's important to realize that almost every temptation to sin is built off of a legitimate, God-given desire. If a temptation were not desirable to us in some way, we wouldn't be bothered by it. Satan knows how to take God's good gifts and mix them with deception and empty promises to entice us.

The allure of temptation is graphically pictured by the word *entice* in James 1:14. It describes a fisherman putting a worm on a hook and throwing it into the water to entice a fish to bite. The fish is looking for a snack, not to become dinner for the fisherman. No mouse goes looking for a mousetrap. What the mouse wants is the cheese attached to the trap. But its lust for cheese deceives the mouse into thinking the cheese is there for the taking, and the trap is sprung.

Most of us are in debt because of deception. We have a desire to buy something that we cannot afford or do not need, but which is presented in such a way that we come to believe we can't live without it. So we step into the debt trap, forgetting that we will be paying for our momentary purchases over many months and even years at a high interest rate.

The Desire Produces Disobedience

The next step downward in temptation is taken when the desire, fueled by Satan's enticement, leads us to disobedience. "Then when lust has conceived, it gives birth to sin" (James 1:15a). Notice that sin doesn't come until the temptation is accepted and acted upon. It's good news to know that it's not a sin to be tempted.

The Bible says that Jesus was "tempted in all things as we are, yet without sin" (Heb. 4:15). So don't let the devil put you on a guilt trip for being tempted. The only people who aren't tempted are in the graveyard. Our response to it determines whether a temptation becomes sin. Jesus talked about someone who "looks at a woman with lust for her" as committing sin (Matt. 5:28). This is looking, and then looking again with the specific purpose of lusting. At this point the will is engaged and the look becomes sinful lust. It's a deliberate act of the will.

Disobedience Produces Death

James tells us there is one more step in the progress of temptation as we move from desire to disobedience. That final step is death. "When sin is accomplished, it brings forth death" (v. 15b). Sin never stops until it brings about death—either eternal death for the unsaved or a rupture in the believer's fellowship with God, which is the essence of death.

Now we don't drop dead physically every time we sin, but death occurs every time we sin. God told Adam and Eve that they would die the day they ate of the forbidden tree, and they did. Their fellowship with God was shattered, and spiritual and physical death were introduced into the human race. For the Christian, the result of yielding to temptation is the loss of fellowship with God and the stunting of spiritual growth, which is why confession of sin is so important.

The problem with sin is that the devil uses false advertising. Sin almost never comes with a sticker that says, "Warning: Will Cause Death." Sin looks attractive, and its price seems reasonable. But it always costs more than the advertised price. It's a rare person who, like Moses, can see beyond "the passing pleasures of sin" (Heb. 11:25) and pass them up in favor of obeying God.

Sin will always take you further than you wanted to go and cost you more than you wanted to pay. It starts off causing us to say, "Ahhh," but ends up causing us to say, "Ohhh." Nothing stunts growth faster than death, and nothing stunts spiritual growth faster than allowing temptation to breed sin and death.

THE SOURCE OF TEMPTATION

Since all of us are vulnerable to temptation, and since yielding to it carries such a heavy price tag, we had better be figuring out where this stuff comes from so we can resist it, as God tells us to do.

The Devil Is the Tempter

The devil is the head of an extremely sophisticated network whose goal is to tempt Christians and lead us into ruin. Satan knows he has lost the battle for our eternal souls, for we are secure forever in Christ. But he can wreak havoc in our lives if we let him.

The devil is the tempter. The Bible even calls him by that name in Matthew 4:3 when he came to Jesus in the wilderness to tempt Him. Now let's pause here and note that the Holy Spirit led Jesus into the wilderness (Matt. 4:1). If God allowed Satan to tempt His own Son, He will allow Satan to tempt you and me. God has given the devil access to this world for the time being.

Satan as the tempter is the thought master. He works in the realm of the mind. He can plant a thought we might never have ourselves. In the guise of the serpent, Satan gave Eve the idea of eating the fruit God had forbidden. He was the one who suggested that she could be like God. Eve wasn't standing there trying to figure out how she could disobey God.

If you are a Christian, you have to understand that the initial thought to do evil is not always from you. The new nature you have from God would not come up with that, because it is perfect. Your sin nature may come up with it but oftentimes the initial thought to disobey God comes from the evil one. We respond sometimes because our new nature is still living in our old sinful flesh, which is part of the enemy we are talking about.

The devil is a master of temptation because he studies and knows you, the way a football coach studies game film of his opponents. The devil knows your tendencies and weak spots. He knows what you are most likely to do and what temptation would have the best chance of success against you. Just as holy angels are assigned to every believer, demons are also assigned to believers to study our game film and report back to the coach. The devil is not all-knowing and all-powerful, so he cannot control us. But he can influence and plant thoughts and hit us where we are the weakest.

Now before you begin to feel defenseless in the face of Satan's temptations, here is a great verse to review and commit to memory. The Bible gives us this assurance: "No temptation has overtaken you but such as is common to man; and God is faithful, who will not allow you to be tempted beyond what you are able, but with the temptation will provide the way of escape also, so that you will be able to endure it" (1 Cor. 10:13).

God will not allow you to be overcome by a temptation that is absolutely beyond your capacity to endure. When you're in the middle of a temptation, you may feel as if you can't handle it. But if a temptation reaches you, you can assume that it has passed through heaven's review and God knows it is within your ability to endure.

The way you know you can handle a temptation is that God provides with it "the way of escape." God builds a back door into every temptation with a lighted "exit" sign over it. The key word here is "with." The way of escape comes *with* the temptation, at the same time.

Someone might say, "But I don't see any exit sign." That's because the person is focused on the temptation instead of looking for the way out. God's promise of escape doesn't mean we won't have to persevere and be faithful to Him. But it does mean that when God's purpose of victory over temptation and spiritual growth through it has been served, He will bring us out.

Satan cannot control you or put you in a place where you can't get out. But he can suggest and entice and put together an attractive looking deal. That's what he did with Jesus during the temptation in the wilderness (Matt. 4:1–11). I want to summarize this encounter and show you how Satan offered Jesus illegitimate means to fulfill legitimate desires.

The first thing Satan offered Jesus was satisfaction. Jesus was hungry, and Satan tempted Him to turn stones into bread. But this was satisfaction without God, because His plan was to feed His Son through the angels.

Then Satan offered Jesus success, but again without God. Satan took Jesus to the top of the temple and said, "Jump off. God will protect You, and everyone will believe You are the Messiah." In other words, Satan was suggesting a way that Jesus could be successful without having to die on the cross. It was an easy way out. But Jesus knew He had to endure the cross in order to get where God wanted Him to be.

Then Satan offered Jesus significance without God by offering Him the kingdoms of the world and their glory if Jesus would just bow down to Satan. But Jesus rebuked Satan with the reminder from Scripture that God alone is worthy of worship.

That's quite a package, because our desires for satisfaction, success, and significance are God-given. But Satan wants us to pursue these without God. As the tempter Satan is head of an evil empire.

The World Is the Devil's Network

Our second enemy in temptation is the world, which is like the devil's sophisticated network, his system. The Bible says, "Do not love the world nor the things in the world. If anyone loves the world, the love of the Father is not in him" (1 John 2:15). That's a serious warning, so we need to ask what God means by the world. The Greek word for world is *cosmos,* the basis of the English word *cosmetic.* The word means to arrange or put in order, so when women say they are going to put on a face with cosmetics, this is what they mean.

When this word is used in a negative sense as in 1 John 2, it refers not to our planet but to a system that leaves God out. We talk about the world of politics or the world of finance. Those are not locations, but orientations or arrangements around a central focus. Spiritually speaking the orientation of the world is away from God. It seeks to subtract God's kingdom from the equation of life.

Now you and I have to live in this world, but we don't have to love it. Satan has a network that consists of people who are his minions and carry out his will, whether they realize it or not. The world is hostile toward God because Satan is calling the shots, and therefore the world is hostile toward us. He tries to tantalize us with all that the world has to offer, and too often believers are falling for it.

No one ever said the world didn't have anything to offer. It seeks to dazzle us through "the lust of the flesh and the lust of the eyes and the boastful pride of life" (1 John 2:16). Satan and the world don't mind you going to church on Sunday, as long as you leave God in church and don't make a big deal out of Him the rest of the week.

Sometimes what the world offers us looks like a lot of fun, and we can be made to feel like we are missing out on it. But the world is also into false advertising, offering you an amusement park full of fun without telling you that you have to stand in line three hours for a ninety-second thrill ride. John said, "The whole world lies in the power of the evil one" (1 John 5:19).

The Flesh Is the Enemy Within

The third enemy we have to battle is our own flesh, our inbred self-centeredness that gives the world and the devil an entry point into our lives. We discussed the flesh in an earlier chapter and the fact that it is the part of us in which "nothing good dwells" (Rom. 7:18). It was his flesh that Paul had in mind when he said, "I see a different law in the members of my body, waging war against the law of my mind and making me a prisoner of the law of sin which is in my members" (v. 23). Paul's struggle was that of a Christian who seeks to live righteously in this world.

Paul's frustration over doing wrong even when he wanted to do right is the battle every believer must wage. You know what it's like to mess up no sooner than you got off your knees making a commitment to God. That's the flesh kicking in, but thanks be to God we are not helpless victims. Paul gave us the formula for victory over the flesh: "Walk by the Spirit, and you will not carry out the desire of the flesh" (Gal. 5:16).

The desires of the flesh won't go away. We will carry them throughout our lives. But we don't have to go around being slaves to our flesh.

The flesh works with the devil and the world to solicit us to sin. Aren't you tired of telephone solicitors calling you day and night? You tell them you're not interested, but they keep talking and make you feel bad for hanging up. That's how the system of evil works to tempt us to sin. The devil, the world, and the flesh are constantly calling us, trying to draw us away from God. But we have another system working for us that can block those calls before they become a problem.

DRESSING FOR SPIRITUAL SUCCESS

Now we get to the good news, because as powerful as our enemies are, they are no match for our Lord. The operative principle for us is: "You are from God, little children, and have overcome them; because greater is He who is in you than he who is in the world" (1 John 4:4). James said it this way: "Resist the devil and he will flee from you" (James 4:7).

Sometimes we may feel like the emperor who didn't have any clothes when it comes to facing the devil and his allies, but that's not the case. The Bible tells us how to dress for spiritual success against Satan and his forces.

Our Strength Is in the Lord

The spiritual wardrobe we need is found in Ephesians 6, one of my favorite passages of Scripture. Paul wrote: "Be strong in the Lord and in the strength of His might. Put on the full armor of God, so that you will be able to stand firm against the schemes of the devil" (vv. 10–11). Forget New Year's resolutions and promises to yourself and God that you'll do better next time. Your strength is in the Lord and His might, not in the limited power of your human will.

The reason we need God's strength is that our battle, according to Paul, "is not against flesh and blood, but against the rulers, against the powers, against the world forces of this darkness, against the spiritual forces of wickedness in the heavenly places" (v. 12). Our battle is supernatural, not natural, so we need the supernatural armor of God, which is available to us in Christ Jesus.

And here's more good news. When we dress ourselves in God's armor, all we have to do is "stand firm" (vv. 11, 13–14). Why does the Bible tell us to stand firm instead of "go fight"? Because in Christ the battle is already over and won. We're not fighting *for* victory, but *from* victory. Jesus won the battle over the world, the flesh, and the devil. All we're doing is mopping up. But just because we are fighting from a position of victory, we should not get too relaxed. The battle is real even though it's over from heaven's perspective. We have to put on God's armor in order to stand firm and "resist in the evil day" (v. 13), which is any day we are under attack.

We Should Put on the Armor of God

I want to take you through the six pieces of God's armor described in Ephesians 6:14–17. Please notice something interesting by way of introduction. The first three pieces of armor are introduced with verbs that indicate a state of being. In other words, these are things we wear all the time. They're part of the daily uniform. But the last three pieces are introduced with the verb *take*, meaning these are things we pick up as needed for the moment. We'll see how this plays out as we go through the armor.

The first piece is the *belt of truth*. "Stand firm therefore, having girded your loins with truth" (v. 14a). We have defined truth as a fixed, nonnegotiable standard to which everything else must adjust. God's Word is that standard.

I was once flying with a friend who explained to me how important it is to trust the airplane's instruments no matter what your senses tell you, because you can easily become disoriented in flight. Your eyes may tell you you're right side up when you are actually upside down and heading for disaster.

A plane crashed in the desert of Africa during World War II, many miles past its destination, because the crew didn't realize they had a strong tailwind and refused to believe what the plane's instruments were telling them. In fact, when the plane was found years later, the instruments were still in perfect working order.

God's Word is the instrument panel, and we have to believe it no matter what our senses or the devil may be telling us. The Bible says, "Let God be found true, though every man be found a liar" (Rom. 3:4).

The second piece of God's armor is *the breastplate of righteousness* (Eph. 6:14b). The breastplate covers your heart, which in the Bible is the center of your consciousness. When you know God's truth, then your heart knows how to beat at the right rhythm. But once you let go of truth, God sets off a warning beeper inside that something is wrong—and it's not wise to ignore warning signals from your heart.

Recently I set off the metal detector at the airport, so I emptied my pockets and went through again. But the alarm sounded, so the guard said, "Sir, you must have metal on you somewhere. We're going to have to check you." By now I was getting evangelically irritated because I had to catch a plane. So I told him, "I don't have anything else in my pockets."

He didn't buy it, of course, and now it was like a contest. He checked me with the wand and found nothing, so I was feeling pretty good. But then he came to my shoes, which unbeknownst to me had a piece of metal in the bottom. The security agent gave me a triumphant look as if to say, "My detector doesn't lie."

When God sets off an alarm in your heart, when your spiritual pulse becomes irregular, He's found something you may not see or even know is there. The Holy Spirit's job is to connect God's truth with your heart so you deal with sin and maintain fellowship with God. The breastplate of righteousness keeps Satan from penetrating your heart with his lies.

The third section of the believer's armor, *the shoes of peace*, confirms God's desire for us to be in fellowship with Him (v. 15a). This peace is the inner tranquility that comes from "the gospel of peace" through which we come into right standing with God.

The imagery of shoes suggests the need to stand firm. The shoes of a Roman soldier, whose armor was the pattern Paul followed, gave him sure footing as he fought on unsteady ground. You don't want to trip and fall when you're engaging the enemy.

Shoes also mean that you are going somewhere. God tells us to stand firm, not stand pat. There is nothing static about the Christian life. Spiritual growth requires movement and development. Don't expect to hear from God if you remain frozen in the same spot all the time. When you move ahead for the Lord, He confirms the rightness of your decision by the peace He gives. You have a firm foundation under you.

The *shield of faith* is the fourth piece of armor and the first we are told to take up as we need it. The shield allows us "to extinguish all the flaming arrows of the evil one" (v. 16b), those missiles called the "fiery darts" of Satan (KJV). Satan's arrows, things like doubt and discouragement, are designed to distract us from the real battle and get us fighting the fires started by the arrows. But faith, which is acting like God is telling the truth, snuffs out those arrows.

Whenever I read this I think of the old West and the battles between the American Indians and the settlers on the wagon trains. The settlers would circle the wagons to repel the Indians' attack, but then the Indians would start shooting flaming arrows into the wagons to set them on fire. They did this because they knew the settlers couldn't fight the fires and the Indians at the same time. The flaming arrows were a huge distraction, and Satan uses the same tactic against us.

If you're under attack and need your shield, you are also going to need the *helmet of salvation* (v. 17a). A helmet protects your brain, or mind, which for the Christian has to do with your new identity or who you are in Christ. Your salvation is not just your ticket out of hell, but it's everything you are in Jesus Christ—a blood-bought, totally forgiven, absolutely redeemed, heaven-bound child of God. Anything else is a false ID.

My daddy ruined many a Saturday night for me. I'd be going out, looking good, ready to get my groove on. But then Dad would say, "Before you leave the house, remember your last name." He was saying, "Son, when you walk out the door, our family's name and identity goes with you. Don't mess up the family name. Don't lose sight of your identity." The helmet of salvation protects your identity in Christ.

The sixth and last piece of armor is the *sword of the Spirit,* "which is the word of God" (v. 17b). This is rich, because the word for Scripture here is not *logos,* but *rhema,* which means an utterance. This refers to our use of God's Word to defeat Satan in battle, using the right Scripture at the right time to deal with the problem at hand.

The best example of the *rhema* of God in action is the way Jesus answered Satan in the wilderness. Three times Satan came at Him, and three times Jesus answered, "It is written" (Matt. 4:4, 7, 10) and then carved Satan up with the sword of God's Word. The devil can out-argue and out-debate you, but he has no answer for the Word of God.

Now let me ask you something. If Jesus, the living incarnate Word of God, needed to use Scripture, the written Word of God, to deal with the enemy, how much more do we need to use the Word? We learn the Bible to use it. When Satan hits us with a temptation, we can answer him with the Word. The sword Paul referred to here is not the big broadsword you see ancient soldiers wielding in the movies, but a short sword for close-in fighting. When Satan gets close, thrust the Word at him.

We Get Dressed through Prayer

I'm glad Paul didn't stop with a description of our armor, because one key to the effectiveness of a soldier's armor was putting it on correctly so the pieces fit together and provided maximum protection. Ephesians 6:18 pertains to our wearing of God's armor: "With all prayer and petition pray at all times in the Spirit, and with this in view, be on the alert with all perseverance and petition for all the saints."

How do you put on the armor of God? By prayer. Praying in the power of the Spirit clothes us for spiritual warfare, which is what we are talking about. I encourage you to pray specifically at the start of every day, asking God to clothe you with each piece of His armor you are supposed to wear at all times and to enable you to take up the pieces of armor you need as the occasion demands. Don't go out for the day spiritually underdressed.

PUTTING ON JESUS

If you want an interesting study, compare each piece of the armor of God to the provisions you have in Christ. For instance, there is the belt of truth. Jesus said He is the truth (John 14:6). We have the breastplate of righteousness, and the Bible says that Jesus has been made to us our righteousness (1 Cor. 1:30). We are to wear the shoes of the gospel of peace, and we read that "[Jesus] Himself is our peace" (Eph. 2:14).

Next is the shield of faith. The Bible declares that Jesus is "the author and perfecter of faith" (Heb. 12:2). What about the helmet of salvation? Jesus' title is Savior. And He is called the Word in John 1:1.

Jesus is our armor, in other words. So when we talk about putting on our armor, we are really talking about putting on Christ. That's why the Bible commands us, "Put on the Lord Jesus Christ, and make no provision for the flesh in regard to its lusts" (Rom. 13:14). That is one of the best verses in the Bible regarding how to win over temptation. Paul mentioned the flesh because it is the only one of our three enemies we can do something about. We can't keep the devil from being himself and the world from throwing its enticements at us, but we don't have to respond to them in our flesh.

Let me tell you what putting on Jesus will do for you. Hebrews 2:18 says that Jesus was tempted as we are tempted so that He can deliver us when we are tempted. When you say, "Jesus, I am being tempted to cheat on this test," Jesus says, "I know what you are going through. The devil tempted Me to cheat on My test by avoiding the cross." And He will come to your aid. What you need to do is keep your eyes fixed on Jesus (Heb. 12:2).

Dog trainers who want to train dogs to listen to them and obey their commands no matter what start a dog's training by throwing a juicy piece of red meat in front of the dog. The untrained dog goes for the meat immediately, but eventually the trainer teaches the dog to keep its attention on him no matter what is put in front of it. If the process is successful, the dog will not take its eyes off its master even with the "temptation" of meat right under its nose.

If you keep your eyes on Jesus Christ, it won't matter what kind of meaty lie Satan throws your way. Every now and then you may want to go for it, but if you keep your eyes on Jesus and listen for His voice alone, you can be victorious over anything.

14

Calling: The Ministry of Kingdom Living

THE SITCOM *SEINFELD* was one of the most popular programs on TV during its multiyear run. The actors involved were good at what they did, and the writers created some crazy characters, but one of the unusual features of *Seinfeld* that contributed to its popularity was the fact that the show's episodes had no plot. The characters simply meandered from situation to situation with no apparent purpose or order to their lives. An analysis was done of the *Seinfeld* audience, and it was discovered that the reason so many people loved the program was that their lives were as aimless and plotless as those of the people on the show.

Far too many people today are living "Seinfeld" lives with no apparent purpose, like hamsters on a wheel inside a cage. These people may be running fast, but they are going nowhere. Their lives flicker like a candle instead of shining with the brilliance of the noonday sun. And the tragedy is that this description of life fits far too many of us Christians who say we believe that God made us and saved us for a purpose.

When I was a boy growing up in Baltimore we used to take Sunday afternoon drives as a family. You may remember those too. We never went anywhere, but we just meandered aimlessly with no destination. Now that may be an acceptable way to kill a few hours on Sunday afternoon, but it's not the way God designed us to live.

Many people have a career, a home, a family, and all the other things our society deems important, but they still feel that life is incomplete. If this is true for you as a Christian, it may be that you have not dealt with the issue of your calling. Until you find that divinely ordained reason for being, you may continue to feel as if you are in the middle of a *Seinfeld* episode—no plot or plan to life.

Finding and living out your calling as a believer is an important part of kingdom living. True fulfillment is discovering the reason that God put you here on earth in the first place.

THE MEANING OF A CALLING

It always helps to define our terms, so let me give you a definition of *calling* that will underlie our study in this chapter. Your calling is *the customized life purpose that God has shaped, fashioned, and equipped for you, in order to expand His kingdom and bring Himself greater glory.*

We learned earlier that we are to live for God's glory as His people. One reason God wants you to grow in your faith is so that you will be able to maximize your calling for your own personal good and the advancement of His kingdom agenda. A calling is one of the grace gifts God has provided to every believer, no exceptions.

Now before we go on, let me address the idea many people in the church have that a calling is a supernatural experience whereby God speaks in a dramatic way, such as Christ appearing to Saul on the road to Damascus. Some people may have a dramatic sense of God's call, but He doesn't speak and appear today the way He did in Bible times, because we have His completed revelation. For most of us, our calling will come as we search the Word and the Holy Spirit impresses God's will on our hearts, often accompanied by the confirming evidence of circumstances.

Your Calling Is from a Good God

The Bible addresses this important issue in a number of places. We are told in Jeremiah 29:11 that God's calling or plan for us is good. "'For I know the plans that I have for you,' declares the Lord, 'plans for welfare and not for calamity to give you a future and a hope.'"

Ephesians 2:10 is another great verse dealing with our calling. This verse often gets overlooked after Paul's famous teaching in verses 8–9 that we are saved by grace through faith as God's gift. But His grace gift does not end with salvation, as we read in verse 10: "For we are His workmanship, created in Christ Jesus for good works, which God prepared beforehand so that we would walk in them." This is a general statement of our calling, which is to produce "good works" that bless and help others and glorify God (Matt. 5:16). So your calling is not just what you do for a living, but your divinely preplanned service for God that is your response to the great grace He has shown you in salvation (Rom. 12:1–8).

Now if our calling comes from the hand of our good God, and its goal is to produce good works, then our calling itself cannot be anything but good, which makes it another provision of God's grace.

Your Calling Has a Divine Purpose

God is also a God of purpose as well as a good Giver. "The counsel of the Lord stands forever, the plans of His heart from generation to generation" (Ps. 33:11). Everything in the universe He created has a purpose behind it, and He made us with that same desire and drive to find a purpose for our existence. I can't tell you how many people have said to me, "I know God put me here for a reason." That's a cry for a calling, a sense of divine purpose.

This desire in us reflects God's orderly nature, which is revealed in Genesis 1 as He assigned each portion of the creation its designated purpose. Light was given to dispel the darkness and keep it in its place. The sun was created to "govern" or give light during the day, and the moon was to "govern" the night (Gen. 1:16).

But it's when we come to Adam and Eve that we find this kingdom purpose: "Be fruitful and multiply, and fill the earth, and subdue it; and rule over the fish of the sea and over the birds of the sky and over every living thing that moves on the earth" (Gen. 1:28). Mankind's purpose is to fulfill God's kingdom dominion over the earth.

If you have ever heard a person strain or stray off the melody trying to sing a song that is outside of his or her natural range, you were probably glad when that singer came back into a more natural range. Even singers who can sing falsetto eventually have to come back down to their normal range.

Too many of us are like singers trying to perform outside their range—straining and getting off-key because we are not fulfilling our divinely ordained purpose. Acts 13:36 makes a very significant statement about King David of Israel: "For David, after he had served the purpose of God in his own generation, fell asleep, and was laid among his fathers." There is no greater epitaph that could be put over your life than to say that you fulfilled God's purpose in your generation.

The worst kind of life to live is a plotless one, a life without purpose stuck in the same loop. Most of us know what that feels like. Every day you get up out of that same old bed and go to the same old bathroom to look at the same old face in the mirror. You go to the same old closet to choose from the same old clothes, then sit down at the same old kitchen table to eat the same old breakfast.

Then you go to that same old garage and get into that same old car to head down that same old road to that same old job. There you work all day for that same old pay, next to those same old people, supervised by that same old manager. Then you get back into that same old car to head back down that same old road to that same old house.

Once you are home you sit down in that same old chair to watch that same old TV. Then you go to that same old table to eat that same old dinner. And at the end of the day, you go to that same old bed and sleep that same old way so you can get up the next morning to start that same old loop all over again. One day you look up and discover that your life is purposeless. You're moving but like a hamster on a wheel, you aren't going anywhere.

THE CHARACTER OF YOUR CALLING

But God did not create us, and He most certainly did not redeem us, to live a plotless, purposeless existence. That should be good news for you, because it means that even if you are searching to find God's calling and purpose for you right now, there is something out there worth the search.

Your Calling Is Tailor-Made for You

One reason you want to grow and maximize your spiritual development as a Christian is to realize your kingdom purpose. I don't know many people who are content just to live and die and have on their tombstone, "Joe was here." We were made for greater things than to occupy space on the planet.

God has a kingdom calling for you, and the beauty of it is that your calling is tailor-made for you. That's why Paul wrote, "Work out your [own] salvation" (Phil. 2:12). It's your salvation, not someone else's. We are all saved by the same Lord and Savior, but our God is infinitely creative.

In the same way that you have unique fingerprints and DNA, you have a unique calling, and I want to challenge you not to be satisfied with anything less. Don't settle for a paycheck, a house, and two cars. That may be the American dream, but God has a dream for you that is bigger than that.

Don't get me wrong. There is nothing wrong with having these things. The problem is when they become all there is to life. Some years ago a popular song asked the question, "Is that all there is?" The song didn't resolve the question, but God has told us the answer. The things around us are not all there is. He has a customized plan just for you, and the wise person makes discovering this plan a priority (Prov. 20:5).

God Gives You a Special Gift

God is so intentional in fashioning a unique purpose for each of His children that the Holy Spirit has equipped every believer with what the Bible calls a spiritual gift, or a divine enablement for service (1 Cor. 12:7, 11). I like the way Peter puts it: "As each one has received a special gift, employ it in serving one another as good stewards of the manifold grace of God" (1 Peter 4:10).

We often hear people say, "Well, I'm not talented." But no Christian can say, "Well, I'm not gifted." When God saved you, He also gifted you for your development and the good of others, and part of your spiritual growth is to discover and employ that gift. In fact, the greatest proof that you understand and are using God's liberating grace is through your service to others (Gal. 5:13).

Now just so we are clear on this, a spiritual gift is not simply a human talent or ability. You don't have to be a Christian to have ability in certain areas. You may use a human talent to help exercise your spiritual gift, but a gift is more than a talent, because a gift is something the Spirit of God uses to promote the kingdom purposes and glory of God through your life.

People may use their talents to glorify themselves and promote their own agenda. The problem is that it is possible for us to use God's gifts to promote and benefit ourselves only. I have seen Christians who have taken God's gifts and settled for using them as human talents. The way you do that is by using your giftedness for your benefit only, and not for God's kingdom and glory. That's a dangerous position to be in, because God will not allow His gifts to be misused. Spiritual gifts are called this because they are given by the Holy Spirit (1 Cor. 12:11) to enable you to fulfill your calling from God and further His program on earth.

One of the reasons many of us are missing our calling is that we're missing our gift. We have settled for a secular definition of why we are here and have missed God's eternal purpose, which is why He has given each of us unique abilities and experiences and desires.

Your calling and your career may or may not be the same, depending on your gifts. As a person who has been called to preach the Word of God, I am fulfilling my calling through my career. Proclaiming God's Word is also my full-time job. Some people's careers support their calling, as in the case of Paul himself. Paul's calling was to preach the gospel to the Gentiles, but he paid the bills by being a tentmaker. His gifts were those of a pastor and teacher and evangelist, but he had a human ability to cut and sew tents together.

Are You a Missing Piece in the Puzzle?

Do you know what God has called you to do? Do you know how God has gifted you? If so, how are you using your giftedness for God's glory?

If you can't answer these questions, or if you are not at least pursuing their answers, your spiritual growth is going to be limited because you are not fulfilling your reason for being.

The kingdom of God is like a gigantic jigsaw puzzle that is made up of many little pieces. I'm sure you have tried to put a puzzle together, only to discover that a piece or two is missing. It's obvious that the puzzle maker had a place for each piece, and the puzzle is incomplete without it.

Now we can't press that too far, because God is not going to allow His kingdom plan to be thwarted by anyone's lack of cooperation. But if you and I are not fulfilling our calling, there is a piece missing from the whole. Many of us also try to fit where God did not design us to fit, which some of us have tried to do with a puzzle piece as we put a puzzle together. But forcing a piece to go where it does not fit only frays the corners of the piece if you keep pushing and jamming it down.

When you discover God's calling you won't have to force yourself to fit anywhere. The Bible says that God has placed each part of Christ's body exactly where He wants it to be (1 Cor. 12:18). Thus your local church should be the primary beneficiary of your gifting, even though you may also serve in other places, such as parachurch ministries, neighborhood programs, and of course in your family and your job. There is tremendous satisfaction in finding that place and knowing that this is where God called you to be.

THE PROPER TIME FOR YOUR CALLING

The Bible is full of people who discovered their calling and tied it to God's eternal purpose. The story of Esther is one classic example, in part because the book of Esther contains one of the Bible's classic statements of our calling.

Your Calling Is Bigger than You

Esther's life reminds us of an important principle concerning our calling as believers, which I mentioned briefly above. That is, since God's calling relates to His kingdom, He has something far bigger in mind for you and me than our own agenda. You may remember that Esther was one of the Jewish exiles living in Persia. Esther was so beautiful that when the king of Persia decided to get rid of his queen and find another, Esther won the royal beauty contest that was held to select a new queen. The king couldn't take his eyes off Esther, but he didn't know that she was Jewish.

Enter a man named Haman, one of the king's top advisers and a hater of Jews after Esther's Jewish relative Mordecai refused to bow to him. Haman determined to exterminate the Jews and even got the king of Persia to issue a decree for their annihilation. Mordecai learned of the edict and went to Esther with a simple message: "Go into the king, tell him who your people are, and plead for the lives of the Jews. Otherwise, we'll all die."

The only problem with this plan is that Esther didn't see it that way. She told Mordecai, "I can't help you. If I go in to the king when he hasn't called for me, I'll be putting my life on the line."

Esther was suffering from the American disease of "personal peace and affluenza." She was living large. She had been just a nobody before, but now she was somebody. She was the first lady of Persia. And it was true that if she went into the king on her own, she could be put to death if he wasn't pleased with her.

But there was too much at stake not to take a risk. Mordecai got a little ticked off and reminded Esther, "Girl, if you don't use your position to save the Jews, God will bring deliverance from some other source, but you and your house will be destroyed" (Esth. 4:14a). Then Mordecai makes this powerful statement in the second half of this verse: "Who knows whether you have not attained royalty for such a time as this?" Esther got the message, appealed to the king, and the Jews were saved from annihilation.

Esther didn't understand at first that God didn't make her beautiful just so she could become queen and live in luxury. It took time and the rebuke of Mordecai for Esther to realize that God had placed her on the throne of Persia at that very time to fulfill a specific calling that involved the preservation of God's people.

Your Calling Involves the Whole Church

Many Christians ask, "How do I find my calling?" The short answer is that God will reveal it to you because He knows your name and where you are, and because He is not playing hide-and-seek with His purpose for you. If you want to know your purpose, don't go looking for your purpose. Go looking for God and your purpose will find you. The opening verses of Acts 13 give us some important insights into the way God calls His people to fulfill His plan:

> Now there were at Antioch, in the church that was there, prophets and teachers: Barnabas, and Simeon who was called Niger, and Lucius of Cyrene, and Manaen who had been brought up with Herod the tetrarch, and Saul. While they were ministering to the Lord and fasting, the Holy Spirit said, "Set apart for Me Barnabas and Saul for the work to which I have called them." (Acts 13:1–2)

Please notice that the Holy Spirit called out Barnabas and Saul, or Paul, by name in the context of the church's corporate worship. We tend to think this kind of calling only happened in biblical days when God gave specific tasks to specific people. But the Holy Spirit still speaks to believers today as we participate in the body of Christ. This is important because God's call on individuals is for the benefit of the body. The church also acts as the confirming agent for the calling of individual believers. The best place to discover your call is at church.

Make no mistake. God has not lost any of His ability to communicate His will clearly to us today. One reason so many believers are missing their calling is that they aren't in the place where God can

228

speak to them objectively through His Word and subjectively through His Spirit, confirmed by His people and even circumstances. They are on the sidelines waiting for something to happen.

In other words, they aren't active in the fellowship of the body of Christ and serving shoulder to shoulder with other believers. Too many of us are sitting on our hands saying, "Well, when God reveals His will to me, I'll get moving." No, God only hits a moving target. This is where your spiritual growth becomes so important. As you grow in the Word, in faith, and in service, you give God a growing target to hit. Don't put off serving the Lord until you find your call. As we will see later, it was not until Moses turned aside to investigate the burning bush that he heard God's explicit purpose for him.

Besides a lack of movement, another problem that can block the realization of God's call is that some people are satisfied with what I refer to as a general calling. These people go to church and hear the Word, but they go away and leave it at that. They don't seek God diligently for His will for their lives.

It's like a quarterback in professional football. They have headsets in their helmets so the coach can call in the specific play he wants. The quarterback may already know the playbook, but that's different from calling out a particular play for a particular situation.

It's one thing to come to church on Sunday and hear the Word of God. But it's another thing to be in the game yourself so the Holy Spirit can call your name in your "headset" and reveal the specific play He wants you to execute.

THE ELEMENTS OF YOUR CALLING

I suggested earlier that God uses a variety of means to reveal His calling. The counsel of His Word is indispensable, and we also need to seek the wisdom of other believers whose spiritual maturity we respect. Since we have entire chapters on how God uses His Word and His body in our spiritual growth, I want to concentrate on the way God uses experiences.

God Uses All of Your Experiences

God also uses your circumstances to prepare you for your calling, even if those circumstances sometimes appear to be a waste of time. But God doesn't waste anything. He can use all of our experiences—the good, the bad, and the ugly—to accomplish His purposes.

Moses grew up in a "foster home" in Egypt as the adopted grandson of Pharaoh. He spent forty years in the palace learning the language and the ways of the Egyptians, because God was going to use him to lead Israel out of Egypt. What better preparation for understanding your enemy than to be raised among them.

But Moses also needed to learn some personal lessons, so God sent him out into the desert for another forty years to tend sheep. The grandson of Pharaoh was now a lowly shepherd. Nothing will humble you more than having to take a job for which you are overqualified, especially when it's your own failure that put you there. Those years in the desert taught Moses what it was like to live on the poor side of town.

Finally, at the age of eighty, Moses was ready to fulfill his calling. God got his attention through a bush that burned but was not consumed. Moses said, "I've got to see this," and while he was looking at this strange sight, God gave him a personal call: "Moses, Moses!" (Ex. 3:4). It was at the burning bush that God revealed to Moses his calling as Israel's deliverer. Even though Moses had some objections, he obeyed God and delivered Israel.

The point is that none of Moses's eighty years of training was wasted. His years in the palace of Pharaoh prepared him to stand in Pharaoh's court and announce that God had sent him to lead the Israelites out. And Moses's forty years alone with God as a shepherd prepared him spiritually for the enormous calling of leading God's people and receiving His law.

The prophet Isaiah received God's call in the midst of a bad situation. It was "the year of King Uzziah's death" (Isa. 6:1). The king was dead, a negative circumstance that drove Isaiah to the house of God, where Isaiah saw the Lord and God called him to speak to His people.

The unfortunate reality is many of us don't know the Spirit's voice. We've never heard Him call our names. I'm not talking about some unusual, out-of-body experience, but the reality of God the Holy Spirit speaking to your heart and clearly communicating with you what He wants you to do.

God Gives You a Passion for Your Calling

Another important element in your calling is passion—a burning desire or fire in your heart to do a particular work for God's glory. Many Christians are afraid to tell God, "I will do whatever You want to me to do," because they are afraid He will send them somewhere they don't want to go or make them do something they don't want to do.

Now don't get me wrong. I'm not saying God never calls us to do some things that are hard. But people who are afraid of what they think their calling might be don't understand that God's will is "good and acceptable and perfect" (Rom. 12:2). What is there to be afraid of in that formula?

Now that doesn't just mean that God's will is good in the objective sense, although it is. God also gives us a passion for His will so that we become as excited about it as He is. With the calling of God comes the fire of God. Jeremiah said that when he tried to quit speaking about God, His word became to the prophet "like a burning fire shut up in my bones" (Jer. 20:9). The apostle Paul had a passion for his calling to preach the gospel where Jesus' name had not been heard (Rom. 15:20). You can't contain a fire that God lights.

A God-given passion for your calling motivates and compels you. It's the fire that cannot be quenched. When He sets your heart ablaze, you begin to see things you never saw before and you get excited about them.

We had our first leadership retreat one year after our church in Dallas began. We had about thirty-five or forty people in the church and a handful of men at the retreat, but I shared with them the vision and calling God had given me, much of which is now a reality. This was before we had any land or buildings or staff. But there was a calling, and with the calling comes the fire. And with the fire comes vision, so that God can take you to places that are not yet in existence. As a church we are now seeing the fulfillment of that divine fire.

A beautiful thing about a calling is that God can even work through your regrets to fulfill it. People in my generation remember Chuck Colson as a figure in the Watergate scandal during Richard Nixon's presidency. Colson was the president's counselor, his "hatchet man," and he was sentenced to prison. But God used Colson's legal troubles to bring him to Himself, and by the time Colson went to prison, he was a believer in Christ. While he was in prison, he saw the tremendous spiritual needs of prisoners. After Colson's release, God laid those needs on his heart until he couldn't do anything but go back into prisons and share Christ. Today, the work Chuck Colson founded, Prison Fellowship, is one of the world's largest prison ministries. God used Chuck Colson's fall from earthly power and imprisonment to ignite within him a passion to see prisoners' lives changed.

The Holy Spirit stands ready to inflame your heart for a calling that is from Him. Sometimes the passion may follow your obedience in doing what you know God wants you to do. It's not likely you'll find much of a passion for anything if you're just sitting on the sidelines waiting for something to happen. Jesus said, "If anyone is willing to do His will, he will know of the teaching" (John 7:17).

Many people have discovered a passion for some area of service after they began doing it. There was that inner sense, "This is what I was made to do." When you have a burning inner reason for doing something, and you know that God is watching and smiling on you, it makes all the difference.

This reminds me of the boy who was on his high school football team. All through his career he goofed off during practice and never really played hard, so he wound up as a fourth-string running back. But in the last game of his senior year, all the other running backs got hurt, and the coach had to put this kid in the game.

Well, to everyone's amazement, this former low performer ran wild, playing his heart out and giving the performance of his career. The coach couldn't believe his eyes, and after the game he asked him, "What in the world happened to make you play like that?"

"I can explain," he said. "My father was blind. But he died last week, so today is the first chance he's had to see me play." When you know your Father is watching, it ignites a passion within you.

A DEFINITION OF TRUE SUCCESS

Another benefit of knowing and fulfilling your calling is that it settles the question of what constitutes true success—which is a big issue for most of us. No one has ever told me that he set out to fail.

A Faulty View of Success

But too many Christians are operating under a faulty definition of success. We have bought into the world's idea that success is measured by how well we do compared to how other people do. Now if you want a surefire formula for stress, anxiety, and unhappiness, start playing the comparison game. The problem is that no matter what you do, someone else will always do more of it, and do it better.

But when you define success in terms of God's calling, the standard changes. True success is not what you have done compared to what others have done, but what you have done compared to what you were supposed to do—which is another way of saying how well you fulfill God's kingdom purpose for your life. Jesus was successful because He completed the work His Father sent Him to do (John 17:4). Paul was successful because he finished his race (2 Tim. 4:5–8).

By this standard, success may mean leaving a lucrative job to follow God's call into the ministry. It may mean using a special gift for God's glory instead of chasing fame and fortune. But whatever it is, once you are in your calling, you can stop comparing yourself to others or wishing you were someone else.

Don't Keep Your Gifts to Yourself

The reverse of this definition of success is also true. We will not be truly successful until we are using our gifts to fulfill our calling. One thing that concerns me as a pastor is seeing Christians use their abilities in their profession, but not for the kingdom. Paul said the Holy Spirit gives us gifts for "the common good" of Christ's body (1 Cor. 12:7).

All of us need to understand that unless and until we are using our gifts to advance God's kingdom agenda, we will not enjoy His divine sense of calling and satisfaction. A paycheck can never take the place of a call. Your calling is the place where you will experience the abundant life Jesus promised (John 10:10).

So let me ask you a few more questions. Just as bowlers are measured by their impact, the number of pins they knock down, what impact are you making for the kingdom of God? What time and talent and energy are you devoting to your purpose? How are you using the gifts God bestowed on you to carry out His kingdom program? How is the body of Christ benefiting from the fact that you are here?

You have been saved for a purpose. God didn't take you to heaven the moment He saved you because He has something for you to do here on earth. Let me suggest a few ways you can get started finding the will and the calling of God for your life.

One way is simply to decide you are going to grow in Christ. You know what it takes to grow, so determine that nothing is going to keep you out of God's Word and off of your knees in prayer. Ask the Holy Spirit to reveal Himself to you and show you the gifts God has given you and the ways He wants you to use them. Totally consecrate yourself to God, and His purpose for you will track you down (Rom. 12:1–2).

Also, do what is before you to do until God shows you the next step. Get busy for God, and you won't have to find your calling. Your calling will find you, because the Holy Spirit knows where you live and knows how to speak without stuttering.

One of the great reasons you want to grow in grace is so that you can say at the end of your life, as Paul said, "I have fought the good fight, I have finished the course, I have kept the faith" (2 Tim. 4:7). The crown goes to those who finish their race.

It's time for you to get on the track and start running. The future may not be completely clear right now, but keep at it. When you discover your calling, you'll know it, because you will be more alive than you ever were before. God's grace will have set you free to become all that you were created to be.

15

Obedience: The Response of Kingdom Living

I HEARD ABOUT A WOMAN who married a very demanding, hard, and unloving man. Her husband made her existence miserable by presenting her with a list of his demands and expectations, such as "You will wash and iron my clothes," and "You will have my meals cooked and ready at the stated times each day." The woman's husband insisted that she follow his list to the letter, and he never thanked her for anything. She complied with his demands, but she hated her life with this man.

The woman endured her miserable marriage for twenty-five years before her husband died. She vowed she would never marry again, but two years later she met a very kind man and got married. Instead of making demands of her, her second husband just loved her. The woman began to experience happiness for the first time, and she found herself enjoying even her routine daily activities.

One day as she was cleaning, she came across the old list of demands that her late husband had given her. She read the list again for the first time in years, and she began to laugh. She discovered she was doing these same things for her second husband, and even more. The difference was that now she was enjoying these things, whereas before she hated them and only did them as a duty. Her new husband's love had radically transformed her attitude.

The way we respond to the expectations that God places upon us as His children is another vital component in kingdom living. Make no mistake, God does have expectations of us. He is not big on suggestions. Obedience to God's will as revealed in Scripture is the standard, and any Christian who wants to please God and grow will seek to be obedient. But God doesn't present us with a "chore list" and then stand by ready to clobber us if we mess up.

I know that for any number of reasons, the very word *obedience* throws some people into a spin. For example, there are those who don't want to obey anybody because it sounds like oppression. These could be people who have had experiences like the woman in our opening story. Other people say they have tried to obey, but they can't keep it up. These are often people who say they leave church on Sunday excited about what they have heard and ready to respond, but something happens as the week goes on and they seem unable to obey.

We don't want to excuse disobedience to God for any reason. But as I studied this subject again, it occurred to me that we often have a mistaken view of what constitutes true biblical obedience. And because we have a wrong view of obedience, we are not able to apply it in terms of our everyday living.

I'm excited to share with you what I discovered, because the issue of obedience is closely related to the new covenant and the new work that God has done in our hearts through Christ's death on the cross. I want to recast the concept of obedience so you can relate to it in a way that may be different from what you have heard before.

A NEW DEFINITION OF OBEDIENCE

The connection between the new nature that God put within us at salvation and our obedience to Him is so vital that I want to establish it first. God announced in Jeremiah 31:31–34 that someday He would relate to human beings in a new way called the new covenant. This covenant is not based on law and animal sacrifice, but on the once-and-for-all sacrifice of Jesus Christ. The main feature of the new covenant is this: "I will put My law within them and on their heart I will write it" (v. 33).

This is a promise of the new nature and new relationship we have with God as believers today. We could also call this nature a new disposition or a heart that is made up of a whole new set of inclinations—which are *built-in desires* we have to draw close to God and obey His Word.

The fact that these desires are built-in, or internal, is crucial, because it revolutionizes our understanding of obedience. Not only has God given us His law, but when He made us new creations in Christ He also gave us the internal desire to obey His law by walking in His ways. This is why Paul could write: "So then, my beloved, just as you have always obeyed, not as in my presence only, but now much more in my absence, work out your salvation with fear and trembling; for it is God who is at work in you, both to will and to work for His good pleasure" (Phil. 2:12–13).

Being Made to Obey

Many Christians grew up memorizing these verses without really understanding what they mean. We know they have to do with obedience and that obedience is somehow tied to God's "good pleasure." But most people would not connect obedience with pleasure at any level.

That's because we are so used to obeying out of necessity or fear.

The worst example is a slave who is forced to obey by a master standing over him with a whip. But even apart from this, we have parents who made us obey because it was the right thing to do, or, sometimes, "Just because I said so." Many people only obey their bosses because they need to in order to keep their jobs.

In other words, most of us equate obedience with the "do it or else" approach. Now please don't misunderstand. It is not wrong for parents to expect obedience from their children and to discipline them for disobedience. A supervisor has the right to take action against uncooperative employees. What I'm saying is that doing what you are told because you are made to, or because you need to, is neither the best definition of obedience nor the highest motivation for obedience.

Instead, the Bible gives us a better definition of obedience, which is doing what you really want to do deep down inside. The element that is missing in so many people's definition of obedience is the "want to" factor, the idea that the desire to obey God is already built into us. This takes our obedience out of the "ought to, have to, better do it or else God will zap me" mode and elevates it to the level of a joyful response to all that God has done for us.

Therefore, Paul can tell us to obey by working out our salvation because of what God has already worked into our new nature. Another way to define biblical obedience is simply the working out of what God has worked in. I contend that most of us as Christians do not look at obedience as the activation and cultivation of something that is already present within us. We consider obedience a responsibility that we have to manufacture, not something we already have the "want to" to perform.

In fact, I'm convinced that what a lot of us call obedience is merely outward compliance. By that I mean we do it, but deep down we really don't want to do it. We're like the boy who misbehaved and was told by his mother to go sit in the corner. After a few minutes she asked him from the other room, "Are you sitting down?"

The boy replied, "I'm sitting down on the outside, but I'm standing up on the inside."

You could call that obedience, but actually it is nothing more than outward compliance without the inward response of eager and joyful obedience. Biblical obedience is joyfully doing on the outside what you really want to do on the inside.

Doing What You Want to Do

This definition of obedience is built on several biblical principles we will examine, the first of which is found in Philippians 2:13. Paul says we can obey because God is at work within us, "both to will and to work for His good pleasure." This means we have both the *desire* and the *ability* to do what God asks us to do. These are the two components necessary for authentic obedience.

A desire is something you want to do, and so Paul can use the word *pleasure* in connection with our responsibility to obey God. It should be pleasurable for us to obey, both because God is pleased by our obedience and because we are pleased knowing that we have made Him happy. If we treat obedience as nothing more than outward compliance divorced from anything that's happening on the inside, then we are not experiencing any joy in what we are doing.

I will never forget Dr. Howard Hendricks, one of my favorite professors at Dallas Seminary, telling us how his fifth-grade teacher tied him to the chair in an attempt to make him behave. When he went to sixth grade, his teacher eyed him and said, "So you're Howard Hendricks. I hear you're a bad boy, but I want you to know that I don't believe a word of it."

Professor Hendricks said he would have done anything for that teacher. Not only did he not give her trouble, but he became a model student who worked hard and did everything she asked of him. He said his former teacher came by his classroom one day and looked in to see this miracle that had come to pass.

The best kind of obedience is that which is tied to a strong, positive relationship. A lot of parents would say, "Wow, I wish I could get that kind of obedience out of my children." I'm a parent, too, and I know that all of us wrestle, or have wrestled at some point, with the challenge of finding the best way to teach our kids how to obey.

No one has all the answers, but here is a principle you can bank on as a parent (or as a teacher, an employer, or anyone else who has people under your direction). The principle is this: rules without relationship lead to rebellion. I know a lot of parents say their children should obey them just because they are in charge. And it's true that there are times when we must make our kids obey whether they like it or not.

But if all we have going for us in child discipline is "Do it or else," or "Do it because I say so," we may get compliance out of our children until they are old enough to stop being scared of us, and then we will get downright rebellion. There's nothing wrong with laying down the rules, but make sure you also cultivate a close relationship with your children so that they respond to your love with a love of their own that makes obedience a delight instead of a duty.

The Pure Joy of Obeying God

When you were young, did you ever feel that having to obey your parents was awful, a heavy weight that you had to carry around? Unfortunately, many people never shed that feeling as they move into adulthood. Talking about obedience, joy, pleasure, and "want to" in the same breath is a contradiction in terms to them.

I'm afraid many Christians feel the same way about their calling to obey God. Let me tell you something. If you feel that God's commands are a wearisome bunch of dos and don'ts that are weighing you down, and if you find that obeying Him is like carrying around a heavy load, then what you are doing and what God is talking about are not the same thing.

Here's another view of obedience. Jesus said, "Come to Me, all who are weary and heavy-laden, and I will give you rest. Take My yoke upon you and learn from Me, for I am gentle and humble in heart, and you will find rest for your souls. For My yoke is easy and My burden is light" (Matt. 11:28–30).

Does Jesus have a yoke for us to bear that includes obedience? Absolutely. Does He intend it to be a wearying, tiring load of responsibility that is so heavy we can barely manage it? Absolutely not. In fact, if your load is too heavy for you, bring it to Jesus and let Him show you the joy of following and obeying Him.

You may say, "If I have this great desire deep down to obey God, why can't I find it?" One reason may be that you and I still have to contend with our flesh that is as adamant against obeying God as the new nature is for obeying Him. We cannot afford to forget that there is a war within us when we seek to obey God.

A second reason many of us don't feel this desire is that it has been covered by calluses built up over years of doing things because we had to. It's a lot like the hard, dry skin that builds up on our feet. That hard layer has to be removed to get to the soft skin underneath. That's usually the first thing a pedicurist has to do when you go in for a treatment on your feet. In much the same way, God the Holy Spirit often has to remove the calluses from our hearts as part of His softening process that makes us receptive to God's will.

OBEDIENCE, THE OVERFLOW OF LOVE

The Holy Spirit has a favorite tool to remove these spiritual calluses. It is called love—specifically our love for Christ in response to what He has done for us.

The apostle John knew something about loving Christ. John was the disciple who called himself the one "whom Jesus loved" (John 13:23), and who leaned on Jesus at the Last Supper. You might expect John to get pretty gushy and flowery when he wrote about loving God.

But in 1 John 5:3 the apostle wrote, "This is the love of [or, for] God, that we keep His commandments, and His commandments are not burdensome." We prove our love for God by obeying Him. Obedience is the natural overflow of love. And notice that when you love someone, obedience is not a burdensome thing. John's statement perfectly reflects what he no doubt heard Jesus say when He taught that His burden is light.

Jesus also said obedience is the proof of love. In that same upper room where John leaned on Jesus, the Lord said, "If anyone loves Me, he will keep My word; and My Father will love him, and We will come to him and make Our abode with him. He who does not love Me does not keep My words" (John 14:23–24a).

Love Makes Doing a Delight

Notice that Jesus did not say, "If you love Me, you had better keep My Word." There is no threat here. The formula is simple. If we love Jesus, the desire to obey will be there. If the desire to obey is lacking, it's because love is lacking. The reason we don't obey enough is that we're not yet in love enough with Jesus.

Now let me emphasize again that we ought to do what is right because it's right. But all of us know what it is to get tired of doing right just because we are supposed to. When we get to that stage, duty has replaced love. I compare it to the way many married men act toward their wives today as opposed to when they were dating.

A man who is trying to woo and win a woman will do anything for her, even if he's dog-tired and what she is asking is inconvenient, painful, expensive—or all three! She will call him and say, "Honey, I know it's late, you're tired, and it's pouring rain. But could you come over here and change the flat tire on my car?"

What does he say? "Sure, baby, be right over." And he comes and changes the tire in the pouring rain with a smile on his face because he is motivated by love.

Fast forward to today. This guy has now been married for ten years, which means he's in the same house with this woman whom he courted and won. But now when she asks him to get up off the couch and do a little errand for her, she has to say it three times and you'd think she'd asked him to cut off his leg the way he moans and groans. Then she gets upset and starts fussing with him because she remembers a time when she didn't have to ask twice. What was a delight has become a duty because the love motivation has cooled off.

You see, our fundamental problem as Christians is not really obedience. Our problem is keeping our love for Christ fervent, for love makes obedience a delight. A decline in obedience is the outgrowth of a decline in love. What we often do is replace grace with law and love with rules, but we don't enjoy the rules because we don't see the love. The new nature functions best when motivated by relationship, not legislation. We said earlier that rules without relationship lead to rebellion. We could add to this that rules without love lead to coldness. When the risen Lord Jesus addressed the seven churches, He commended the church at Ephesus for its hard work and obedience. But He also said, "But I have this against you, that you have left your first love" (Rev. 2:4). In other words, "You don't love Me the way you used to love Me." Christ commanded this church to return to the point where they had fallen, which was where they let their love for Him slip.

Relationship Changes Everything

Keeping love alive and strong requires an intimacy of relationship that also affects the way we live. John made this critical link when he wrote, "The one who says he abides in [Christ] ought himself to walk in the same manner as He walked" (1 John 2:6). To abide is to maintain an intimate relationship with the Lord, out of which obedience flows.

This connection between our love relationship with Christ and our obedience is important because, if you'll recall, biblical obedience is not being coerced or threatened to behave. Instead, it is responding to the desire we already have within us to obey and please God. Let me state it again. True obedience for the Christian is doing what we truly want to do in our new nature, where God has written His law and given us the Holy Spirit to empower us.

Too many men are harsh and demanding with their wives, who often comply with their husbands' demands just to keep them from getting mad. But when a wife feels loved, when that intimacy of relationship is present in the marriage, that changes everything. A woman blossoms in this kind of atmosphere because women are wired to be responders.

A wise husband will shower his wife with love, attention, and a sense of her value. She, in turn, will respond in love. Then all the arguments about who is supposed to do what and who forgot to do what will begin to dissipate, because love animates proper action. If we will bask in God's perfect love, we won't have any problem doing the things that He asks us to do.

A BIBLICAL PATTERN FOR OBEDIENCE

I don't want you going away from this chapter saying, "Tony, this all sounds great. But you didn't show me how to get my obedience kicked into high gear." Well, hang on because here we go.

When we're looking for practical application of biblical truth, we often wind up in the book of James. I like James because he is an in-your-face kind of guy. He looks right at us and says, "This is the truth. What are you going to do about it?" Here are some ways we can respond to God's Word.

Seek God's Mind at All Times

In the first chapter of his letter, James makes this statement: "Everyone must be quick to hear, slow to speak and slow to anger; for the anger of man does not achieve the righteousness of God" (James 1:19–20). He makes it clear later in the chapter that he is talking about being quick to hear God's Word. In other words, the first question we need to ask in any situation is, What does God say about this in His Word? What is His mind on this?

Along with seeking God's mind and will, James says we need to be slow in our response. By this he means don't be too quick to jump in and react. You probably know people who barely let you get the words out of your mouth before they start rebutting you. When you learn what God says, don't react in the flesh, because your flesh does not want to obey God. Getting angry doesn't do any good, either, because you aren't going to change God's mind, and when it's all over, you still need to obey.

Remove Hindrances to Obeying

Once you have heard the Word and are ready to respond, James 1 says the first step is to remove the things that would hinder you from obeying. "Therefore, putting aside all filthiness and all that remains of wickedness, in humility receive the word implanted, which is able to save your souls" (v. 21).

The hindrances James mentions are general categories for sin, the works of the flesh that act like calluses on our hearts and keep us from obeying the Lord. We need to remove these so the soft flesh of the new nature can be revealed, which is where the "want to" for obeying God is located. Heartfelt confession, as described in 1 John 1:9, removes these hindrances and prepares the way for the Word to "save" us. This is not salvation, but the transformation that comes when the Holy Spirit is free to apply God's Word to our lives.

See Yourself in the Word

I love these next verses of James 1, where he compares our response to the Word with a man looking at himself in a mirror. The goal of seeing ourselves in God's Word is to become "doers of the word, and not merely hearers who delude themselves" (v. 22). In other words, we are supposed to do something about what we see, because the Bible is like a mirror that shows you and me what we really look like.

The opposite of someone who obeys the Word is the person described in verses 23–24: "For if anyone is a hearer of the word and not a doer, he is like a man who looks at his natural face in a mirror; for once he has looked at himself and gone away, he has immediately forgotten what kind of person he was."

The word translated "man" in this passage is the Greek word for a male, so we know James is talking about the way men use a mirror as opposed to women. Things haven't changed much in the last two thousand years, because even back then men used a mirror pretty much the way we use it today. Most men just glance in the mirror long enough to get the basics done—shave, brush the teeth, comb the hair—and then they are gone. But some women are so intent on looking at themselves that they carry a mirror with them in their purse. They can find out any time of the day how they look.

The point is not the difference in the way men and women use a mirror, but the difference between taking a quick glance at yourself and hanging out in front of the mirror until you have fully seen who you are. When we read God's Word or hear it taught or preached, the

Holy Spirit uses it to hold up a mirror before us. A doer of the Word, or a Christian who wants to grow, not only wants to read the Bible or hear it preached. He wants to see himself in the Bible so he can make whatever adjustments are necessary.

This is the person James is referring to in verse 25: "One who looks intently at the perfect law, the law of liberty, and abides by it, not having become a forgetful hearer but an effectual doer, this man will be blessed in what he does." When you look intently into the Word in order to find out what God wants from you, you are on your way to an exciting adventure with Christ.

As a pastor, I have some people tell me my sermon was nice. I appreciate the kind words, but I really get excited when someone says, "Pastor, you were talking to me today." What the person means is that he saw himself in the Word as the Holy Spirit connected what he read on the page or heard with his new nature, the part of a believer that deeply wants to obey and please God. James says the Word of God is already implanted within us, written on our hearts. Real spiritual growth happens when the Spirit shows us ourselves and stirs us to act on the Word.

Continue to Abide in the Word

What we are talking about here requires a response to God's Word that may be different from what you are accustomed to. The person God blesses is the one who "abides" in His Word. Did you catch that word in James 1:25? *Abide* means to hang out, to stick around. The psalmist said that the person who meditates on God's Word "day and night" will be blessed (Ps. 1:2). When you look into the mirror of Scripture, you not only see yourself, but you see what God wants you to become.

Paul used a similar idea when he wrote, "But we all, with un-veiled face, beholding as in a mirror the glory of the Lord, are being transformed into the same image from glory to glory, just as from the Lord, the Spirit" (2 Cor. 3:18). When we look into the Word, we behold the glory of God. And since bringing God glory is our primary purpose for being on earth, He wants to change us so as to reflect His glory more and more.

But this can't happen if we are in the habit of just grabbing a Bible verse here and there or quickly skimming through a passage. If your prayer in coming to the Word is, "God, show me how I can glorify You today through my obedience to You," then you are going to hang out with the Word until the Holy Spirit connects with your spirit and brings about a change within you. That's when spiritual growth breaks out.

If you have ever left dishes in the sink until the food was dried on, you know those dishes need to "abide" in some hot, soapy water for a while before you can get all the junk off. The water and soap soften the hard stuff so the dishes will come clean. We need to soak our minds in the Word until that junk James calls "all filthiness and all that remains of wickedness" (James 1:21) begins to melt away. This is not just gross outward sin, but inner attitudes and other things that keep us from growing in the grace and knowledge of Jesus Christ.

James says if we will abide in the Word, looking intently into the law that sets us free and acting on what we see, we will be blessed. Our new nature has been "programmed" to want to obey God, much the way a calculator has been programmed to compute numbers. All you have to do is feed a calculator the right information to get the right response. Your new nature has been set up to give you the right response when you feed it with the Word of God.

Growing Christians are like sunflowers, which are so named because they follow the sun. When the sun rises in the east, the sunflower points east. When the sun sets in the west, the sunflower points west. Sunflowers throw off a lot of seeds and produce new flowers because they are always looking for the sun.

When you and I look for the Son the way the sunflower looks for the sun, His rays will soften our hearts so we can throw off new seeds and produce new life. Pursue obeying God in concert with your new nature and in response to His love, and you'll see the transformation you've been looking for.

16

Maturity:
The Goal of
Kingdom Living

OVER THE PAST COUPLE DECADES, a number of family and child development experts, both Christian and secular, have come forward to identify a problem that seems to be unique to modern Western culture in general and America in particular. This syndrome is often called "the hurried child," and it refers to the tendency for parents in our fast-paced society to rush their children through childhood and hurry them along to adulthood.

There are various reasons this problem occurs, not the least of which is the determination on the part of many parents today to push their children to excel in every area, often to the point that a child never has a chance to enjoy being a kid. Even activities that are supposed to be fun, such as community sports and extracurricular activities at school, become hotbeds of competition with children feeling great pressure to win or be first.

Jam-packed schedules that allow for little or no relaxed family time at home also contribute to the "hurried-child syndrome." So does the fact that a lot of parents want their children to hurry and grow up because the parents don't want to be bothered with the inconveniences of childhood. But what we are discovering is that you cannot skip the stages of childhood development and expect to produce mature, healthy adults.

Now don't misunderstand. Good parents are concerned about the growth and development of their children. They want to see their children achieve their maximum physical, emotional, and intellectual potential. The idea of the hurried-child syndrome reminds us that each stage of the process is important and has its own developmental challenges that cannot be overlooked.

The same is true with the process of our spiritual growth toward maturity. Spiritual birth, childhood, and adolescence are stages along the way to our becoming mature in Christ, not the final destination. I don't think I've ever met a Christian who is genuinely content to remain in spiritual nursery school drinking from a sealed cup and playing childish games.

My assumption, as I stated at the beginning of this book, is that you want to grow spiritually and reach "the measure of the stature which belongs to the fullness of Christ" (Eph. 4:13). We've covered a lot of ground along the way to that goal, and in this final chapter I want to bring it home and help you reach for the goal of kingdom living which is maturity.

I want to help you be a mature Christian because that's what God wants for you too. Paul issued this challenge to the often-infantile Corinthians: "Brethren, do not be children in your thinking; yet in evil be infants, but in your thinking be mature" (1 Cor. 14:20). We can define spiritual maturity as *the ability to consistently view and live life from the perspective of the Spirit rather than the flesh, with the result that we maximize our God-given capacity to bring Him glory.*

Now this is something that we will be pursuing and living out all of our lives, because we will never do it perfectly in this body. Thus there will always be capacity for more growth, but spiritual growth does have a definable goal called maturity that we need to be moving toward. And there are definable stages along the way, although the good news is that, unlike physical development, you can grow spiritually just as fast as you want to grow.

Our focus on this quest for spiritual maturity is an amazing passage of Scripture in the epistle of 1 John, a letter that was written to help Christians develop true, life-changing fellowship or intimacy with God, which are just two other terms for spiritual maturity. John stated his goal in the opening verses of his letter:

> What was from the beginning, what we have heard, what we have seen with our eyes, what we have looked at and touched with our hands, concerning the Word of Life—and the life was manifested, and we have seen, and testify and proclaim to you the eternal life, which was with the Father and was manifested to us—what we have seen and heard we proclaim to you also, so that you too may have fellowship with us; and indeed our fellowship is with the Father, and with His Son Jesus Christ. (1 John 1:1–3)

I've included John's introduction for a reason. He reminded his readers that he had heard and seen and touched Jesus—most of them probably had not, since this was about sixty years after Jesus' crucifixion. John's message was that he was transferring to them the truth he learned from Jesus. Therefore, even though his readers had not known Jesus in the flesh, they could still enjoy the same intimacy with God that John knew, because fellowship with God is through the Spirit and not the flesh.

John was answering the question of someone who might ask him, "Since Jesus isn't here physically as He was with you, how can we get to know Him as intimately as you know Him?" We could ask the same question today, and the answer would be the same. We are not missing anything because Jesus is not here. In fact, our fellowship is actually more intimate, because when Jesus left, He sent us the Holy Spirit to live within us and be ever present with us (John 14:17).

THREE LEVELS OF SPIRITUAL DEVELOPMENT

With this background set, John went on to address three groups of Christians who represent three levels or stages of spiritual growth in the process of our becoming more like Jesus Christ and bringing God greater glory. These stages correspond to the childhood, adolescence or teenage years, and adulthood of physical life, so we will use these familiar terms. John doesn't keep the three stages in perfect chronological order in the text, but we will discuss them in that order.

Each of these stages is important, as we have indicated. No one is born mature, and children can't skip their teenage years—as much as parents sometimes wish they could! The early stages of spiritual growth need not take as many years as physical and emotional growth do, but the problem is that believers can get stuck along the way.

This is how we get the phenomenon of a person who has been saved for forty years and is still in first grade in terms of spiritual maturity. My goal in this discussion is not to make you feel bad about your level of spiritual development, but to help you determine where you are so you can move on. Once again, the assumption is that you want to "press on to maturity" (Heb. 6:1).

The Stage of Spiritual Childhood

The first stage of spiritual development John addresses is the Christian who is in childhood. "I am writing to you, little children, because your sins have been forgiven you for His name's sake" (1 John 2:12). At the end of verse 13 we read, "I have written to you, children, because you know the Father." New Christians know God as their Father, but not in the intimate way that is characteristic of mature Christians, as we will see below.

We aren't going to try to figure out the exact ages in each stage, because that isn't possible and it's not the issue anyway. The Greek term for "little children" basically refers to a toddler, so we'll say this is a baby Christian whose new birth was fairly recent. People at this stage of spiritual growth are still coming to grips with the exciting fact that Jesus Christ has forgiven all their sins and they have been rescued from judgment and eternal death.

Why did John mention the forgiveness of sins as characteristic of little children? Because it's basic, ABC spiritual truth, which is all that new Christians can handle at this early stage. They are limited in their understanding, and there is nothing wrong with that if they are truly new to the faith. There's a reason that most Sunday school curriculum for toddlers doesn't include the Melchizedek priesthood of Christ.

A friend of mine, who is also a graduate of Dallas Theological Seminary, said he was taken aback at first when he and his wife began teaching a Sunday school class of two-year-olds at their church. This man had never taught children this young before, and he was used to seminary-level material.

So when he saw an entire lesson whose only point was to teach "Jesus loves me," he thought it was too simple—until he began to realize what an important truth that is for two-year-olds to grasp. He says one thing that helped wise him up was that one of the children in the class was his own, and he began to see firsthand how two-year-olds learn.

Baby Christians are dependent on others. They need someone to feed them and help them make their way along in the spiritual life. A baby or young child cannot function on their own. Baby Christians don't know how to live life yet because they haven't been alive in Christ long enough to know how to live.

Spiritual infancy is also marked by instability. For baby Christians, stability or the lack thereof is dictated by their circumstances. If things are fine, so are they. But when times get tough, they are far from fine. They have not yet made the crucial connection between trials and spiritual development.

Another typical characteristic of new Christians is that they function based on the externals instead of the internals. By that I mean they may listen to a sermon and hear the preacher's voice, but they are not attuned to hear the voice of God speaking to them from the general instruction of the Word to others.

Now I am not saying that those who are children in the faith cannot do anything. If you are saying, "Well, I can't witness to anyone yet because I've only been a Christian for a year," you have the wrong idea. Young Christians are often effective witnesses for Christ, and they can tell someone else what God has been teaching them. Baby Christians can be spiritual as opposed to fleshly, and that is certainly what is desired. But spiritual children are more dependent on the ministry and input of others than more mature Christians are.

There's nothing wrong with that if you are new in the faith. But if you have been a Christian for years and you are still completely dependent on someone else to feed you, your growth is going to be severely limited unless some changes are made.

The difference between new Christians and believers whose spiritual lives are simply stunted is seen in 1 Corinthians 3, where Paul rebuked the Corinthians for being "infants" in Christ who were "still fleshly" (vv. 1, 3). He said that because these people had been saved for at least five years by this time, yet they were still drinking from the bottle and wearing diapers. They should have at least been able to pick up a spoon and feed themselves, spiritually speaking, by this time.

If you realize that you are a baby Christian, make sure you are feeding regularly on "the pure milk of the word, so that by it you may grow in respect to salvation" (1 Peter 2:2).

Becoming a Spiritual Young Person

The apostle John addressed Christians in a second stage of spiritual growth when he wrote: "I am writing to you, young men, because you have overcome the evil one" (1 John 2:13b). And again, "I have written to you, young men, because you are strong, and the word of God abides in you, and you have overcome the evil one" (v. 14b).

I call this stage becoming a spiritual young person or adolescent, which can reach from the teenage years into the early years of what the world considers young adulthood. This period of life is marked by conflict and the need to become spiritually strong and learn how to overcome the devil. At this stage a young person is coming to grips with the realities of the Christian life and is often engaged in real combat with the devil. These are the years of the Christian life when we first learn how to use the sword of the Spirit, God's Word, to counter the attacks of the enemy.

Now there is a complicating factor at work in this stage of our spiritual development. If you have ever had teenagers, you know that people in this stage of life are making a growth transition from childhood to adulthood, and it can be a pretty bumpy trip. Many teenagers and young people often clash with their parents and other authority figures because they are moving from dependence to independence, and they wrestle with conflicting feelings of wanting their freedom, and yet sometimes not really wanting it—especially if Dad and Mom are still paying the bills at home or at college.

When I was about fourteen years old, I started using a particular line on my dad when I perceived that he was interfering with my freedom and treating me like a child. I would want to do something that he didn't think I was ready for, and I would say, "But I'm almost a man." Now I didn't have a job or anything, and Dad was providing for my needs. But I felt that I was ready to have a man's privileges. Let's just say my father was not impressed with my arguments.

I experienced some of this same thing years ago when my son Jonathan, who was in college, complained about coming home because he said he was embarrassed to have to still call in at midnight at the age of twenty-one to let me know where he was. You see, if you are in my house and you are a young person with the same last name as mine who is being supported in school, you have to call in at night because I am not going to lie awake staring at the ceiling at midnight wondering where you are. I at least want to know where you are.

Jonathan said he was out on a date and he was embarrassed having to tell his date, "I have to call my dad." Now we wouldn't go through all of this except that Jonathan still called me for money. As long as he needed my money, he would also get my guidance.

I tell you that story to illustrate that what is true in the physical world is also true in the spiritual. That is, while young Christians are learning to be strong and overcome the devil with the Word of God, they still need the support and guidance of mature Christians to help them handle the conflicts, whether they think so or not. Adolescent Christians want to move forward in these experiences, and they often feel they can take on the world, the flesh, and the devil all by themselves. But they need help and direction to become strong.

If you are in this stage of your spiritual development, there are times when you will fail and be overcome rather than overcome. In those times of defeat you especially need support and guidance from more mature Christians so you can learn how to avoid the enemy's trap the next time. You also need instruction and training in the Word to sharpen your sword and keep it battle ready at all times. And as a growing, adolescent Christian, you need mature Christians to provide you with opportunities to serve and take leadership so you can gain battle experience.

So a spiritual adolescent is a person who is learning to depend on the Word of God to overcome the evil one. A baby Christian does not have practice in handling the Word of God (Heb. 5:11–14). If you are able to use the Word in conflict to overcome the devil, you have grown out of your spiritual childhood.

Becoming a Mature Adult

No teenager wants to be an adolescent forever, and the same is true in the Christian life. The objective of spiritual growth is to reach the level of maturity that John described in the text we're studying as being a father. "I am writing to you, fathers, because you know Him who has been from the beginning" (1 John 2:13). John then repeated his message for these people: "I have written to you, fathers, because you know Him who has been from the beginning" (v. 14).

What makes you a spiritual adult, or a mature Christian? It's very simple, yet profound. The mature believer knows God, and not just that He forgives sin or gives power for spiritual battle. The mature believer knows God in a depth of intimacy that has been developing over time. That's why John added the interesting phrase "who has been from the beginning." The idea is that the mature believer is tapping into a deeper understanding of God and His eternal nature, a process that certainly suggests the passage of time.

In other words, John was not just making a theological statement here. God is definitely from the beginning, or eternal. But the context of 1 John 2 is not theological argument, but personal spiritual experience and growth. A mature Christian has come to know God over time— through the growth process and the scars obtained in spiritual battle.

A mature believer still needs to grow in Christlikeness, because that's a lifetime job. And there are still battles with the enemy to fight and win. But a mature Christian's life has a quality of depth about it that can only be gained by going through the process of growing and battling.

We could say that the mature Christian has a personal testimony of God's faithfulness and goodness. If you are mature in your faith, you don't have to listen to other people tell how good and faithful God is for you to understand it. An adolescent Christian cannot yet say, "I know God is real because I have walked with Him all these years and proved Him faithful."

This description of a mature Christian raises a question. How do you know when you know God in such an intimate way? The short answer is that your spirit is able to commune with God at such a deep level that you pick up signals that other folk miss.

Now let me explain that answer and show you from Scripture how it works. Your spirit is the deepest part of your being, and it gives you the ability to connect with God. You relate to the world through your body and to yourself through your soul, but you relate to God and other people through your spirit.

When you accepted Christ, a union occurred between your human spirit and the Holy Spirit, who made you alive in Christ. This union can be compared to a marriage between two people that produces one new life out of two lives. At salvation your spirit became one with God and you received a new nature from Him that is perfect.

Now the ideal in a marriage is that the two people involved fall so in love and become so close over the years that they know what the other person is thinking and feeling without a word having to be spoken. If you have ever been around a married couple like that, or if your own marriage enjoys that kind of intimate communication of spirit to spirit, you know how incredible it is, and you also know it is not developed overnight. It's the product of time and commitment producing true maturity.

Transferring that concept to the Christian life, you will find that a growing and developing Christian who has been communing with the Lord for many years enters a higher level of spiritual awareness. Paul described this in 1 Corinthians 2 when he wrote about "things which eye has not seen and ear has not heard, and which have not entered the heart of man, all that God has prepared for those who love Him. For to us God revealed them through the Spirit" (vv. 9–10).

Paul was not writing about heaven here, but about the things that God reveals to us down here on earth. Notice that these are not the things we could ever come up with on our own, because they are taught by the Holy Spirit, the only One who knows the thoughts of God (v. 11).

Now go on to verses 15–16, where we read, "He who is spiritual appraises all things" because he has "the mind of Christ." This means that the mature believer, another term for one "who is spiritual," is able to receive the "all things" that the Holy Spirit searches and reveals.

In other words, mature Christians see things that the human eye can't see. They hear things that the most acute hearing on earth cannot detect. And they have thoughts that they did not originate on their own because the Holy Spirit is helping them think God's thoughts. You will know you are spiritually mature when God lets you pick up on spiritual truths and insights from His Word that go far beyond what someone told you or what you heard in a sermon. The Holy Spirit is free to send His message clearly and directly to you.

The promise to a person who is listening to the Spirit is that he or she will "know the things freely given to us by God" (1 Cor. 2:12). These are the things we receive from God through His grace, but we have to be close enough to hear Him speak. It has to do with the intimacy of your relationship with God. If you are going to church, praying, and reading your Bible, but you're not getting closer to God, you will not see and hear the things that human eyes and ears cannot receive. Spiritual activities and programs can never replace spiritual intimacy.

What I am talking about here is the kind of spiritual intimacy and maturity that allows you to hear God speaking directly to you through His Word. You see, a lot of people come to church with the wrong focus. They want to know what the pastor's subject is, which is not the issue. What they should be focusing on is a prayer like this: "Lord, whatever the preacher is preaching on today, I need Your Holy Spirit to speak to my spirit through Your Word so that I will know what Your will is for my situation."

When hearing from God is your focus, then God can take even a side comment in a sermon and reveal His will to you. If you have ever had a thought relating to the Lord and wondered, *Where did that come from?* you know what it is like to hear from heaven. When God's Word is coming alive for you in ways that change your life and take you in a direction you would never have discovered for yourself, you know what it is like to be on the same vibe as the Holy Spirit, whose job it is to declare to us the Father and the Son who live within us (John 16:13–15).

Now this puts you in another world from the mass of people, and even from many Christians. Paul said in 1 Corinthians 2:14 that the "natural man," or unbeliever, can't grasp anything from God because his spirit is dead. In fact, the things of God are "foolishness" to this person. So a mature believer is worlds removed from the understanding of the unsaved person.

But not even other Christians always understand the mature believer. Paul said this person "is appraised by no one" (v. 15). People can't figure mature believers out, because they have the mind of Christ and thus intimacy with God, which is rare in the body of Christ even though the mind of Christ is God's will for, and is available to, every believer. Spiritually mature Christians have a passion to pursue and know God, and they aren't satisfied until they are in intimate fellowship with Him.

THE EVIDENCE OF YOUR INTIMACY WITH GOD

Now the last time I checked, you can't be a father without becoming intimate with someone. You don't stand at a distance or just have a parenting desire and get the privilege of being a father. And when intimacy occurs, a new life is created and will soon become evident as it grows inside the mother and then produces a child who bears the image and DNA of the parents. The evidence that you are mature will be the offspring you produce. A father is someone with children. If you are spiritually mature, you will have spiritual children.

It's impossible to keep a growing life hidden for very long, because life by its very nature wants to express itself. So it is with our spiritual life and growth. As you grow in the grace and knowledge of Christ, as stated in our theme verse for this book (2 Peter 3:18), your growth will manifest itself first to you and then to others. God will increasingly make Himself real to you, and your joy will be full as you come to know God in the intimacy of mature fellowship.

I love Jesus' answer to Philip at the Last Supper when Philip said to Him, "Lord, show us the Father, and it is enough for us" (John 14:8). Jesus answered, "Have I been so long with you, and yet you have not come to know Me, Philip? He who has seen Me has seen the Father" (v. 9).

That exchange tells me that it's possible to be a believer and yet not really know God in the way we have been talking about. My prayer for you is that you will grow into such close communion of heart and mind with God that whenever you hear or read His Word, it will have your name on it. And when you pray, your spirit will discern the Spirit of God revealing the mind and heart of God to you. Intimacy breeds communication. The Holy Spirit speaks another language from the inside, even though He may use external things to deliver it to the inside.

If you want to know God, then everything you do must have that as its driving goal. In the meantime, you have to go through the childhood and adolescent stages, and you may be a little wobbly and unsure at times. But that's when you have to go to the Word and say, "Lord, this is what You say and what I want to do. But I need You to make it real to me, because I need it deep down right now."

How quickly and solidly you grow depends on how hungry you are for growth. Therefore, your passion must be to increase your hunger for God. The formula for spiritual growth is simple: rate multiplied by time equals distance. The diligence with which you use your time to pursue God will determine the speed at which you arrive at your destination of maturity. This is why it is possible for people who have been Christians for five years to be more spiritually mature than people who have been saved for twenty-five years. The first group advanced through the stages of spiritual growth much faster.

Wherever you are on your journey with Christ, the best place to start growing is right where you are. You can't go back to yesterday, but today is a brand-new day to draw close to the Lord and hear from Him so that He can guide you on the fulfilling path of kingdom living.

Conclusion

PRIOR TO THE ADVENT OF digital photography, all of us had to take our film to the developer so the negatives could be turned into photos that documented the changes in our families. Our home is filled with photo albums that show the changes and growth in our family over the years.

Such is the process of spiritual growth. When we came to Christ we handed over to the negatives of our lives to God. He, the supreme Developer, took those negatives into His special laboratory of grace to transform them into beautiful pictures of His marvelous grace as we are transformed "from glory to glory" into the image of Christ.

As we continue our journey of spiritual growth with Christ, we will have an album of grace showing how God changed us into something beautiful. Then one day we will enter into His presence and no longer be negative prints waiting to be developed. Instead, like a digital photograph, the process will be completed instantaneously, for in heaven there will be nothing to interfere with our understanding of what it means to be sons and daughters of God. The apostle John said it best:

> See how great a love the Father has bestowed on us, that we would be called children of God; and such we are. For this reason the world does

not know us, because it did not know Him. Beloved, now we are children of God, and it has not appeared as yet what we will be. We know that when He appears, we will be like Him, because we will see Him just as He is. And everyone who has this hope fixed on Him purifies himself, just as He is pure. (1 John 3:1–3)

As we look to and live under the Lordship of the risen Christ as His kingdom disciple, we will continually and progressively grow in our faith. We will become spiritual images of our Savior. What better hope could we have as we seek to advance God's kingdom in our time on earth.

Scripture Index

Appendix:
The Urban Alternative

The Urban Alternative (TUA) equips, empowers, and unites Christians to impact *individuals, families, churches,* and *communities* through a thoroughly kingdom agenda worldview. In teaching truth, we seek to transform lives.

The core cause of the problems we face in our personal lives, homes, churches, and societies is a spiritual one; therefore, the only way to address it is spiritually. We've tried a political, social, economic, and even a religious agenda.

It's time for a **kingdom agenda**.

The kingdom agenda can be defined as the visible manifestation of the comprehensive rule of God over every area of life.

The unifying central theme throughout the Bible is the glory of God and the advancement of His kingdom. The conjoining thread from Genesis to Revelation—from beginning to end—is focused on one thing: God's glory through advancing God's kingdom.

When you do not recognize that theme, the Bible becomes disconnected stories that are great for inspiration but seem to be unrelated in purpose and direction. Understanding the role of the kingdom in Scripture increases the relevancy of this several thousand-year-old text to your day-to-day living, because the kingdom is not only then; it is now.

The absence of the kingdom's influence in our personal lives, family lives, churches, and communities has led to a deterioration in our world of immense proportions:

- People live segmented, compartmentalized lives because they lack God's kingdom worldview.

- Families disintegrate because they exist for their own satisfaction rather than for the kingdom.

- Churches are limited in the scope of their impact because they fail to comprehend that the goal of the church is not the church itself, but the kingdom.

- Communities have nowhere to turn to find real solutions for real people who have real problems because the church has become divided, ingrown, and unable to transform the cultural and political landscape in any relevant way.

The kingdom agenda offers us a way to see and live life with a solid hope by optimizing the solutions of heaven. When God is no longer the final and authoritative standard under which all else falls, order and hope leaves with Him. But the reverse of that is true as well: as long as you have God, you have hope. If God is still in the picture, and as long as His agenda is still on the table, it's not over.

Even if relationships collapse, God will sustain you. Even if finances dwindle, God will keep you. Even if dreams die, God will revive you. As long as God and His rule are still the overarching standard in your life, family, church, and community, there is always hope.

Our world needs the King's agenda. Our churches need the King's agenda. Our families need the King's agenda.

We've put together a three-part plan to direct us to heal the divisions and strive for unity as we move toward the goal of truly being one nation under God. This three-part plan calls us to assemble with others in unity, address the issues that divide us, and to act together for social impact. Following this plan, we will see individuals, families, churches, and communities transformed as we follow God's kingdom agenda in every area of our lives. You can request this plan by emailing info@tonyevans.org or by going online to tonyevans.org.

In many major cities, there is a loop that drivers can take when they want to get somewhere on the other side of the city but don't necessarily want to head straight through downtown. This loop will take you close enough to the city so that you can see its towering buildings and skyline, but not close enough to actually experience it.

This is precisely what we, as a culture, have done with God. We have put Him on the "loop" of our personal, family, church, and community lives. He's close enough to be at hand should we need Him in an emergency, but far enough away that He can't be the center of who we are.

We want God on the "loop," not the King of the Bible who comes downtown into the very heart of our ways. Leaving God on the "loop" brings about dire consequences as we have seen in our own lives and with others. But when we make God, and His rule, the centerpiece of all we think, do, or say, it is then that we will experience Him in the way He longs for us to experience Him.

He wants us to be kingdom people with kingdom minds set on fulfilling His kingdom's purposes. He wants us to pray, as Jesus did, "Not my will, but Thy will be done." Because His is the kingdom, the power, and the glory.

There is only one God, and we are not Him. As King and Creator,

God calls the shots. It is only when we align ourselves underneath His comprehensive hand that we will access His full power and authority in all spheres of life: personal, familial, ecclesiastical, and governmental.

As we learn how to govern ourselves under God, we then transform the institutions of family, church, and society using a biblically based kingdom worldview.

Under Him, we touch heaven and change earth.

To achieve our goal, we use a variety of strategies, approaches, and resources for reaching and equipping as many people as possible.

BROADCAST MEDIA

Millions of individuals experience *The Alternative with Dr. Tony Evans* through the daily radio broadcast playing on nearly **1,400 Radio outlets** and in over **130 countries**. The broadcast can also be seen on several TV networks, and is available online at tonyevans.org. You can also listen or view the daily broadcast by downloading the Tony Evans app for free in the app store. Over thirty million message downloads/streams occur each year.

LEADERSHIP TRAINING

The Tony Evans Training Center (TETC) facilitates a comprehensive discipleship platform which provides an educational program that embodies the ministry philosophy of Dr. Tony Evans as expressed through the kingdom agenda. The training courses focus on leadership development and discipleship in the following five tracks:

- Bible & Theology
- Personal Growth
- Family & Relationships
- Church Health & Leadership Development
- Society & Community Impact Strategies

The TETC program includes courses for both local and online students. Furthermore, TETC programming includes course work for non-student attendees. Pastors, Christian leaders, and Christian laity, both local and at a distance, can seek out The Kingdom Agenda Certificate for personal, spiritual, and professional development. For more information, visit TonyEvansTraining.org.

The Kingdom Agenda Pastors (KAP) provides a *viable network* for *like-minded pastors* who embrace the kingdom agenda philosophy. Pastors have the opportunity to go deeper with Dr. Tony Evans as they are given greater biblical knowledge, practical applications, and resources to impact individuals, families, churches, and communities. KAP welcomes *senior and associate pastors* of all churches. KAP also offers an annual Summit held each year in Dallas with intensive seminars, workshops, and resources. For more information, visit KAFellowship.org.

Pastors' Wives Ministry, founded by the late Dr. Lois Evans, provides *counsel, encouragement,* and *spiritual resources* for pastors' wives as they serve with their husbands in the ministry. A primary focus of the ministry is the KAP Summit that offers senior pastors' wives a safe place to *reflect, renew,* and *relax* along with training in personal development, spiritual growth, and care for their emotional and physical well-being. For more information, visit LoisEvans.org.

KINGDOM COMMUNITY IMPACT

The outreach programs of The Urban Alternative seek to provide positive impact to individuals, churches, families, and communities through a variety of ministries. We see these efforts as necessary to our calling as a ministry and essential to the communities we serve. With training on how to initiate and maintain programs to adopt schools, or provide homeless services, or partner toward unity and justice with the local police precincts, which creates a connection between the police and our community, we, as a ministry, live out God's kingdom agenda according to our *Kingdom Strategy for Community Transformation.*

The Kingdom Strategy for Community Transformation is a three-part plan that equips churches to have a positive impact on their communities for the kingdom of God. It also provides numerous practical suggestions for how this three-part plan can be implemented in your community, and it serves as a blueprint for unifying churches around the common goal of creating a better world for all of us. For more information, visit tonyevans.org and click on the link to access the 3-Point Plan. A course for this strategy is also offered online through the Tony Evans Training Center.

Tony Evans Films ushers in positive life change through compelling video-shorts, animation, and feature-length films. We seek to build kingdom disciples through the power of story. We use a variety of platforms for viewer consumption and have over 120 million digital views. We also merge video-shorts and film with relevant Bible study materials to bring people to the saving knowledge of Jesus Christ and to strengthen the body of Christ worldwide. *Tony Evans Films* released the first feature-length film, *Kingdom Men Rising*, in April 2019 in over eight hundred theaters nationwide, in partnership with Lifeway Films. The second release, *Journey with Jesus*, is in partnership with RightNow Media and was released in theaters in November 2021.

RESOURCE DEVELOPMENT

We are fostering lifelong learning partnerships with the people we serve by providing a variety of published materials. Dr. Evans has published more than 125 unique titles based on over fifty years of preaching whether that is in booklet, book, or Bible study format. He also holds the honor of writing and publishing the first full-Bible commentary and study Bible by an African American, released in 2019. This Bible sits in permanent display as a historic release, in The Museum of the Bible in Washington, DC.

For more information, and a complimentary copy of Dr. Evans's devotional newsletter, call (800) 800–3222 *or* write TUA at P.O. Box 4000, Dallas TX 75208, *or* visit us online.

tonyevans.org

WHERE HAVE ALL THE
DISCIPLES GONE?

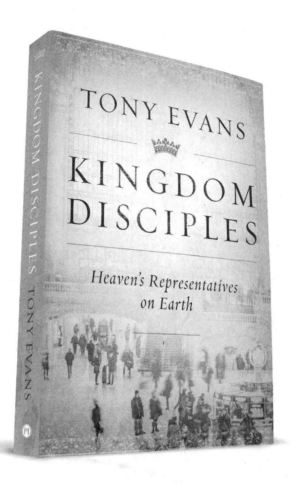

Christians often know the *theory* of the Spirit-filled life but not the joy-filled *experience*.

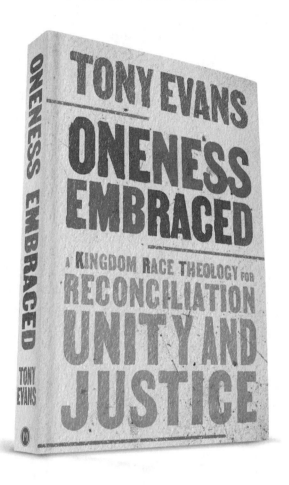